Redeeming
the
Time

Redeeming
the
Time

Russell Kirk

edited with an introduction
by Jeffrey O. Nelson

Intercollegiate Studies Institute
Wilmington, Delaware
2006

Library of Congress Cataloging-in-Publication Number
    96-077112

ISBN 1-882926-21-8

Published in the United States by:

    Intercollegiate Studies Institute
    3901 Centerville Rd.
    P.O. Box 4431
    Wilmington, DE 19807-0431

Manufactured in the United States of America

...the fountain sprang up and the bird sang down
Redeem the time, redeem the dream....

—*T. S. Eliot*

Dedication

To Andrew Scott Carman and Isabel Annette Nelson, whose grandfather, the author of this book, now embarked upon that otherworld journey, has no doubt set strong ghosts to watch over them—"the communication of the dead is tongued with fire beyond the language of the living."

Contents

Acknowledgments

The contents of this book were public lectures sponsored by the Heritage Foundation in the Foundation's auditorium. Thanks go especially to those associated with the Heritage Lecture series for their hospitality and farsightedness in sponsoring such lectures. In addition to being presented in Washington, versions were presented elsewhere. "Criminal Character and Mercy" was delivered at Georgia State University; "Regaining Historical Consciousness" at Indiana University; and the "Libertarians" at a conference sponsored by the Liberty Fund and the Intercollegiate Studies Institute. Other audiences to hear some altered form of these essays include: Pepperdine University; Texas Agricultural and Mechanical University; Grand Valley State University; Hillsdale College; Albion College; Alma College; Christendom College; Kirtland Community College; The McCallie School; Charlotte Latin School; the Intercollegiate Studies Institute; and the Philadelphia Society. Versions of some of the following have been published in periodicals: "Three Pillars of Order," "Libertarians," "Criminal Character and Mercy," "The Age of Sentiments," "Civilization without Religion?," "The Wise Men Know What Wicked Things Are Written on the Sky," "The Age of Sentiments," and "Can Virtue Be Taught?" in *Modern Age*; "The Perversity of Recent Fiction: Reflections on the Moral Imagination" in *Literature and Belief*; and a version of "The Tension of Order and Freedom" appeared in *Order, Freedom, and the University*, edited by James R. Wilburn. Chapters 3, 4, 5, 9, 12, 13, 17, and 22 appeared in *The Wise Men Know What Wicked Things Are Written on the Sky*; Chapters 6, 7, 8, 18, 19, 20 appeared first in *Reclaiming a Patrimony*.

Many thanks to Brooke Daley, Catherine Lulves, and Mary Slayton for their able editorial assistance, and to my wife, Cecilia Kirk Nelson, for her thoughtful editorial input and her unflagging support and encouragement in this and many other projects.

Introduction

The writings collected here were delivered originally as public lectures at The Heritage Foundation in Washington, D.C., over a period of fourteen years—from 1980 until the author's death on April 29, 1994. Part of what follows first appeared in two long out-of-print books: *Reclaiming a Patrimony* and *Wise Men Know What Wicked Things Are Written on the Sky*. Much, though, is unique to this book.

Redeeming the Time is intended to be a companion volume to the highly acclaimed *The Politics of Prudence*—another collection of popular Heritage lectures. Together, these two books comprise nearly the complete Kirk lecture series sponsored by that eminent Washington policy institute. Heritage President Edwin J. Feulner, Jr., has said of Kirk's Washington lectures that, "In a city of constant change, Kirk reminded opinion leaders, journalists, legislators, and staffers of prudence and taking the long view." These lectures, Feulner observed, were "masterpieces of clear thought and eternal truth," and insure that "Kirk's influence in Washington will continue to be far greater than many of the transient politicians who descend upon this city, cycle after cycle."

In the pages that follow, Kirk counsels us to direct our energies toward cultural renewal. Arguing that our civilization stands in peril, he exhorts those who believe that life is worth living to address themselves to means by which a restoration of our culture may be achieved.

*   *   *

While the reader of *Redeeming the Time* will detect the immense range of Kirk's interests, he viewed himself principally as an historian of ideas and literary critic. He endeavored "to wake the moral imagination through the evocative power of humane letters." Indeed, he was, above all else, a man of humane letters. As the distinguished literary critic George A. Panichas has pointed out, Kirk's strength of character and sense of moral obligation elevated the man of letters to his true stature—that is, to one who points the way to first principles.

Kirk's role as he saw it was that of "guardian of the Word." Men of letters, teachers, and all who labor in educational vineyards, are entrusted with an almost sacred duty to preserve and transmit as intact as they are able a shared cultural and intellectual patrimony to the generation in ascendance. "We need to remind ourselves," Kirk wrote,

> that men of letters and teachers of literature are entrusted with a social responsibility: they have no right to be nihilists or fantastic or neoterists, because the terms on which they hold their trust are conservative. Whatever the immediate political opinions of the guardians of the Word, his first duty is conservative in the larger sense of that adjective: his work, his end, is to shelter and promul-

gate an inherited body of learning and myth. The man of letters and teacher of literature have no right to be irresponsible dilettantes or reckless iconoclasts; they are placed in their high dignity so that they may preserve the ideas that make all men one.

In 1953, Kirk, recently awarded the degree D.Litt. from St. Andrews University in Scotland and a young professor at Michigan State University, published his magnum opus, *The Conservative Mind*. Before that time social critics like Lionel Trilling could perceive no trace of conservative imagination to challenge the hegemony of liberalism. But Kirk "tossed into the stagnant pond of intellectualism" his *Conservative Mind*, and its waves are still being felt. Kirk's book was reviewed at length in *The New York Review of Books* and *Time*, as well as in countless other publications. Publication of *The Conservative Mind* launched not only one man's distinguished career, but an American political movement.

Kirk, however, did not immediately fancy himself part of a "conservative movement." He wouldn't be pigeonholed by words such as "Right" or "Left"—labels that tend to lead "one into the trap of ideological infatuation." As he observed in his memoir *The Sword of Imagination*, those eminent post-war literary figures who abjured the official liberal ideology and who seldom thought in political categories

> may better be described as the literary party of order. It was order in the soul that chiefly interested them; but they knew, most of them, that the commonwealth too requires principles of order. Some of them were willing to be called conservatives, others not; labels are of no great consequence; they were no ideologues, no politicizers of humane letters.

If Kirk joined the lists of the "literary party of order," his sworn opponents were those adherents of the "literary party of disorder." Kirk stood forthright against the purveyors of disorder, those "nihilists, fanatic ideologues, and purveyors of violent sensation" who "present us with the image of man unregenerate and triumphant in his depravity." By the end of the 1950s, due in no small part to Kirk's efforts, the climate of opinion in America was slowly changing.

Kirk labored in the tiny village of Mecosta, Michigan, far from the centers of "publishing, book reviewing, and literary cocktail parties." Though he avoided the allure of certain literary circles, by the mid-1950s Kirk was a prolific man of letters. In addition to *The Conservative Mind* and *Randolph of Roanoke*, his first book, Kirk published *A Program for Conservatives* (later entitled *Prospects for Conservatives*), *Beyond the Dreams of Avarice*, *St. Andrews*, *Academic Freedom*, *The Intelligent Woman's Guide to Conservatism*, and *The American Cause*. Additionally, he founded, in collaboration with the publisher Henry Regnery and a few others, the quarterly *Modern Age*—which to this day remains what Kirk intended it to be: "an American protest against the illusions of the age."

His growing influence was felt abroad as well as at home. Throughout his life, Kirk was numbered among the company of the leading literary figures of Europe. T. S. Eliot, Roy Campbell, Wilhelm Roepke, Wyndham Lewis, Otto von Habsburg, all were friends and allies, men of letters, as Kirk put it, turned "tailors in the West, doing what they might to stitch together once more that serviceable old suit variously called 'Christian Civilization,' 'Western Civilization,' 'North Atlantic Community,' or 'the free world.'"

Kirk learned much from contemporary European literary figures—particularly T. S. Eliot. Like his friend Eliot, Kirk, too, "had sworn fealty to the permanent things, understanding that these permanent things are not the creations of men merely." Of T. S. Eliot, Kirk wrote, "What Eliot's revolution in literature gave to his age was a renewal of moral imagination—with social consequences potentially." In his age, Russell Kirk effected a similar revolution in politics and humane letters—with social consequences actually.

By the 1960s, Kirk was an established author and public personality; by the 1980s he was hailed as the father of modern American conservatism and was among the speakers most in demand on college campuses. Kirk lived to see the intellectual movement to which he had contributed so much from its haphazard beginnings become "a popular cause—nay, a high tide in the affairs of men."

Over the last thirty years, Kirk added more than twenty books to the ones aforementioned, including major works such as *T. S. Eliot and His Age*, *Edmund Burke: A Genius Reconsidered*, *Enemies of The Permanent Things*, *The Roots of American Order*, *America's British Culture*, and *The Politics of Prudence*. He was also a master in the art of storytelling, particularly of ghostly tales, and could count among his achievements an acclaimed corpus of fiction, including *A Creature of the Twilight*, *Lord of the Hollow Dark*, *The Surly Sullen Bell*, *Watchers at the Strait Gate*, *The Princess of all Lands*, and *Old House of Fear*. Kirk would note with satisfaction in his 1963 collection *Confessions of a Bohemian Tory*, that "without design or strong exertion, I have fallen into the best of lives, that of the independent man of letters—a dying breed, but one capable still of a shrewd cut or thrust before twilight."

*   *   *

Redeeming the Time is the first collection of Kirk essays to appear posthumously. These essays distill, in prose characteristically lively and graceful, many of the tenets central to Kirk's brand of humane conservatism: the nature of culture, the precariousness of order, justice, and freedom, the true purpose of education, the dangers of rapacious ideology, the importance of beauty, and the centrality of the imagination. Together with its immediate predecessor, *The*

Politics of Prudence, one will find this volume an excellent introduction to the thought of this seminal twentieth-century thinker. But for the full depth and sophistication of Kirk's thought on the range of political, literary, and cultural matters he discusses, the reader is encouraged to consult his weightier works, such as the ones already listed.

While Kirk considers here a congery of themes in several disciplines, a thread of continuity nevertheless joins these writings: the patrimony of culture and of order, justice, and freedom that Americans have inherited—but often neglected to renew. Kirk's wide and deep reading made him painfully cognizant that the freedoms we Americans have enjoyed may not be maintained in perpetuity, that our "new order of the ages" may not endure forever. As he cautiously notes in the second chapter: "It is by no means certain that our present moral and constitutional order is providing sufficiently for its own future. Modern men pay a great deal of attention to material and technological means, but little attention to the instruments by which any generation must fulfill its part in the contract of eternal society."

It was this task of reflection upon the problem of how to conserve, and then of discerning ways to renew, our cultural patrimony that was central to nearly all of Kirk's books—and, as the title suggests, it is the primary concern of *Redeeming the Time*.

At the heart of his analysis of the current state of culture is the concern that a proper relationship exist between faith, freedom, and order—with particular attention paid to the question of order. In the early pages of his treatise *The Roots of American Order*, Kirk defines this word "order" as "a systematic and harmonious arrangement—whether in one's character or in the commonwealth. Also 'order' signifies certain duties and the enjoyment of certain rights in a community: thus we use the phrase civil social order." Before men can live tolerably well with each other, Kirk taught, there must be order.

While for Kirk (as for Simone Weil) "order is the first need of all," it does not follow that he considers freedom to be a secondary good. Rather, as he states in "The Tension of Order and Freedom in the University," freedom is intricately bound up with order, they co-exist necessarily in a healthy tension. Order and freedom are not paradoxical, they are the flip-side of the same coin, and so Kirk advances "ordered freedom" as the ideal of the commonwealth.

The glue that holds order and freedom together in healthy tension is, Kirk argues, religion. "[I]t seems to me that a high degree of ordered, civilized freedom is linked closely with religious belief.... If the great troubles of our time teach mankind anything, surely we ought now to recognize that true freedom cannot endure in a society which denies a transcendent order." For Kirk, the America of the early Republic typified this ideal of a union between order and freedom.

> Our constitutions were established that order might make possible true freedom. Despite all our American talk of private judgment, dissent, and individualism, still our national character has the stamp of respect for the moral order ordained by religion, and for the prescriptive political forms that we, more than any other people in the twentieth century, have maintained little altered. We would work immense mischief to our freedom if we ceased to respect our established order, running instead after an abstract, Jacobin liberty.

If we are to redeem our time, we must seek out imaginative ways to renew our understanding of and commitment to our prescriptive freedoms and our inherited moral and constitutional order. This is certainly a grand challenge, but we are reminded in these pages that "every grand question has to be argued afresh in every generation."

Kirk is the ablest of guides for those unsure of foot and in need of orientation in this delicate process of cultural renewal. Each of the succeeding chapters addresses a component integral to the process of civil social reinvigoration. For instance, in "Civilization without Religion?" Kirk argues forcefully that "culture can be renewed only if the cult is renewed"; and at the center of the cult is religious belief: "If a culture is to survive and flourish, it must not be severed from the religious vision out of which it arose." In "The Conservative Purpose of a Liberal Education" he underscores the importance of education in social and personal renewal: "[T]he function of liberal education is to conserve a body of received knowledge and to impart an apprehension of order to the rising generation." In "Renewing a Shaken Culture" Kirk exhorts the reader to "resist manfully and womanfully the thoughtless central-ization of political and economic power." In "The American Mission" he counsels us to take a fresh look at that "champion of ordered freedom," Orestes Brownson, who argued that the central problem of politics was the reconciling of authority and liberty, and who discerned that it was this country's mission "to present to mankind a political model: a commonwealth in which order and freedom exist in a healthy balance or tension." In "The Case For and Against 'Natural Law'" Kirk encourages a reconsideration of that much-maligned doctrine, contending that the natural law "is meant for the governance of persons...that we may restrain will and appetite in ordinary walks of life"—and in that way it may have the salutary effect, too, of helping to "form the opinions of those who are lawmakers." In "Three Pillars of Order" the reader is presented with eighteenth-century exemplars who resisted fanatic ideology and defended the old moral order against the rebellious innovators of their time.

In the midst of these thoughtful expositions of conservative belief and counsels for reform, Kirk takes issue with a host of enemies of ordered freedom and authentic cultural renewal. "In any age," he argues in the ensuing pages, "some people revolt against their own inheritance of order.... Near the end of the twentieth century, the number of such enemies to order has become alarming.... To the folk who rebel against their patrimony of moral and constitutional order, that legacy seems a burden—when in truth it is a footing."

Those "enemies of ordered freedom" drawing particular attention include the libertarians, who "dream of an absolute private freedom" and advance a theory of "ravening liberty"; the multiculturalists, who "would pull down the whole elaborate existing culture of this country in order to make everybody equal—that is equal in ignorance"; the egalitarians, who "would discourage or suppress enterprising talents—which would result in social stagnation"; the technocrats, who "seem calculated to enfeeble the individual reason and to make most of us dependent upon an elite of computer programmers"; the sentimentalists, who "feel" with projected images "that rouse *sentiments* rather than reflections"; the educrats, who consider education to be nothing higher "than an instrument of public policy"; the democratists, who refuse to acknowledge that "the American Constitution is not for export"; the legal positivists, who deny "any source for justice except the commands of the sovereign state"; and the sham architects and perverse literati, who war against the "normative purpose" of art and letters, proffering instead unparalleled dreariness, uniformity, violence, and servility—a "barrenness of soul and mind."

This combination of sober reflection, thoughtful analysis, and tempered optimism, or rather hope, make *Redeeming the Time* the perfect guide for those in search of intelligent conservative reform. These essays of diagnosis and prognosis, penned during the last years of Kirk's life, resonate with the wisdom of the ages, as well as with the wisdom of an aging seer. The reader discouraged by the prospects of returning a modicum of order and justice and freedom to this bent world should turn to the final chapter of this collection. Therein Kirk's genuine cheerfulness sheds light on the darkness of

our cultural landscape. Concurring with Napoleon that "imagination rules the world," and understanding that we "are not the slaves
of some impersonal force called Destiny or History," Kirk rallies the
reader, charging that

> it is not inevitable that we submit ourselves to a social life-
> in-death of boring uniformity and equality. It is not
> inevitable that we indulge all our appetites to fatigued
> satiety. It is not inevitable that we reduce our schooling
> to the lowest common denominator. It is not inevitable
> that obsession with creature-comforts should sweep away
> belief in a transcendent order. It is not inevitable that the
> computer should supplant the poet.

But how are we to reverse our slide into the darkness of cultural
decadence? In the end, Kirk puts his trust in Providence and his
hope in the rising generation: that the "children of light may labor
with fortitude, knowing that the struggle availeth."

Thankfully, we are not left to labor alone. Rather, those among
us who work to restore our inherited cultural patrimony can look
over our shoulders for energy and direction, to those giants who
have labored before us. Kirk himself counseled that it is from the
memorable dead that we look for "the energy that sustains people
in a time of tribulation." "The order, inner and outer, of our
common culture," he contended, "is defended not by the living
merely, but by the valiant dead as well." Russell Kirk is now counted
among those valiant dead who give us energy. The incandescence
of his immortal soul shines through this work, and enlightens and
emboldens us in our efforts to redeem the time.

—Jeffrey O. Nelson

Section I

Renewing the Cultural Order

I

Civilization without Religion?

Sobering voices tell us nowadays that the civilization in which we participate is not long for this world. Many countries have fallen under the domination of squalid oligarchs; other lands are reduced to anarchy. "Cultural revolution," rejecting our patrimony of learning and manners, has done nearly as much mischief in the West as in the East, if less violently. Religious belief is attenuated at best, for many—or else converted, after being secularized, into an instrument for social transformation. Books give way to television and videos; universities, intellectually democratized, are sunk to the condition of centers for job certification. An increasing proportion of the population, in America especially, is dehumanized by addiction to narcotics and insane sexuality.

These afflictions are only some of the symptoms of social and personal disintegration. One has but to look at our half-ruined American cities, with their ghastly rates of murder and rape, to perceive that we moderns lack the moral imagination and the right reason required to maintain tolerable community. Writers in learned quarterlies or in daily syndicated columns use the terms "post-Christian era" or "post-modern epoch" to imply that we are breaking altogether with our cultural past, and are entering upon some new age of a bewildering character.

Some people, the militant secular humanists in particular, seem pleased by this prospect; but yesteryear's meliorism is greatly weakened in most quarters. Even Marxist ideologues virtually have ceased to predict the approach of a Golden Age. To most observers, T. S. Eliot among them, it has seemed far more probable that we are stumbling into a new Dark Age, inhumane, merciless, a totalist political domination in which the life of spirit and the inquiring intellect will be denounced, harassed, and propagandized against: Orwell's *Nineteen Eighty-Four,* rather than Huxley's *Brave New World* of cloying sensuality. Or perhaps Tolkien's blasted and servile land of Mordor may serve as symbol of the human condition in the twenty-first century (which, however, may not be called the twenty-first century, the tag *Anno Domini* having been abolished as joined to one of the superstitions of the childhood of the race).

*   *   *

Some years ago I was sitting in the parlor of an ancient house in the close of York Minster. My host, Basil Smith, the Minster's Treasurer then, a man of learning and of faith, said to me that we linger at the end of an era; soon the culture we have known will be swept into the dustbin of history. About us, as we talked in that medieval mansion, loomed Canon Smith's tall bookcases lined with handsome volumes; his doxological clock chimed the half-hour musically; flames flared up in his fireplace. Was all this setting of culture, and much more besides, to vanish away as if the Evil Spirit had condemned it? Basil Smith is buried now, and so is much of the society he ornamented and tried to redeem. At the time I thought him too gloomy; but already a great deal that he foresaw has come to pass.

The final paragraph of Malcolm Muggeridge's essay "The Great Liberal Death Wish" must suffice as a summing-up of the human predicament at the end of the twentieth century.

"As the astronauts soar into the vast eternities of space," Muggeridge writes, "on earth the garbage piles higher; as the groves of academe extend their domain, their alumni's arms reach lower; as the phallic cult spreads, so does impotence. In great wealth, great poverty; in health, sickness, in numbers, deception. Gorging, left hungry; sedated, left restless; telling all, hiding all; in flesh united, forever separate. So we press on through the valley of abundance that leads to the wasteland of satiety, passing through the gardens of fantasy; seeking happiness ever more ardently, and finding despair ever more surely."

Just so. Such recent American ethical writers as Stanley Hauwerwas and Alasdair MacIntyre concur in Muggeridge's verdict on the society of our time, concluding that nothing can be done, except for a remnant to gather in little "communities of character" while society slides toward its ruin. Over the past half-century, many other voices of reflective men and women have been heard to the same effect. Yet let us explore the question of whether a reinvigoration of our culture is conceivable.

*　　　*　　　*

Is the course of nations inevitable? Is there some fixed destiny for great states? In 1796, a dread year for Britain, old Edmund Burke declared that we cannot foresee the future; often the historical determinists are undone by the coming of events that nobody has predicted. At the very moment when some states "seemed plunged in unfathomable abysses of disgrace and disaster," Burke wrote in his *First Letter on a Regicide Peace,* "they have suddenly emerged.

They have begun a new course, and opened a new reckoning; and even in the depths of their calamity, and on the very ruins of their country, have laid the foundations of a towering and durable greatness. All this has happened without any apparent previous change in the general circumstances which had brought on their distress. The death of a man at a critical juncture, his disgust, his retreat, his disgrace, have brought innumerable calamities on a whole nation. A common soldier, a child, a girl at the door of an inn, have changed the face of fortune, and almost of Nature."

The "common soldier" to whom Burke refers is Arnold of Winkelreid, who flung himself upon the Austrian spears to save his country; the child is the young Hannibal, told by his father to wage ruthless war upon Rome; the girl at the door of an inn is Joan of Arc. We do not know why such abrupt reversals or advances occur, Burke remarks; perhaps they are indeed the work of Providence.

"Nothing is, but thinking makes it so," the old adage runs. If most folk come to believe that our culture must collapse—why, then collapse it will. Yet Burke, after all, was right in that dreadful year of 1796. For despite the overwhelming power of the French revolutionary movement in that year, in the long run Britain defeated her adversaries, and after the year 1812 Britain emerged from her years of adversity to the height of her power. Is it conceivable that American civilization, and in general what we call "Western civilization," may recover from the Time of Troubles that commenced in 1914 (so Arnold Toynbee instructs us) and in the twenty-first century enter upon an Augustan age of peace and restored order?

To understand these words "civilization" and "culture," the best book to read is T. S. Eliot's slim volume *Notes Towards the Definition of Culture*.

Once upon a time I commended that book to President Nixon, in a private discussion of modern disorders, as the one book which he ought to read for guidance in his high office. Man is the only creature possessing culture, as distinguished from instinct; and if culture is effaced, so is the distinction between man and the brutes that perish. "Art is man's nature," in Edmund Burke's phrase; and if the human arts, or culture, cease to be, then human nature ceases to be.

From what source did humankind's many cultures arise? Why, from cults. A cult is a joining together for worship—that is, the attempt of people to commune with a transcendent power. It is from association in the cult, the body of worshippers, that human community grows. This basic truth has been expounded in recent decades by such eminent historians as Christopher Dawson, Eric Voegelin, and Arnold Toynbee.

Once people are joined in a cult, cooperation in many other things becomes possible. Common defense, irrigation, systematic agriculture, architecture, the visual arts, music, the more intricate crafts, economic production and distribution, courts and government—all these aspects of a culture arise gradually from the cult, the religious tie.

Out of little knots of worshippers, in Egypt, the Fertile Crescent, India, or China, there grew up simple cultures; for those joined by religion can dwell together and work together in relative peace. Presently such simple cultures may develop into intricate cultures, and those intricate cultures into great civilizations. American civilization of our era is rooted, strange though the fact may seem to us, in tiny knots of worshippers in Palestine, Greece, and Italy, thousands of years ago. The enormous material achievements of our civilization have resulted, if remotely, from the spiritual insights of prophets and seers.

But suppose that the cult withers, with the elapse of centuries. What then of the culture that is rooted in the cult? What then of the civilization which is the culture's grand manifestation? For an answer to such uneasy questions, we can turn to a twentieth-century parable. Here I think of G. K. Chesterton's observation that all life being an allegory, we can understand it only in parable.

*   *   *

The author of my parable, however, is not Chesterton, but a quite different writer, the late Robert Graves, whom I once visited in Mallorca. I have in mind Graves's romance *Seven Days in New Crete*—published in America under the title *Watch the North Wind Rise*.

In that highly readable romance of a possible future, we are told that by the close of the "Late Christian epoch" the world will have fallen altogether, after a catastrophic war and devastation, under a collectivistic domination, a variant of Communism. Religion, the moral imagination, and nearly everything that makes life worth living have been virtually extirpated by ideology and nuclear war. A system of thought and government called Logicalism, "pantisocratic economics divorced from any religious or national theory," rules the world—for a brief time.

In Graves's words:

> Logicalism, hinged on international science, ushered in a gloomy and anti-poetic age. It lasted only a generation or two and ended with a grand defeatism, a sense of perfect futility, that slowly crept over the directors and managers of the regime. The common man had triumphed over his spiritual betters at last, but what was to follow? To what could he look forward with either hope or fear? By the abolition of sovereign states and the disarming of even the police forces, war had become impossible. No one who cherished any religious beliefs whatever, or was interested in sport, poetry, or the arts, was allowed to hold a position of public responsibility. 'Ice-cold logic' was the most valued civic quality, and

those who could not pretend to it were held of no account. Science continued laboriously to expand its over-large corpus of information, and the subjects of research grew more and more beautifully remote and abstract; yet the scientific obsession, so strong at the beginning of the third millennium A. D., was on the wane. Logicalist officials who were neither defeatist nor secretly religious and who kept their noses to the grindstone from a sense of duty, fell prey to colobromania, a mental disturbance....

Rates of abortion and infanticide, of suicide, and other indices of social boredom rise with terrifying speed under this Logicalist regime. Gangs of young people go about robbing, beating, and murdering, for the sake of excitement. It appears that the human race will become extinct if such tendencies continue; for men and women find life not worth living under such a domination. The deeper longings of humanity have been outraged, so that the soul and the state stagger on the verge of final darkness. But in this crisis an Israeli Sophocrat writes a book called *A Critique of Utopias,* in which he examines seventy Utopian writings, from Plato to Aldous Huxley. "We must retrace our steps," he concludes, "or perish." Only by the resurrection of religious faith, the Sophocrats discover, can mankind be kept from total destruction; and that religion, as Graves describes it in his romance, springs from the primitive soil of myth and symbol.

Graves really is writing about our own age, not of some remote future: of life in today's United States and in the former Soviet Union. He is saying that culture arises from the cult; and that when belief in the cult has been wretchedly enfeebled, the culture will decay swiftly. The material order rests upon the spiritual order.

So it has come to pass, here in the closing years of the twentieth century. With the weakening of the moral order, "Things fall apart; / ...Mere anarchy is loosed upon the world...." The Hellenic and the Roman cultures went down to dusty death after this fashion. What may be done to achieve reinvigoration?

*   *   *

Some well-meaning folk talk of a "civil religion," a kind of cult of patriotism, founded upon a myth of national virtue and upon veneration of certain historic documents, together with a utilitarian morality. But such experiments of a secular character never have functioned satisfactorily; and it scarcely is necessary for me to point out the perils of such an artificial creed, bound up with nationalism: the example of the ideology of the National Socialist Party in Germany, half a century ago, may suffice. Worship of the state, or of the national commonwealth, is no healthy substitute for communion with transcendent love and wisdom.

Nor can attempts at persuading people that religion is "useful" meet with much genuine success. No man sincerely goes down on his knees to the divine because he has been told that such rituals lead to the beneficial consequences of tolerably honest behavior in commerce. People will conform their actions to the precepts of religion only when they earnestly believe the doctrines of that religion to be true.

Still less can it suffice to assert that the Bible is an infallible authority on everything, literally interpreted, in defiance of the natural sciences and of other learned disciplines; to claim to have received private revelations from Jehovah; or to embrace some self-proclaimed mystic from the gorgeous East, whose teachings are patently absurd.

In short, the culture can be renewed only if the cult is renewed; and faith in divine power cannot be summoned up merely when that is found expedient. Faith no longer works wonders among us: one has but to glance at the typical church built nowadays, ugly and shoddy, to discern how architecture no longer is nurtured by the religious imagination. It is so in nearly all the works of twentieth-century civilization: the modern mind has been secularized so thoroughly that "culture" is assumed by most people to have no connection with the love of God.

How are we to account for this widespread decay of the religious impulse? It appears that the principal cause of the loss of the idea of the holy is the attitude called "scientism"—that is, the popular notion that the revelations of natural science, over the past century and a half or two centuries, somehow have proved that men and women are naked apes merely; that the ends of existence are production and consumption merely; that happiness is the gratification of sensual impulses; and that concepts of the resurrection of the flesh and the life everlasting are mere exploded superstitions. Upon these scientistic assumptions, public schooling in America is founded nowadays, implicitly.

This view of the human condition has been called—by C S. Lewis, in particular—reductionism: it reduces human beings almost to mindlessness; it denies the existence of the soul. Reductionism has become almost an ideology. It is scientistic, but not scientific: for it is a far cry from the understanding of matter and energy that one finds in the addresses of Nobel prize winners in physics, say. Popular notions of "what science says" are archaic, reflecting the assertions of the scientists of the middle of the nineteenth century; such views are a world away from the writings of Stanley Jaki, the cosmologist and historian of science, who was awarded the Templeton Prize for progress in religion.

As Arthur Koestler remarks in his little book *The Roots of Coincidence,* yesterday's scientific doctrines of materialism and mechanism ought to be buried now with a requiem of electronic music. Once more, in biology as in physics, the scientific disciplines enter upon the realm of mystery.

Yet the great public always suffers from the affliction called cultural lag. If most people continue to fancy that scientific theory of a century ago is the verdict of serious scientists today, will not the religious understanding of life continue to wither, and civilization continue to crumble?

*   *   *

Perhaps; but the future is unknowable. Conceivably we may be given a Sign. Yet such an event, if it is to occur at all, is in the hand of God. Meanwhile, some reflective people declare that our culture must be reanimated, by a great effort of will.

More than forty years ago, that remarkable historian Christopher Dawson, in his book *Religion and Culture*, expressed this hard truth strongly. "The events of the last few years," Dawson wrote, "portend either the end of human history or a turning point in it. They have warned us in letters of fire that our civilization has been tried in the balance and found wanting—that there is an absolute limit to the progress that can be achieved by the perfectionment of scientific techniques detached from spiritual aims and moral values.... The recovery of moral control and the return to spiritual order have become the indispensable conditions of human survival. But they can be achieved only by a profound change in the spirit of modern civilization. This does not mean a new religion or a new culture but a movement of spiritual reintegration which would restore that vital relation between religion and culture which has existed at every age and on every level of human development."

Amen to that. The alternative to such a successful endeavor, a conservative endeavor, to reinvigorate our culture would be a series of catastrophic events, the sort predicted by Pitirim Sorokin and other sociologists, which eventually might efface our present sensate culture and bring about a new ideational culture, the character of which we cannot even imagine. Such an ideational culture doubtless would have its religion: but it might be the worship of what has been called the Savage God.

Such ruin has occurred repeatedly in history. When the classical religion ceased to move hearts and minds, two millennia ago, thus the Graeco-Roman civilization went down to Avernus. As my little daughter Cecilia put it unprompted, some years ago looking at a picture book of Roman history, "And then, at the end of a long summer's day, there came Death, Mud, Crud."

Great civilizations have ended in slime. Outside the ancient city of York, where York Minster stands upon the site of the Roman praetorium, there lies a racecourse known as the Knavesmire. Here in medieval time were buried the knaves—the felons and paupers. When, a few years ago, the racecourse was being enlarged, the diggers came upon a Roman graveyard beneath, or in part abutting upon, the medieval burial ground. This appeared to have been a cemetery of the poor of Romano-British times. Few valuable artifacts were uncovered, but the bones were of interest. Many of the people there interred, in the closing years of Roman power in Britain, had been severely deformed, apparently suffering from rickets and other afflictions—deformed spines and limbs and skulls. Presumably they had suffered lifelong, and died, from extreme malnutrition. At the end, decadence comes down to that, for nearly everybody.

It was at York that the dying Septimius Severus, after his last campaign (against the Scots), was asked by his brutal sons, Geta and Caracalla, "Father, when you are gone, how shall we govern the empire?" The hard old emperor had his laconic reply ready: "Pay the soldiers. The rest do not matter." There would come a time when the soldiers could not be paid, and then civilization would fall to pieces. The last Roman army in Italy—it is said to have been composed entirely of cavalry—fought in league with the barbarian general Odoacer against Theodoric, King of the Ostrogoths, in the year 491; on Odoacer's defeat, the Roman soldiers drifted home, nevermore to take arms: the end of an old song. Only the earlier stages of social decadence seem liberating to some people; the last act, as Cecilia Kirk perceived, consists of Death, Mud, Crud.

In short, it appears to me that our culture labors in an advanced state of decadence; that what many people mistake for the triumph of our civilization actually consists of powers that are disintegrating our culture; that the vaunted "democratic freedom" of liberal society in reality is servitude to appetites and illusions which attack religious belief; which destroy community through excessive centralization and urbanization; which efface life-giving tradition and custom.

> *History has many cunning passages, contrived corridors*
> *And issues, deceives with whispering ambitions,*
> *Guides us by vanities.*

So Gerontion instructs us, in T. S. Eliot's famous grim poem. By those and some succeeding lines, Eliot means that human experience lived without the Logos, the Word; lived merely by the asserted knowledge of empirical science—why, history in that sense is a treacherous gypsy witch. Civilizations that reject or abandon the religious imagination must end, as did Gerontion, in fractured atoms.

*   *   *

In conclusion, it is my argument that the elaborate civilization we have known stands in peril; that it may expire of lethargy, or be destroyed by violence, or perish, from a combination of both evils. We who think that life remains worth living ought to address ourselves to means by which a restoration of our culture may be achieved. A prime necessity for us is to restore an apprehension of religious insights in our clumsy apparatus of public instruction, which—bullied by militant secular humanists and presumptuous federal courts—has been left with only ruinous answers to the ultimate questions.

What ails modern civilization? Fundamentally, our society's affliction is the decay of religious belief. If a culture is to survive and flourish, it must not be severed from the religious vision out of which it arose. The high necessity of reflective men and women, then, is to labor for the restoration of religious teachings as a credible body of doctrine.

"Redeem the time; redeem the dream," T. S. Eliot wrote. It remains possible, given right reason and moral imagination, to confront boldly the age's disorders. The restoration of true learning, humane and scientific; the reform of many public policies; the renewal of our awareness of a transcendent order, and of the presence of an Other; the brightening of the corners where we find ourselves—such approaches are open to those among the rising generation who look for a purpose in life. It is just conceivable that we may be given a Sign before the end of the twentieth century; yet Sign or no Sign, a Remnant must strive against the follies of the time.

II

The Fraud of Multiculturalism

What is called *order*, a word signifying harmonious arrangement, has two aspects when we discuss the diverse cultures of humankind. The first of these is order in the soul: what is called moral order. The second of these is order in the commonwealth: what is called constitutional order. In both its aspects, order stands endangered today, requiring vigorous defense.

Six decades ago in *The Revolt of the Masses*, José Ortega y Gasset wrote that American civilization could not long survive any catastrophe to European society. This remains true, and particularly true with respect to Britain. America's higher culture, and the American civil social order, are derived from institutions and concepts that arose to the east of the Atlantic Ocean. Americans are part of a great continuity and essence.

America and Britain and their cultural dependencies share a common religious heritage, a common history in large part, a common pattern of law and politics, and a common body of great literature. Yet American citizens and British subjects cannot be wholly confident that their order will endure forever. It is possible to exhaust moral and social capital; a society relying altogether upon its patrimony soon may find itself bankrupt. With civilization, as with the human body, conservation and renewal are possible only if healthful change and reinvigoration occur from age to age. It is by no means certain that our present moral and constitutional order is providing sufficiently for its own future. Modern men pay a great deal of attention to material and technological means, but little attention to the instruments by which any generation must fulfill its part in the contract of eternal society.

*   *   *

Twentieth-century mankind, in Britain and in America, have tended to be contemptuous of the past; yet they contribute little enough of their own, except in technology and applied sciences, toward the preservation of a tolerable order, let alone its improvement. The facile optimism of the nineteenth and early twentieth centuries is much diminished nowadays, but this does not signify that naive notions of inevitable Progress have been supplanted by serious reflection on the problem of how to conserve and to renew our cultural patrimony. The present threat to the inner order and the outer order comes as much from indifference, empathy, and selfishness as it comes from totalist political powers. Pessimism for pessimism's sake is as fatuous as is optimism for optimism's sake. Grim symptoms may be discerned of an absolute decline of the higher culture in both America and Britain, and also symptoms of a decline of the ties that have joined the English-speaking cultures on either side of the Atlantic. How may decay be arrested?

In any age, some people revolt against their own inheritance of order—and soon find themselves plunged into what Edmund Burke called "the antagonist world of madness, discord, vice, confusion, and unavailing sorrow." Near the end of the twentieth century, the number of such enemies to order has become alarming. A spirit of defiance or biting criticism that may be healthful, when confined to a creative minority, can become perilous if it is taken up unimaginatively by a popular majority. To the folk who rebel against their patrimony of moral and constitutional order, that legacy seems a burden—when in truth it is a footing. Cultural restoration, like charity, begins at home; and so I touch here upon symptoms of neglect of the common inheritance of America.

Religious faith, whether Catholic, Protestant, or Judaic, seems enfeebled in the United States. Many of the clergy tend markedly toward a sentimental and humanitarian application of religious teachings; they incline toward the radical alteration of society at the expense of the transcendent ends of religion and of any personal obedience to moral teachings.

As for the legacy of ordered liberty, there, too, one finds cause for misgiving. Even among judges and lawyers, one encounters a growing disregard of the old principles of justice and jurisprudence; and one encounters, too, an overwhelming tendency toward concentration of power in centralized governments.

*   *   *

The causes of such drifts may be found, in part, in the gradual substitution of "pragmatic" standards for old principles of jurisprudence and inherited political institutions. With few exceptions, schools of law have encouraged this progress. There may come to pass the triumph of what Eric Voegelin called "theoretical illiteracy" in law and politics. A university student of considerable native intelligence inquires of me why checks and balances are at all desirable in politics. Why should we not simply train up an elite of governmental administrators, he inquires, trust to their good will and abilities, and let them manage the concerns of the nation?

This growing naïveté, born of an ignorance of the political and legal institutions of the British-American culture, too often passes unchallenged by disciples of the pragmatic and technical method-ologies dominant in schools of public administration and in gov-ernmental research. This simplicity also reflects a wondrous un-awareness of human nature and of statecraft. It is the attitude that Lord Percy of Newcastle denominated "totalist democracy"—a trust in an abstraction called The People, combined with an unquestioning faith in The Expert.

Theoretical illiteracy in politics and jurisprudence is paralleled by a decline of true apprehension of humane letters. In the Anglo-American culture, the study of great literature has pursued an ethical end through an intellectual means. The improvement of reason and conscience for the person's own sake, and the incidental improvement of society thereby, was the object of the traditional literary disciplines. The present generation of schoolchildren is expected, instead, to "learn to live with all the world, in one global village"—a consummation to be achieved, perhaps, by scissors-and-paste projects.

When poetry is replaced by "communication skills" and narrative history by vague sociological generalizations, the intricate patri-mony of general culture is threatened. There exist professors of education who argue that no young person ought to read any book more than half a century old. The imaginative and rational disci-plines, so painfully cultivated over centuries, can be permanently injured by a generation or two of neglect and contempt.

*   *   *

Modern men and women live in an age in which the expectation of change often seems greater than the expectation of continuity. In any order worthy of the name, men and women must be something better than the flies of a summer; generation must link with generation. Some people, in this closing decade of the twentieth century, are doing what is in their power to preserve a common heritage. This is not a work that can be accomplished through fresh

positive laws or through the creation of new international commis-
sions. Yet if a people forget the ashes of their fathers and the temples
of their gods, the consequences soon will be felt in the laws and in
international affairs. Cultural continuity lacking, there remains
small point in political tinkering with a body social that has become
exhausted spiritually and intellectually.

A French aphorism instructs us that the more things change, the
more they are the same. We fight over again, generation after
generation, the battle to maintain the inner order and the outer. As
T. S. Eliot wrote, there are no lost causes because there are no
gained causes. Say not the struggle naught availeth. In defense of
the order into which we have been born, one may reaffirm the
counsel of Edgar, in *King Lear:*

> *Take heed o' th' foul fiend; obey thy parents; keep thy word
> justly; swear not; commit not with man's sworn spouse; set
> not thy sweet heart on proud array.... Keep thy foot out of
> brothels, thy hand out of plackets, thy pen from lender's books,
> and defy the foul fiend.*

From Shakespeare, as from other most memorable dead, comes
the energy that sustains people in a time of tribulation. The order,
inner and outer, of our common culture is defended not by the living
merely, but by the valiant dead as well.

*   *   *

From time to time, during this twentieth century, some American
voices have been raised in dispraise of America's inheritance of
British culture. One such assault occurred about the middle forties;
it was renewed a decade later. Even some American scholars of
good repute suggest that it would be well to drop from formal

instruction most of our baggage of British literature, and to concentrate instead upon native American verse and prose; certain language associations embrace this line; buy the homegrown product! In effect these literary nationalists advocate a cultural Tariff of Abominations.

Dr. Louis B. Wright, then director of the Folger Shakespeare Library in Washington, took up his cudgel about 1952 in defense of a civilized heritage, against academic allies of barbarism. In his lively book *Culture on the Moving Frontier,* Dr. Wright repeatedly and persuasively digressed from his narrative to point out the essentially British character of American institutions and the American realm of reason and of art. He wrote in his first chapter:

> Modern America is so polyglot, and social historians have devoted so much attention in recent years to analyzing and describing the multifarious European, Asiatic, and African influences in the development of American life that we are now in danger of underestimating and even forgetting the oldest, the most persistent, and the most vigorous strain in our cultural inheritance. Great Britain's influence is still so strong that it subtly determines qualities of mind and character in Americans who cannot claim a drop of Anglo-Saxon blood.... If there were no other legacy from the past except the English language and its literature, that alone would be sufficient to explain the durability and strength of the tradition.

Four decades after Professor Wright reproved thus the Goths and Vandals within the Ivory Tower, a new horde of adversaries is bent upon deconstructing the edifice of Anglo-American culture. The principal accrediting associations of the United States, indeed, have menaced colleges and universities with disaccreditation unless they promptly proceed to enter upon programs of multiculturalism, permeating the whole curriculum. And various academic presidents and deans have supinely submitted to this intellectual bullying.

One encounters in today's American education, truly, a great deal of dullness, at every level; and much intellectual provinciality, too. Ever since the Second World War, indeed, oddly enough, American schooling, from kindergarten through graduate school, has sunk farther and farther into the provinciality of place and time, so that the rising generation grows up unicultural, notably ignorant of other countries and other cultures, despite the tremendous ascendancy of the United States in world affairs.

*   *   *

Six decades ago, when I was enrolled in a public grade school not far from great railway yards outside Detroit, nobody thought of demanding multiculturalism: we already possessed that in our school. In geography class, we learned a great deal about the cultures of five continents; we were very interested. Many of us, a few years later, enrolled (during high school) in three years of history: ancient, modern, and American. At least half of us took two years of language, either Latin or French, with corresponding instruction about Roman civilization or French culture; some pupils finished four years of foreign language. Our intelligent courses in English and American literature helped to redeem us from what T. S. Eliot called "the provincialism of time." We were much aware of diversity in the world and in our own country.

Today the radical multiculturalists complain, or rather shout, that African, Asian, and Latin American cultures have been shamefully neglected in North America's schools. In that they are correct enough. In many primary, intermediate, and high schools nowadays—aye, in colleges, too—the offering in the discipline of history amounts only to a whirlwind "Survey of World History" (with

Good Guys and Bad Guys occasionally pointed out by the teacher, amidst the violent dust storm), and perhaps a year of American history, often ideologically distorted. As for geography, that virtually has gone by the board; at least one famous state university, a few years ago, swept away altogether its department of geography. Even at boarding schools of good repute and high fees, the teaching of humane letters is very nearly confined to reading and discussing some recent ephemeral novels.

Sixty years ago, most school pupils were taught a good deal about the people and the past of Bolivia, Morocco, China, India, Egypt, Guatemala, and other lands. They even learnt about Eskimo and Aleut cultures. Nowadays pupils are instructed in the disciplines of sexology, driver education, sex education, and the sterile abstractions of Social Studies. Formerly all pupils studied for several years the principal British and American poets, essayists, novelists and dramatists—this with the purpose of developing their moral imagination. Nowadays they are assigned the prose of "relevance" and "current awareness" at most schools. Indeed a great deal of alleged "education," either side of the Ocean Sea, requires medication or surgery.

*   *   *

But what the curious sect of multiculturalists prescribe, in Britain as in America, is poison. There is reason to suspect that such multiculturalists as Leonard Jeffries, a black radical professor at the City College of New York, hope to bring down the whole edifice of pedagogy—so as to hold among the ruins perpetual "rap sessions" about indignities once suffered by blacks.[1]

Yet suppose that the multiculturalists were sincere in their professions of desire to redress the balance by reducing emphases upon Eurocentric and British culture, and introducing new programs to describe other cultures that have affected the United States—why, how might the thing be accomplished? The number of hours in an academic day is limited. How would a multicultural curriculum deal with the worthy contributions of Armenians, Syrians, Lebanese, Iraqi Chaldeans, Russians, Ukrainians, Poles, Serbs, Maltese, Croats, Puerto Ricans, Czechs, Chinese, Vietnamese, Mexicans, Hungarians, and a score of other "minorities" that inhabit the city of Detroit, say? Early in 1991, the Detroit School Board instructed publishers of textbooks that the Board would give short shrift to any school manuals that did not fully emphasize the contributions of Afro-Americans to American culture. Are textbooks for instruction, or are they to become merely devices for "increasing the self-esteem" of ethnic groups?

*   *   *

Even before multiculturalism was taken seriously by anybody, it was sufficiently difficult to publish a textbook that objectively dealt with its subject. A decade ago, I was editing a series of social science manuals. In a history textbook, it had been found prudent to insert a chapter on the Mongols—giving those devastators equal space and classroom time with Hellenes and Romans. In that chapter appeared the phrase "the charge of the barbarian horsemen." Our textbooks were printed and distributed by a commercial textbook publisher, acting for our council. A woman editor of that firm instructed me, "There may have been women among them. Change your phrase to 'the charge of the barbarian horsepersons.'" I replied to her that in historical fact, the ferocious cavalry of Genghis Khan included no females; and that I knew of no American woman who would be gratified by being labeled a "barbarian horseperson." Such are the difficulties that arise when objective scholarship is subject to the whims of all "minorities"—and, moreover, those "minorities" are engaged in endless warfare, one against another.

It is well to learn much about distant cultures. When a sophomore in college, this present writer spent a whole year reading rare works about travels in Africa, borrowed from the shelves of the

Library of the State of Michigan—considerably to the neglect of the conventional disciplines for which he was being graded at his college. But to neglect or to repudiate the central and pervasive British culture in America would be to let the whole academic and social enterprise fall apart, "The centre cannot hold; / Mere anarchy is loosed upon the world...."

May the Anglo-American culture, so battered by the pace of change during the twentieth century, so damaged by ideological assaults these past several decades, be restored to health? (It is one culture, really, that complex of literature and law and government and mores which still makes civilization possible in both the United States and Britain. Of the three major poets in the English language during the twentieth century—T. S. Eliot, Robert Frost, William Butler Yeats—two were American-born, a fact suggesting that British and American cultures have coalesced.) No culture endures forever: Of those that have vanished, some have fallen to alien conquerors, as did Roman Britain; but most have expired in consequence of internal decay. When the cult failed, the culture presently crumbled to powder. Will the American culture and the British expire jointly "not with a bang, but a whimper"? One thinks of the Chorus in Sir Osbert Sitwell's long poem "Demos the Emperor":

> *We are the modern masters of the world,*
> *The arbiters, the heirs*
> *Of Egypt, Greece and Italy*
> *(We have no time for art*
> *But we know what we like!)*
> *We are the fulfillment of Man's Promise*
> *The Cup-tie Final and the paper cap;*
> *We are the Soul of the Cash Register,*
> *The Secret of the Hire-Purchase System,*
> *The Vacuum, and the Vacuum-Cleaner.*[2]

Perhaps. And yet, great cultures commonly pass through alternating periods of decay and renewal, flickering out finally after many centuries. Byzantine Civilization is our clearest instance of this process. The culture from which Anglo-American culture developed extends back more than three thousand years, to Moses and Aaron. Cultures cannot be deliberately created; they arise, rather, from the theophanic events that bring cults into existence. It remains conceivable, nevertheless, that cultures may be *reinvigorated.*

*   *   *

If America's British culture is to be reinvigorated, its roots must be watered. The twentieth-century guardians of that culture must reject such silliness as the multiculturalist ideology, which does nothing more than gratify little ethnic vanities. Those guardians—who are the whole class of tolerably educated Americans—must resist those ideologues of multiculturalism who would pull down the whole elaborate existing culture of this country in order to make everybody culturally equal—that is equal in ignorance. On this point, Louis B. Wright deserves to be quoted a final time:

> For better or for worse, we have inherited the fundamental qualities in our culture from the British. For that reason we need to take a long perspective of our history, a perspective which views America from at least the period of the first Tudor monarchs and lets us see the gradual development of our common civilization, its transmission across the Atlantic, and its expansion and modification as it was adapted to conditions in the Western Hemisphere. We should not overlook other influences which have affected American life, influences from France, Holland, Spain, Germany, Scandinavia, and the rest of Europe, and also influences from Asia and

Africa. But we must always remember that such was the vigor of British culture that it assimilated all others. That is not to say that we have been transmogrified into Englishmen, or that we are even Anglophile in sentiment. But we cannot escape an inheritance which has given us some of our sturdiest and most lasting qualities.

Arnold Toynbee instructs us that cultures develop, and civilizations arise, by the process of challenge and response. Some threat to a culture's survival may occur; if that culture vigorously surmounts that challenge, the culture will grow in strength. But if the challenge is so formidable as to damage or distort the culture—why, the threatened culture becomes stunted and possibly succumbs altogether.

The ideology called multiculturalism might benefit American society, after all—in the sense that it is a challenge (if a foolish challenge) to the friends of America's inherited culture. If the response to the multiculturalist threat is healthy, it should rouse again among Americans an apprehension of the high merits of the literature, the language, the laws, the political institutions, and the mores that Americans have received, in the course of four centuries, from the British people. For if a civilization never is challenged, that civilization tends to sink into apathy—and slowly to dissolution.

Multiculturalism is animated by envy and hatred. Some innocent persons have assumed that a multicultural program in schools would consist of discussing the latest number of *The National Geographic Magazine* in a classroom. That is not at all what the multiculturalists intend. Detesting the achievements of Anglo-American culture, they propose to substitute for real history and real literature—and even for real natural science—an invented myth that all things good came out of Africa and Asia (chiefly Africa).

Intellectually, multiculturalism is puny—and anti-cultural. Such power as the multiculturalist ideologues possess is derived from political manipulation: that is, claiming to speak for America's militant "minorities" (chiefly those of African descent). These ideologues take advantage of the sentimentality of American liberals, eager to placate such "minorities" by granting them whatever they demand. But what fanatic ideologues demand commonly is bad for the class of persons they claim to represent, as it is bad, too, for everybody else. To deny "minorities" the benefits of America's established culture would work their ruin.

"Culture, with us, ends in headache," Ralph Waldo Emerson wrote of Americans in 1841. Should the multiculturalists have their way, culture, with us Americans a century and a half later, would end in heartache—and in anarchy. But to this challenge of multiculturalism, presumably the established American culture, with its British roots, still can respond with vigor—a life-renewing response. Love of an inherited culture has the power to cast out the envy and hatred of that culture's adversaries.

Notes

1. Jeffries drafted the report "A Curriculum of Inclusion" to submit to the New York Board of Regents. In 1991, Mr. Jeffries indulged himself in denunciation of the Jews, some of them having been obstacles in his deconstructive path; his epithets opened the eyes of persons who had fancied that multiculturalism was merely an endeavor to inform the rising generation about the contributions made to American civilization by folk from many lands.

2. Published in 1949.

III

The Tension of Order and Freedom in the University

Universities were founded to sustain faith by reason—and to maintain order in the soul and in the commonwealth. My own university, St. Andrews, was established in the fifteenth century by the Scottish Inquisitor of Heretical Pravity, to resist the errors of the Lollards, the levellers of that age. The early universities' teaching imparted both order and freedom to the intellect; and that was no paradox, for order and freedom exist necessarily in a healthy tension.

But in our day, as in various earlier times, many universities have lost any clear general understanding of either freedom or order, intellectually considered. So it seems worthwhile to review here the relationship between order and freedom, and the part of a university in maintaining the tension between the two.

Indulge me first in some observations concerning the connections among faith, order, and freedom, all of which are intertwined in university studies. In recent generations, many professors have failed to apprehend the connections. Let us commence with that popular but vague term "freedom."

Freedom is normal for mankind. I mean that ordered liberty is natural for truly human persons. Yet human freedom, like much else in human normality, is denied at least as often as it is affirmed.

The word "normal" does not really mean "average" or "generally accepted": it means "enduring standard." Human beings have the power either of observing the norms of their nature, or of violating them. So it is that the periods of true social freedom, throughout the course of history, have been shorter than the periods of servitude. Men and women have the privilege and the peril of choosing the life they will lead. Much of the time, in ages past as today, men have used their moral freedom to choose slavery or anarchy instead of ordered liberty.

Living as we Americans do in a nation still substantially free, and perhaps at the end of what has been called the "liberal era," many of us take for granted a degree of freedom which has been bestowed upon us by the painful labors and experiences of our ancestors, over many generations—and which may be ruined in the space of a few years, by folly or neglect. Freedom already has vanished from much of the modern world, and in many lands it never took root. Unless we understand the origins and ends of our liberty, we Americans may learn what it is to lose freedom in a fit of absence of mind. And if the nature of freedom is misunderstood in the universities, it will be misunderstood everywhere.

As I read history, it seems to me that a high degree of ordered, civilized freedom is linked closely with religious belief. Most liberals of the eighteenth and nineteenth centuries were willing enough to agree that there existed some connection between liberty and property. Yet many of those liberals ignored or denied the bond between religious faith and ordered freedom. "We learn from history that we learn nothing from history," Hegel wrote, in irony. If the great troubles of our time teach mankind anything, surely we ought now to recognize that true freedom cannot endure in a society which denies a transcendent order. A university that ridicules the claims of the transcendent must end without intellectual coherence—and without genuine intellectual freedom.

The first people to be freed from the spiritual bondage of the ancient empires were the Hebrews. It was consciousness of their duty and their hope as children of God which gave them resolution to withstand the life-in-death of the great nations that surrounded them.

A degree of personal freedom still higher was achieved by certain Greek peoples in the sixth and fifth centuries before Christ. This noble freedom decayed when the old Greek religion and morality gave way to sophistry, and "the rude son might strike the father dead." The genius of Socrates, Plato, and Aristotle did not suffice to restore the Greek freedom of spirit and law, once belief in the divine ordering of things had dissolved.

Among the Romans, freedom endured so long as the high old Roman virtue prevailed: so long as the Roman piety moved men, the disciplines of *labor, pietas, fatum.* Yet out of the ruins of Rome grew the highest order of liberty man has known: Christian freedom. The depressed masses of the proletariat were given hope by the promise of Christ; the barbarians were taught restraint by the Word. Humanity learnt the lesson of the suffering servant, and came to know that the service of God is perfect freedom.

Medieval liberties, in great part, were the product of Christian belief. The rights of the towns, the independence of the guilds, the code of chivalry—these arose out of faith in what Burke was to call "the contract of eternal society."

So modern freedom is not the recent creation of a few enthusiastic revolutionaries. Rather, it is a heritage laboriously developed in suffering. Freedom cannot endure unless we are willing to nurture that religious understanding which is its sanction; unless we maintain the springs of ordered liberty. It is worth remarking that the nineteenth-century ideology of "liberalism" generally ignored its religious sources. Some of these liberals, deficient in understanding of the sources, thought of freedom as wholly secular and utilitarian, man-made. Others thought of freedom as a political abstraction, unrelated to religious concepts or to ancient usages. Both these "liberal" views have been hostile toward the Christian idea of the "person" under God. Such liberalism has dominated the universities for a century and more—and not state universities merely.

As we near the end of the twentieth century, when much of the world is subject to arbitrary dominations, it is the urgent duty of the university to restore an apprehension of the sources of freedom. Even among a people who boast of their liberty, freedom may be lost at the moment of its seeming triumph. Stand upon the Acropolis of Athens, or on the Roman Capitoline, or on the Rock of Athena at Agrigento, and look upon the ruins. The material splendor of those societies was at its height not long before the collapse of faith and liberty. In the name of democracy, of equality, of social justice, it is possible to overturn speedily the genuine order and justice and freedom of modern civilization. "And that house fell; and great was the fall of that house." The university—which Dante called one of the three powers governing society, along with church and state—can ignore the true character of freedom only at the university's grave peril. So let me turn to some brief observations on the relationship between freedom and order, considered intellectually and socially.

*   *   *

"Orders and degrees," John Milton says, "jar not with liberty, but well consist." I believe that we will be unable, in the university or out of it, to maintain any successful defense of our freedoms until we recognize afresh those principles of order under which freedom in our heritage acquired real meaning. Every right is married to a duty; every freedom owes a corresponding responsibility; and there cannot be genuine freedom unless there exists also genuine order, in the moral realm and in the social realm.

I am saying this: in any just society, there subsists a healthy tension between the claims of order and the claims of freedom. When that tension is well maintained, it is possible to obtain a large measure of justice. This clear understanding was the principal contribution of Edmund Burke to political theory; and the attempt to achieve such a tension or balance is the principal problem of modern practical politics.

Order, in the moral realm, is the realizing of a body of transcendent norms—indeed a hierarchy of norms or standards—which give purpose to existence and motive to conduct. Order, in society, is the harmonious arrangement of classes and functions which guards justice and obtains willing consent to law and ensures that we all shall be safe together. Although there cannot be freedom without order, in some sense there occurs always a conflict between the claims of order and the claims of freedom. Often we express this conflict as the competition between the desire for liberty and the desire for security.

Modern technological developments and modern mass democracy have made this struggle more intense. President Washington observed that "individuals entering into a society must give up a share of their liberty to preserve the rest." Yet doctrinaires of one ideology or another, in our time, continue to cry out for absolute security, absolute order; or for absolute freedom, power to assert the ego in defiance of all convention. During the past two decades, this clash was readily observed on the typical American campus.

I suggest that in asserting freedom as an absolute, somehow divorced from order, we repudiate our heritage of practical liberty and expose ourselves to the peril of absolutism—whether that absolutism be what Tocqueville calls "democratic despotism" or what recently existed in Germany and Russia, and now stands triumphant in China and other countries. "To begin with unlimited freedom," Dostoevski wrote in *The Devils*, "is to end with unlimited despotism."

When some people—E. H. Carr in England, for instance, or David Lilienthal in America—talk of "freedom," they seem to mean, really, "material prosperity for the many." Now material prosperity, pure "economic security," is not the same thing as either freedom or order. Nor is it the same thing as happiness. An Athenian slave might be more comfortable than many a freeman, but he was not free.

It is quite possible that the person who desires freedom and the benefits of order must be prepared to sacrifice a degree of security. A slave, in Aristotle's definition, is a being who allows others to make his choices for him. It is quite possible for a man to be materially prosperous, freed from the necessity of choice, and yet servile. It also is possible that such a man may suffer no outrageous personal oppression. But he must always lack one thing, this servile man, and that is true manhood, the dignity of man. He remains a child; he never comes into man's birthright, which is the pleasure and the pain of making one's own choices.

Some of these problems of freedom upon which I have touched glancingly here are examined by John Stuart Mill in his essay *On Liberty*—a little treatise that has done much to confuse universities' discussion of freedom, from his day to ours. There may be found value in that essay; but I think there also is weakness in it, and peril; and adulation of Mill tends to confuse serious discussion of the difficulties of liberty today. We live in the twentieth century, not the nineteenth, and we now experience distresses to which Mill never was exposed. Yet Dr. Henry Steele Commager, not many years ago, informed us that "we cannot too often repair to John Stuart Mill's *On Liberty*," implying that this essay, like the laws of the Medes and the Persians, is immutable. Mill was unaware of any difficulty in closely defining "liberty"—unlike Cicero, who saw the necessity for distinguishing between *libido* and *voluntas*. To Mill, "liberty" might mean "doing as one likes" or "pursuing one's own good in one's own way" or acting "according to one's own inclination and judgment."

At present, Mill's arguments are being employed interestingly by persons who pretend to believe in an absolute freedom that no society ever has been able to maintain—and this in an age which requires the highest degree of cooperation, when "the great wheel of circulation" upon which our economy and our security depend necessarily is more to us than ever before. Such use of the writings of Mill—or those of a different sort of philosopher, Rousseau— may be encountered among enthusiasts of the New Left, and also among zealots of the "libertarian" Right. Some of these persons curiously archaic in their opinions—although they pride themselves upon their preoccupation with "relevance"—are oldfangled Benthamite liberals, dedicated to economic individualism in the age of the atomic pile; others (and these the more ominous) are the newfangled collectivistic liberals, desirous of receiving everything from the state, but insistent that they owe nothing in return—not even loyalty.

So my general argument is this: liberty, prescriptive freedom as we Americans have known it, cannot endure without order. Our constitutions were established that order might make possible true freedom. Despite all our American talk of private judgment, dissent, and individualism, still our national character has the stamp of a respect for order almost superstitious in its power: respect for the moral order ordained by religion, and for the prescriptive political forms that we, more than any other people in this twentieth century, have maintained little altered. We would work immense mischief to our freedom if we ceased to respect our established order, running instead after an abstract, Jacobin liberty.

What is deficient in the thought of Mill and his disciples, it seems to me, is an adequate understanding of the principles of order. First, any coherent and beneficial freedom, surely, must have the sanction of moral order: it must refer to doctrines, religious in origin, that establish a hierarchy of values and set bounds to the ego. Second, any coherent and beneficial freedom must know the check of social order: it must accord with a rule of law, regular in its operation, that recognizes and enforces prescriptive rights, protects minorities against majorities and majorities against minorities, and gives meaning to the concept of human dignity.

Freedom as an abstraction is the liberty in whose name crimes are committed. But freedom, as realized in the separate, limited, balanced, well-defined rights of persons and groups, operating through historical development within a society moved by moral principles, is the quality which makes it possible for men and women to become fully human.

These things have been said often before. But every grand question has to be argued afresh in every generation—especially in the universities. We need, I repeat, to refresh the understanding of "freedom" even among the learned, or perhaps especially among the learned.

For when many people, professors included, employ nowadays this word "freedom," they use it in the sense of the French Revolutionaries: freedom from tradition, from established social institutions, from religious doctrines, from prescriptive duties. One thinks of Robert Louis Stevenson's little exercise in mockery, "The Four Reformers":

"Four reformers met under a bramble bush. They were all agreed that the world must be changed. 'We must abolish property,' said one.

"'We must abolish marriage,' said the second.

"'We must abolish God,' said the third.

"'I wish we could abolish work,' said the fourth.

"'Do not let us get beyond practical politics,' said the first. 'The first thing is to reduce men to a common level.'

"'The first thing,' said the second, 'is to give freedom to the sexes.'

"'The first thing,' said the third, 'is to find out how to do it.'

"'The first step,' said the first, 'is to abolish the Bible.'

"'The first thing,' said the second, 'is to abolish the laws.'

"'The first thing,' said the third, 'is to abolish mankind.'"

This mood is what Santayana mordantly called "freedom from the consequences of freedom," confounding nihilism with liberation. For we do not live in an age that is oppressed by the dead weight of archaic establishments and obsolete customs. The peril in our time, rather, is that the foundations of the great deep will be broken up, and that the swift pace of alteration will make it impossible for generation to link with generation. Our era, necessarily, should be what Matthew Arnold called an epoch of concentration. Or, at least, the thinking American, in the university as out of it, needs to turn his talents to concentration, the reconstruction of our moral and social heritage. This is an age not for anarchic freedom, but for ordered freedom.

There survive older and stronger concepts of freedom than that proclaimed by the Jacobins; and more consistent concepts than that of Mill. In Christian teaching, freedom is submission to the will of God. This is no paradox. As he who would save his life must lose it, so the person who desires true freedom must recognize an order that gives all freedoms their sanction. This lacking, freedom becomes at best the liberty of those who possess power at the moment to do as they like with the lives and the property of persons whose interests conflict with theirs.

In the Christian understanding, as in the Judaic tradition and the Stoic philosophy and in Indic thought, there subsists also the conviction that freedom may be attained through abstinence. Not to lust after the things of the flesh, or after power, or after fame: this is true freedom, the freedom of Stilbo confronting the conqueror, or of Socrates before the Athenian jury. This is the freedom of

Diogenes asking Alexander to stand out of the sun. The man who has made his peace with the universe is free, however poor he may be; the man bent upon gratifying his appetites is servile, however rich he may be. This freedom from desire, once taught within universities, has a strange ring in universities of our day.

Personal freedom must be found within a moral order. And public freedom must be found within a well-maintained social order; it must be the product of a common historical experience, of custom, of convention. We live in an age which, for good or ill, has come to depend upon the highest degree of cooperation and discipline ever known to civilization. Our economy, our very political structure, might not abide for twenty-four hours the triumph of that "absolute liberty" of the individual preached by Lamartine and other political enthusiasts of the nineteenth century. As Simone Weil put it, "Order is the first need of all."

*　　　*　　　*

Within today's university, collectivistic prejudices and libertarian prejudices frequently coexist within the same professor, an insane conjunction. Both collectivism and libertarianism are the enemies of ordered freedom.

Once upon a time, the university maintained authority; indeed, the university was authority. But today a great many people within the Academy will submit to no authority, temporal or spiritual. They desire to be different, in morals as in politics. In our highly tolerant society, such extreme individualism seems an amusing pose. Its consequences may become unamusing.

Against license, anarchy, and chaos, the university was raised up, to restrain passion and prejudice through right reason. What the university offers to intellects is discipline and order. Through such intellectual order and discipline, rational liberty of the person and of the society is made possible. This is true of the humane and the social studies; it is quite as true of the physical sciences. The university is one important response to the universal menace of chaos. I think of some sentences written by an English biologist, Lyall Watson.

"Chaos is coming," Dr. Watson reminds us. "It is written in the laws of thermodynamics. Left to itself, everything tends to become more and more disorderly until the final and natural state of things is a completely random distribution of matter. Any kind of order, even that as simple as the arrangement of atoms in a molecule, is unnatural and happens only by chance encounters that reverse the general trend. These events are statistically unlikely, and the further combination of molecules into anything as highly organized as a living organism is wildly improbable. Life is a rare and unreasonable thing.

"The continuance of life depends on the maintenance of an unstable situation. It is like a vehicle that can be kept on the road only by continual running repairs and by access to an endless supply of spare parts. Life draws its components from the environment. From the vast mass of chaotic probability flowing by, it extracts only the distinctive improbabilities, the little bits of order among the general confusion. Some of those it uses as a source of energy, which it obtains by the destructive process of digestion; from others, it gets the information it needs to ensure continued survival. This is the hardest part, extracting order from disorder, distinguishing those aspects of the environment that carry useful information from those which simply contribute to the overall process of decay. Life manages to do this by a splendid sense of the incongruous." So Watson puts this truth in his chapter entitled "Cosmic Law and Order."

The university is meant to assist in life's struggle for survival, by extracting order from disorder. Studies in seventeenth-century literature and ancient history and quantum mechanics all are paths to order. And also they are paths to freedom: for the unexamined life is a servile existence, not worth living. The university is not intended to be a staging-ground for the destruction of order in personality and order in society; on the contrary, the university's mission (to paraphrase John Henry Newman) is to impart a philosophical habit of mind.

Men and women of a philosophical habit of mind are free intellectually. If their influence upon a society is strong, that society is free politically. Such private and public freedom is made possible by the ordering of mind and conscience. For the university, as for society generally, freedom and order are ends of equal importance, existing at once in symbiosis and in tension. So it is that when a university forgets the ordering and integrating of knowledge, it impairs the freedom of the mind. And then chaos rushes upon us. In our campus disorders of the 'Sixties and 'Seventies, graduate students in the disciplines of philosophy, humane letters, and history were interestingly active in the disruption of classes, the burning of books, and the harassing of professors—which suggests our degree of success, in the typical American university, in this enterprise of developing a philosophical habit of mind. Intellectual chaos promptly brings on social chaos.

Out of faith arises order; and once order prevails, freedom becomes possible. When the faith that nurtured the order fades away, the order disintegrates; and freedom no more can survive the disappearance of order than the branch of a tree can outlast the fall of the trunk. Doubtless there will be technical schools called universities, in the twenty-first century. But whether any institutions resembling genuine universities may be found a hundred years from now—why, like much else, that will depend upon whether fidelity to a mundane order is sustained by renewed belief in a transcendent order. Meanwhile, various eminent professors are cleverly engaged in sawing off the particular limb of the tree of learning upon which they are perched; while a few scholars, aware that the dead tree gives no shelter, have grown concerned for the tree's parched roots.

IV

The Conservative Purpose of a Liberal Education

Our term "liberal education" is far older than the use of the word "liberal" as a term of politics. What we now call "liberal studies" go back to classical times; while political liberalism commences only in the first decade of the nineteenth century. By "liberal education" we mean an ordering and integrating of knowledge for the benefit of the free person—as contrasted with technical or professional schooling, now somewhat vaingloriously called "career education."

The idea of a liberal education is suggested by two passages I am about to quote to you. The first of these is extracted from Sir William Hamilton's *Metaphysics:*

> Now the perfection of man as an end and the perfection of man as a mean or instrument are not only not the same, they are in reality generally opposed. And as these two perfections are different, so the training requisite for their acquisition is not identical, and has, accordingly,

been distinguished by different names. The one is styled liberal, the other professional education—the branches of knowledge cultivated for these purposes being called respectively liberal and professional, or liberal and lucrative, sciences.

Hamilton, you will observe, informs us that one must not expect to make money out of proficiency in the liberal arts. The higher aim of "man as an end," he tells us, is the object of liberal learning. This is a salutary admonition in our time, when more and more parents fondly thrust their offspring, male and female, into schools of business administration. What did Sir William Hamilton mean by "man as an end"? Why, to put the matter another way, he meant that the function of liberal learning is to order the human soul.

Now for my second quotation, which I take from James Russell Lowell. The study of the classics, Lowell writes, "is fitly called a liberal education, because it emancipates the mind from every narrow provincialism, whether of egoism or tradition, and is the apprenticeship that every one must serve before becoming a free brother of the guild which passes the torch of life from age to age."

To put this truth after another fashion, Lowell tells us that a liberal education is intended to free us from captivity to time and place: to enable us to take long views, to understand what it is to be fully human—and to be able to pass on to generations yet unborn our common patrimony of culture. T. S. Eliot, in his lectures on "The Aims of Education" and elsewhere, made the same argument not many years ago. Neither Lowell nor Eliot labored under the illusion that the liberal discipline of the intellect would open the way to affluence.

So you will perceive that when I speak of the "conservative purpose" of liberal education, I do not mean that such a schooling is intended to be a prop somehow to business, industry, and established material interests. Neither, on the other hand, is a liberal education supposed to be a means for pulling down the economy and the state itself. No, liberal education goes about its work of conservation in a different fashion.

I mean that liberal education is conservative in this way: it defends order against disorder. In its practical effects, liberal education works for order in the soul, and order in the republic. Liberal learning enables those who benefit from its discipline to achieve some degree of harmony within themselves. As John Henry Newman put it, in Discourse V of his *Idea of a University*, by a liberal intellectual discipline, "a habit of mind is formed which lasts through life, of which the attributes are freedom, equitableness, calmness, moderation, and wisdom; of what.... I have ventured to call the philosophical habit of mind."

The primary purpose of a liberal education, then, is the cultivation of the person's own intellect and imagination, for the person's own sake. It ought not to be forgotten, in this mass-age when the state aspires to be all in all, that genuine education is something higher than an instrument of public policy. True education is meant to develop the individual human being, the person, rather than to serve the state. In all our talk about "serving national goals" and "citizenship education"—phrases that originated with John Dewey and his disciples—we tend to ignore the fact that schooling was not originated by the modern nation-state. Formal schooling actually commenced as an endeavor to acquaint the rising generation with religious knowledge: with awareness of the transcendent and with moral truths. Its purpose was not to indoctrinate a young person in civics, but rather to teach what it is to be a true human being, living within a moral order. The person has primacy in liberal education.

Yet a system of liberal education has a social purpose, or at least a social result, as well. It helps to provide a society with a body of people who become leaders in many walks of life, on a large scale or a small. It was the expectation of the founders of the early American colleges that there would be graduated from those little institutions young men, soundly schooled in old intellectual disciplines, who would nurture in the New World the intellectual and moral patrimony received from the Old World. And for generation upon generation, the American liberal-arts colleges (peculiar to North America) and later the liberal-arts schools and programs of American universities, did graduate young men and women who leavened the lump of the rough expanding nation, having acquired some degree of a philosophical habit of mind.

You will have gathered already that I do not believe it to be the primary function of formal schooling to "prepare boys and girls for jobs." If all schools, colleges, and universities were abolished tomorrow, still most young people would find lucrative employment, and means would exist, or would be developed, for training them for their particular types of work. Rather, I believe it to be the conservative mission of liberal learning to develop right reason among young people.

Not a few members of the staffs of liberal-arts colleges, it is true, resent being told that theirs is a conservative mission of any sort. When once I was invited to give a series of lectures on conservative thought at a long-established college, a certain professor objected indignantly, "Why, we can't have that sort of thing here: this is a *liberal* arts college!" He thought, doubtless sincerely, that the word "liberal" implied allegiance to some dim political orthodoxy, related somehow to the New Deal and its succeeding programs. Such was the extent of his liberal education. Nevertheless, whatever the private political prejudices of professors, the function of liberal education is to conserve a body of received knowledge and to impart an apprehension of order to the rising generation.

Nor do I think it the function of genuine schooling to create a kind of tapioca-pudding society in which everybody would be just like everybody else—every young person, perhaps, to be the recipient eventually of a doctoral degree, even if quite innocent of philosophy. Instead, a highly beneficial result of liberal education, conservative again, is that it gives to society a body of young people, introduced in some degree to wisdom and virtue, who may become honest leaders in many walks of life.

At this point in my remarks, someone at this friendly gathering may mutter, knowingly, "An elitist!" Living as we do in an age of ideology, nearly all of us are tempted to believe that if we have clapped a quasi-political label to an expression of opinion, we have blessed or damned it; we need not examine the expression on its own merits. In educationist circles, "elitism" is a devil-term, for isn't everybody just like everybody else, except for undeserved privilege?

Yet actually I am an anti-elitist. I share T. S. Eliot's objections to Karl Mannheim's theory of modern elites. I object particularly to schemes for the governance of society by formally-trained specialized and technological elites. One of my principal criticisms of current tendencies in the higher learning is that, despite much cant about democratic campuses, really our educational apparatus has been rearing up not a class of liberally-educated young people of humane outlook, but instead a series of degree-dignified elites, an alleged meritocracy of confined views and dubious intellectual and moral credentials, puffed up by that little learning which is most truly described by that mordant Tory Alexander Pope as a dangerous thing. We see such elites at their worst in "emergent" Africa and Asia, where the ignorant are oppressed by the quarterschooled; increasingly, if less ferociously, comparable elites govern us even in America—through the political structure, through the public-school empire, through the very churches.

Such folk were in George Orwell's mind when he described the ruling elite of *Nineteen Eighty-Four:*

> ...made up for the most part of bureaucrats, scientists, technicians, trade-union organizers, publicity experts, sociologists, teachers, journalists, and professional politicians. These people, whose origins lay in the salaried middle class and the upper grades of the working class,

had been shaped and brought together by the barren world of monopoly industry and centralized government.

Now it is not at all my desire that university and college should train up such elites. When I say that we experience an increased need for truly liberal learning, I am recommending something to leaven the lump of modern civilization—something that would give us a tolerable number of people in many walks of life who would possess some share of right reason and moral imagination; who would not shout the price of everything, but would know the value of something; who would be schooled in wisdom and virtue.

I am suggesting that college and university ought not to be degree-mills: they ought to be centers for genuinely humane and genuinely scientific studies, attended by young people of healthy intellectual curiosity who actually show some interest in mind and conscience. I am saying that the higher learning is meant to develop order in the soul, for the human person's own sake. I am saying that the higher learning is meant to develop order in the commonwealth, for the republic's sake. I am arguing that a system of higher education which has forgotten these ends is decadent; but that decay may be arrested, and that reform and renewal still are conceivable. I am declaring that the task of the liberal educator, in essence, is a conservative labor.

The more people who are humanely educated, the better. But the more people we have who are half-educated or quarter-educated, the worse for them and for the republic. Really educated people, rather than forming presumptuous elites, will permeate society, leavening the lump through their professions, their teaching, their preaching, their participation in commerce and industry, their public offices at every level of the commonwealth. And being educated, they will know that they do not know everything; and that there exist objects in life besides power and money and sensual gratification; they will take long views; they will look forward to posterity and backward toward their ancestors. For them, education will not terminate on commencement day.

Not long ago I spoke at a reputable liberal-arts college on the subject of the order and integration of knowledge. There came up to me after my lecture two well-spoken, well-dressed, civil graduating seniors of that college; probably they were "A" students, perhaps *summa cum laude*. They told me that until they had heard my talk, they had been unable to discover any pattern or purpose in the college education that they had endured for four years. Late had they found me! Where might they learn more?

I suggested that they turn, first of all, to C. S. Lewis' little book *The Abolition of Man;* then to Michael Polanyi's *Personal Knowledge,* and to William Oliver Martin's *Order and Integration of Knowledge.* Were I speaking with them today, I should add an important book I have read since then, Stanley Jaki's *The Road to Science and the Ways to God.*

Those two young men went off in quest of wisdom and virtue, of which they had heard little at their college, and I have not beheld them since. I trust that they have read those good books and have become members of that unknowable Remnant (obscure, but influential as Dicey's real shapers of public opinion) which scourges the educational follies of our time.

If college and university do nothing better than act as pretentious trade-schools; if their chief service to the person and the republic is to act as employment agencies—why, such institutions will have dehumanized themselves. They will have ceased to give us young people with reason and imagination who leaven the lump of any civilization. They will give us instead a narrow elite governing a monotonous declining society, rejoicing in a devil's sabbath of whirling machinery. If we linger smug and apathetic in a bent world, leaving the works of reason and imagination to molder, we all come to know servitude of mind and body. The alternative to a liberal education is a servile schooling. And when the floodwaters of the world are out, as they are today, it will not suffice to be borne along by the current, singing hallelujah to the river god.

Some of you may have seen the edition of Irving Babbitt's *Literature and the American College* which I brought out under the auspices of the National Humanites Institute, and the edition of Babbitt's *Democracy and Leadership* which I brought out through Liberty Press. Babbitt's warning, in 1908, about the decay of liberal education has taken on grimmer significance since he wrote. Permit me to quote here the concluding sentences of his *Literature and the American College*:

> Our colleges and universities could render no greater service than to oppose to the worship of energy and the frantic eagerness for action an atmosphere of leisure and reflection. We should make large allowance in our lives for 'the eventual element of calm,' if they are not to degenerate into the furious and feverish pursuit of mechanical efficiency.... The tendency of an industrial democracy that took joy in work alone would be to live in a perpetual devil's sabbath of whirling machinery and call it progress....The present situation especially is not one that will be saved—if it is to be saved at all—by what we have called humanitarian hustling.... If we ourselves ventured on an exhortation to the American people, it would be rather that of Demosthenes to the Athenians: 'In God's name, I beg of you to *think*.' Of action we shall have plenty in any case; but it is only by a more humane reflection that we can escape the penalties sure to be exacted from any country that tries to dispense in its national life with the principle of leisure.

By "leisure," Babbitt meant opportunity for serious contemplation and discussion. On the typical campus today—particularly the vast confused campus of what I call Behemoth University —there is opportunity aplenty for hustling or for idleness, but the claims of true academic leisure are neglected. Much more has been forgotten, too, especially the notion of the philosophical habit of mind.

Perhaps I have been somewhat abstract. Permit me, then, to suggest briefly the relevance of liberal education, in its conservative function, to our present discontents.

*   *   *

Nowadays I frequently visit Washington—this city of which Joseph de Maistre said that it never could become a capital. In one sense, de Maistre is vindicated: Washington remains a dormitory town rather than a true national capital, no center for right reason and imagination, a confused and confusing locus of administration, rather than of decision. A good many friends of mine—some about my own age, but most of them a generation younger—have taken office recently; they profess their eagerness for guidance.

They find themselves struggling to act decisively within a vast proliferating bureaucracy, interested seemingly in its own power and preferment. There is urgent need for great decisions; but thought is painful; and the bureaucracy prefers boondoggles and stagnation. Great decisions cannot be long postponed, for the foreign and domestic concerns of the United States will not stay long for an answer.

You may recall the medieval legend of Friar Bacon and Friar Bungay. Bacon had constructed a head of brass, which he expected to speak and reveal the secret of defending England against England's enemies. But exhausted by his labors, Friar Bacon found it necessary to nap while waiting for the brazen lips to part; so he appointed his apprentice, Friar Bungay, to wake him the moment the Head should utter a word.

As the great scientist slept, the brazen oracle commenced to function. "Time will be!" it pronounced. Friar Bungay, terrified, addressed the Head foolishly. "Time is!" the Head proclaimed. Still Bungay babbled. Then the Head exclaimed "Time was!" and burst into a thousand fragments. When Bacon awoke, the opportunity was lost forever.

So matters stand in Washington nowadays. Irrevocable decisions must be reached before that tide in the affairs of men has begun to ebb. Those of my friends who are possessed of a liberal education have the sort of reason and imagination calculated to provide us with prudent and far-reaching decisions. But they stand a small minority among the specialists and technicians, the elite, who dominate the operation of the enormous federal machinery. And sooner than we expect, the Brazen Head may thunder, "Time was!"

Some years ago, President Nixon, in the course of an hour's conversation, asked me, "What one book should I read?" He added that he had put that inquiry, more than once, to Daniel Patrick Moynihan and Henry Kissinger; but they had given him lists of a dozen books, and the President, under the pressures of his office, could find time for only one seminal book. What should it be?

"Read T. S. Eliot's *Notes towards the Definition of Culture,*" I told Mr. Nixon. He wanted to know why.

"Because Eliot discusses the ultimate social questions," I replied. "He deals with the relationships that should exist between men of power and men of ideas. And he distinguishes better than anyone else between a 'class' of truly educated persons and an 'elite' of presumptuous specialists—remarking how dangerous the latter may become."

President Nixon discovered not long later that the elite of his administration were deficient in that wisdom and that virtue so much needed in America. A liberally educated man learns from Plato and from Burke that in a statesman the highest virtue is prudence. The sort of high prudence required in great affairs of state has not frequently been encountered in Washington during the past several decades. One reason for this deficiency has been our American neglect of liberal education, as defined by John Henry Newman. I remind you now of Newman's definition:

> This process of training, by which the intellect, instead of being formed or sacrificed to some particular or accidental purpose, some specific trade or profession or study or science, is disciplined for its own sake, for the perception of its own object, and for its own highest culture, is called Liberal Education; and though there is no one in whom it is carried as far as is conceivable, yet there is scarcely any one but may gain an idea of what real training is, and at least look toward it, and make its true scope, not something else, his standard of excellence.

True liberal education, that standard of excellence, that conservator of civilization, is required not in Washington alone, but everywhere in our society. Most possessors of a liberal education never come to sit in the seats of the mighty. Yet they leaven the lump of the nation, in many stations and occupations; we never hear the names of most of them, but they do their conservative work quietly and well.

I mention here my grandfather, Frank Pierce, a bank-manager. Although he spent only one term at college—studying music at Valparaiso University—he was a liberally educated gentleman; for liberal education may be acquired in solitude, if necessary. On the village council and the school board, he was a pillar of probity and intelligence. From his example I came to understand the nature of wisdom and virtue.

Frank Pierce, possessing four tall cases of good books—chiefly humane letters and historical works—was able to reflect upon the splendor and the tragedy of the human condition. He was no prisoner of the provinciality of place and circumstance, nor of time.

Such conservative people, endowed with a liberal understanding, have taken a large part in giving coherence and direction to our American society. I do not know what we Americans might have become, had we not such men and women among us. I do not know what we will do if they vanish from our midst. Perhaps then we will be left to celebrate "a devil's sabbath of whirling machinery," supervised by specialists—an elite without moral imagination, and deficient in their understanding of order, justice, and freedom. And after that, chaos.

Much needs to be conserved in these closing decades of the twentieth century, when often it seems as if "Whirl is king, having overthrown Zeus." One benefit of a liberal education is an understanding of what Aristophanes meant by that line—and of how Aristophanes, and Socrates, retain high significance for us. If you have studied Thucydides and Plutarch, you will apprehend much about our present time of troubles; and if you cannot order the state, at least a liberal education may teach you how to order your own soul in the twentieth century after Christ, so like the fifth century before him.

If, in a way that is at once conservative and radical and reactionary, we address ourselves to the renewal of liberal learning, conceivably we may yet live a life of order and justice and freedom. But if we linger smug and apathetic in a bent world, increasingly dominated by squalid oligarchs, we shall come to know servitude of mind and body. If our patrimony is cast aside, Edmund Burke reminded his age, "The law is broken, nature is disobeyed, and the rebellious are outlawed, cast forth, and exiled from this world of reason, and order, and peace, and virtue, and fruitful penitence, into the antagonist world of madness, discord, vice, confusion, and unavailing sorrow."

When liberal education is forgotten, we grope our way into that antagonist world—if you will, from space to anti-space, into Milton's "hollow dark."

V

Can Virtue Be Taught?

Are there men and women in America today possessed of virtue sufficient to withstand and repel the forces of disorder? Or have we, as a people, grown too fond of creature-comforts and a fancied security to venture our lives, our fortunes, and our sacred honor in any cause at all? "The superior man thinks always of virtue," Confucius told his disciples; "the common man thinks of comfort." Such considerations in recent years have raised up again that old word "virtue," which in the first half of this century had sunk almost out of sight.

I venture first to offer you a renewed apprehension of what "virtue" means; and then to suggest how far it may be possible to restore an active virtue in our public and our private life. If we lack virtue, we will not long continue to enjoy comfort—not in an age when Giant Ideology and Giant Envy swagger balefully about the world.

The concept of virtue, like most other concepts that have endured and remain worthy of praise, has come down to us from the

Greeks and the Hebrews. In its classical signification, "virtue" means the power of anything to accomplish its specific function; a property capable of producing certain effects; strength, force, potency. Thus one refers to the "deadly virtue" of the hemlock. Thus also the word "virtue" implies a mysterious energetic power, as in the Gospel According to Saint Mark: "Jesus, immediately knowing that *virtue* had gone out of him, turned him about in the press, and said, Who touched my clothes?" Was it, we may ask, that virtue of Jesus which left its mark upon the Shroud of Turin?

Virtue, then, meant in the beginning some extraordinary power. The word was applied to the sort of person we might now call "the charismatic leader." By extension, "virtue" came to imply the qualities of full humanity: strength, courage, capacity, worth, manliness, moral excellence. And presently "virtue" came to signify, as well, moral goodness: the practice of moral duties and the conformity of life to the moral law; uprightness; rectitude.

In recent decades, many folk seemingly grew embarrassed by this word virtue; perhaps for them it had too stern a Roman ring. They made the word "integrity" do duty for the discarded "virtue." Now "integrity" signifies wholeness or completeness; freedom from corruption; soundness of principle and character. You will gather that "integrity" is chiefly a passive quality, somewhat deficient in the vigor of "virtue." People of integrity may be the salt of the earth; yet a rough age requires some people possessed of an energetic virtue.

When we say that a man or a woman is virtuous, what do we mean? Plato declared that there are four chief virtues of the soul: justice, prudence, temperance, and fortitude. (Of these, the virtue most required in a statesman is prudence, Plato remarked.) To these classical virtues, Saint Paul added the theological virtues: faith, hope, and charity. These constitute the Seven Virtues of the Schoolmen. Against them are set the Seven Deadly Sins: pride, avarice, lust, anger, gluttony, envy, and sloth. Incidentally, there was a more specific medieval list of "the sins that cry out to heaven for vengeance": oppression of the poor, willful murder, sodomy, and defrauding a laborer of his wages.

Such formulas of the cardinal and the theological virtues have been fixed in the minds of many of us, either through church teachings or through humane letters. Yet virtue is something more than the sum of its seven parts. From the sixth century before Christ down to the twentieth century, this word "virtue" carried with it the strong suggestion of public leadership. The truly virtuous man would assume public duties, the ancients believed. Take these words from Cicero's *Republic:* "What can be more noble than the government of the state by virtue? For then the man who rules others is not himself a slave to any passion, but has already acquired for himself all those qualities to which he is training and summoning his fellows. Such a man imposes no laws upon the people that he does not obey himself, but puts his own life before his fellow-citizens as their law."

By the "virtuous man," that is, the classical writers meant a leader in statecraft and in war, one who towered above his fellow citizens, a person in whom courage, wisdom, self-restraint, and just dealing were conspicuous. They meant a being of energy and force, moved almost by a power out of himself.

How was this virtue, this conspicuous merit and talent to lead, acquired by men and women? That question provoked the famous debate between Socrates and Aristophanes. Socrates argued that virtue and wisdom at bottom are one. When first I read Socrates' argument, I being then a college freshman, this seemed to me an insupportable thesis; for we all have known human beings of much intelligence and cleverness whose light is as darkness. After considerable experience of the world and the passage of more than four decades, to me Socrates' argument seems yet more feeble.

And so it seemed to Aristophanes. The sophists—that is, the teachers of rhetoric and prudence, Socrates among them—professed that they could teach virtue to the rising generation. Through development of the private rationality, those teachers declared, they could form talented leaders within the state: men of virtue, or charismatic power, endowed with the talents required for private and public success.

To the great comic poet, this notion seemed a dangerous absurdity. Greatness of soul and good character are not formed by hired tutors, Aristophanes maintained: virtue is natural, not an artificial development. Who possesses virtue? Why, not some presumptuous elite of young men trailing effeminately after some sophist or other. The true possessors of virtue are the men of the old families, reared to righteousness and courage, brought up in good moral habits, from their earliest years accustomed to discipline and duty. Their prudence and their daring defend the state. Just how far the hero-poet Aristophanes believed virtue to be inherited, and how far he took it to be nurtured by family example and tradition, we do not know at this remove. But it is clear that Aristophanes laughed to scorn the thesis that virtue may be imitated by school-masters.

The Greek teachers of philosophy, nevertheless, Plato and Aristotle eminent among them, refused to abandon their attempt to impart virtue through appeal to reason. A kind of compromise was reached in Aristotle's *Ethics*. There Aristotle argues that virtue is of two kinds: moral and intellectual. Moral virtue grows out of habit *(ethos)*; it is not natural, but neither is moral virtue opposed to nature. Intellectual virtue, on the other hand, may be developed and improved through systematic instruction—which requires time. In other words, moral virtue appears to be the product of habits formed early in family, class, neighborhood; while intellectual virtue may be taught through instruction in philosophy, literature, history, and related disciplines.

The experience of the Romans during their republican centuries may serve to delineate the two different kinds of virtue. So late as the period of Polybius, the Roman citizens retained their "high old Roman virtue," the product of tradition and deference to example, of habits acquired within the family. They maintained the virtues of reverence, seriousness, equitableness, firmness of purpose, tenacity, hard work, steadiness, frugality, unselfishness, self-restraint— and other virtues besides. All these were habits that grew into virtues.

Then came to Rome the Greek philosophers, with much abstract talk of virtue. But the more the sophists praised an abstract virtue, the more did the *mores maiorum,* the ancient manners or habits of Rome, sink into neglect. Ancestral ways diminished in power; ethical speculation spread. Although the high old Roman virtue was not altogether extinguished until the final collapse of *Romanitas* before the barbarian wanderers, by the time of Nero and Seneca there had come to exist, side by side, a fashionable array of ethical teachings, derived from Greek sources—and a general decay of public and private morals, from the highest social classes to the lowest.

This Roman experience seems to justify the argument of Aristophanes that virtue cannot be taught in schools. Rather, the sprig of virtue is nurtured in the soil of sound prejudice; healthful and valorous habits are formed; and, in the phrase of Burke, "a man's habit becomes his virtue." A resolute and daring character, dutiful and just, may be formed accordingly.

During the Korean war, only one American soldier taken prisoner and confined in North Korea succeeded in escaping and making his way back to his own lines—a sergeant named Pate, set down in his captors' records as a "reactionary." Sergeant Pate, an unlettered man, was possessed of the Roman virtues of *discipline, firmitas, constantia,* and *frugalitas.* His father, Pate remarked, had taught him only two principles: first, if a man calls you a liar, knock him down; if he calls you a son of a bitch, kill him. Ethical instruction in casuistry might have made Sergeant Pate less resistant to Communist indoctrination and less resolute in his daring escape: that is, less virtuous. For virtue, we should remember, is energy of soul employed for the general good.

Intellectual virtue divorced from moral virtue may wither into a loathsome thing. Robespierre was called by his admirers "the voice of virtue"; certainly Robespierre (who justified the slaughter of his opponents by coining the aphorism that one can't make an omelet without breaking eggs) was forever prating of virtue. "Virtue was always in a minority on the earth," said that murderous prig, the "Sea-Green Incorruptible." That sort of intellectual virtue, an aspect of what I have called defecated rationality, still rises up perennially in Paris, and is exported to Ethiopia, to Cambodia, to any national soil that seems ready-furrowed for this poisonous seed. Intellectual virtue, genus Robespierre, is a kind of delusory ethical snobbery, ferocious and malicious, annihilating ordinary human beings because they are not angels.

The abstract intellectual virtue of the Parisian coffee-house intellectual, I am suggesting, is a world away from the habitual high old Roman virtue. The virtues of the statesmen and soldiers of the early American Republic were not at all allied to the bloody fanatical "virtue" that was to arise during the French Revolution. So if we aspire to renew American virtue near the close of the twentieth century, surely we will do well to look with skepticism upon proposals for some sort of abstract "civil religion." An arid virtue that is intellectual only must be unreliable at best, and dangerous often. From time to time in recent years, various educational instrumentalists and progressivists have advocated the public teaching of a "religion of democracy"—that is, a public ethic founded upon idelogical premises. Such an artificial intellectual contraption, with no better footing, would be mischievous in its consequences.

A false, carping, malicious "virtue" is worse than no virtue at all. The urgent need of the United States of America, near the end of the twentieth century, is for a virtue arising from habit and affection, rather than from ideological preaching. Without such a renewed true virtue, our commonwealth may not endure. I think of the words of Simone Weil concerning our era, in her "Reflections on Quantum Theory":

> It is as though we had returned to the age of Protagoras and the Sophists, the age when the art of persuasion—whose modern equivalent is advertising slogans, publicity, propaganda meetings, the press, the cinema, and radio—took the place of thought and controlled the fate of cities and accomplished coups d'etat. So the ninth book of Plato's *Republic* reads like a description of contemporary events. Only today it is not the fate of Greece but of the entire world that is at stake. And we have no Socrates or Plato or Eudoxus, no Pythagorean tradition, and no teaching of the Mysteries. We have the Christian tradition, but it can do nothing for us unless it comes alive in us again.

Just so. It is not propaganda nor productivity nor intellectuality that has power to invigorate America at the crisis of the nation's fate. By virtue are nations defended. But virtue in this land of ours seemingly never lay at a lower ebb. The instruments of false persuasion listed by Simone Weil—the tools of the philodoxers, the purveyors of delusory opinion—have been increased in cleverness since she wrote, by the triumph of television. In no previous age have family influence, sound early prejudice, and good early habits been so broken in upon by outside force as in our own time. Moral virtue among the rising generation is mocked by the inanity of television, by pornographic films, by the twentieth-century cult of the "peer group." By example and precept, until quite recently, grandparents and parents conveyed to young people—or a considerable part of them—some notion of virtue, even if the word itself was not well understood. The decay of family, worked by modern affluence and modern mobility, has mightily diminished all that. As for the influence of the churches—why, more is left of it in the United States than in most countries; but in the typical "main line" church an amorphous humanitarianism has supplanted the emphasis upon virtue that runs through the Christian tradition.

And so we return, finding ourselves in circumstances very like those of the Greeks of the fifth century, to the ancient question, "Can virtue be taught?"

*   *   *

Let me confess at once my inability to provide any simple formula, promptly applicable, for the widespread renewal of the pursuit of virtue. Some people fancy that if only schools would turn their attention systematically and earnestly to this problem, relief soon would follow. But it will not do to become so sanguine.

For Aristophanes was right, I believe, in proclaiming (in *The Clouds* and elsewhere) that moral virtue is not learnt in schools. If good moral habits are acquired at all, they are got ordinarily within the family, within the neighborhood, within the circle of close associates in youth; often good moral habits, or bad ones, are fixed by the age of seven, little more than a year after school has begun for the typical child. The early life of the household and the early life of the streets count for immensely much; and I need not try your patience by expatiating mightily on the sort of character (or lack thereof) formed by the childhood associations and impressions of a large part of our urban population—or, for that matter, our suburban population. I do not refer to the ADC slums merely. In the affluent household too, when parents' opinions and tastes are shaped by incessant watching of television, we need not wonder that children learn the price of everything and the value of nothing.

Boys and girls will model themselves, if they can, upon exemplars. But what sort of exemplars? Rock stars, and the fancied personalities of the heroes and heroines of the soap operas, have become the exemplars for a multitude of American young people in their most formative years. Rarely are such persons, or pseudopersons, admirable mentors.

Enjoying the good fortune to grow up before television did, I found, when a boy, another sort of exemplar, who taught me of virtue by example, and to a lesser extent by precept: my grandfather, Frank Pierce, whom I mentioned briefly in the last chapter. He was a generous and popular bank manager and local public man, who had a short way (several times) with bank robbers. Also he possessed important books, and read them and good periodicals, and helped to develop my own relish for reading. My grandfather was endowed with the cardinal and the theological virtues (if the latter in a form somewhat skeptical and heterodox). By conversing with him and watching him (he all unaware, probably, of the power of his influence upon me), I learned what it is to be a man.

At no time could every family provide such an exemplar; yet time was when emulation within the family amounted to more than it does nowadays. My relationship with my grandfather made it easy for me to understand Aristophanes' implicit argument that virtue arises easily, if mysteriously, among families. My grandfather had many virtues and no vices. I assumed then, somewhat naïvely, that the Republic had sufficient such leaders and molders of opinion as my grandfather, and would have enough such always.

But I digress. My point is this: the recovery of virtue in America depends in great part upon the reinvigoration of family. It would be vain for us to pretend that schools and colleges somehow could make amends for all the neglect of character resulting from the inadequacies of the American family of the 'Eighties and 'Nineties. With some few exceptions, men and women have acquired their virtues or their vices quite outside the classroom. (There comes into my mind's eye a glimpse of Catholic young men, at a Jesuit university, diligently cheating during an examination concerning Aquinas' "On Truth.")

If the family continues to decay in its functions, so will virtue continue to decline in our society. I offer no placebo, in either the liturgical or the medicinal signification of that word. *Placebo Domino in region vivorum?* Nay, but the man or woman brought up without moral virtue shall not be acceptable to the Lord in the land of the living.

Having turned liturgical for the moment, I venture a few words about the churches. Rather as some people expect too much from the schools concerning virtue, so other people count overly upon churches and clergymen as molders of virtuous character.

For Jeremy Bentham notwithstanding, the Church is not a moral police force. What the Church always has been meant to do, really, is to offer a pattern for ordering the soul of the believer; and to open a window upon the transcendent realm of being. It is true that mastery of the theological virtues ought to follow upon sincere belief, and that sometimes it does so follow. Certainly there would be little virtue in our civilization, and quite possibly there would exist no modern civilization at all, were it not for Christian preaching of the theological virtues. From the discipline of the theological virtues issue saints from time to time, as from the discipline of the cardinal virtues issue heroes. Yet it will not do to expect priest or minister to fill the vacuum left by the disappearance of family exemplar or mentor.

Now the churches of America, nevertheless, ought to do far more good work toward the renewal of virtue among persons than they actually are performing nowadays. I do not mean that the Church should become censorious as it was in Scotland in Knox's day, or as it was in New England in my great-great-great-great-great-great-great-great-grandfather's years at Plymouth. I do mean that the Church ought to address itself less to prudential considerations of the hour's politics—at which business the Church usually demonstrates its incompetence—and much more to showing the pertinence of the theological virtues to our present discontents, private and public. Certain developments within theological colleges, here and there, encourage me to think that such an alteration of approach has commenced. And it is altogether possible that a general widespread renewal of faith in the supernatural and transcendent character of Christian belief may come to pass within the next few years—a phenomenon more tremendous than the Great Awakening ushered in by Wesley and others two centuries ago. But to pursue that possibility here would lead me to the mysteries of the Shroud of Turin; I must stick to my last.

However that may be, the present influence of the Christian churches is not calculated to bring about much revival of the concept or the practice of the virtues, theological or cardinal. Most graduates of seminaries seem incapable today of discussing virtue, or particular virtues, with much historical or philosophical insight. For the moment, we must not look to institutional Christianity for rousing moral virtue; as Simone Weil suggests in the passage I quoted earlier, the Christian moral tradition lies dormant (at best) in modern hearts; if it is to come alive again, probably it must be revivified by some outer power.

The moral virtue which grows out of habit being difficult of attainment in our era, people turn their attention to intellectual virtue. It was so in the fifth and fourth centuries before Christ. The whole great philosophical achievement of Socrates, Plato, and Aristotle, indeed, was an endeavor to impart intellectual virtue to the rising generation, moral virtue having shrivelled in an age when "the rude son may strike the father dead." Far from having much immediate practical effect upon the young people of their time, the effort of Socrates, Plato, and Aristotle was a failure. (The fact that Aristotle schooled in philosophy a future great king did not produce any general alteration of minds and hearts.) Finding the old Greek religion and morality enfeebled, and moral habits much impaired,

Socrates endeavored to substitute for habitual moral virtue the identification of virtue with wisdom: intellectual virtue. The immediate benefits of this venture were not obvious: Alcibiades and Critias were among Socrates' more successful disciples. Virtue of a sort was theirs; but not the virtue of moral worth.

Yet there have been times when intellectual virtue has been imparted successfully. Such, in British North America, was the second half of the eighteenth century, when there was developed a class of able persons (enduring as a class so late as the 1830s) who knew the meaning of virtue. Theirs was the schooling of English gentlemen of the age, deliberately intended to bring home the idea and the reality of virtue to those members of the rising generation presumably destined to be leading men of their society—whether (in Burke's phrases) "men of actual virtue" or "men of presumptive virtue." (This distinction is one between "enterprising talents" and inherited rank and wealth.)

And how were such young persons schooled in virtue? They were required to read carefully, in the classical languages (chiefly in Latin), certain enduring books that dealt much with virtue. In particular, they studied Cicero, Vergil, and Plutarch, among the ancients. They memorized Cicero's praise of virtuous Romans; they came to understand Vergil's *labor, pietas, fatum;* they immersed themselves in the lives of Plutarch's Greeks and Romans "of excellent virtue"—men in whom the energy of virtue had flamed up fiercely.

It does not follow that we, in our time, could produce such a generation of leaders as signed the Declaration and wrote the Constitution, were we suddenly to sweep all rubbish and boondoggle and driver training out of the typical American school curriculum, and install instead the required reading of 1787, say. For that study and reflection necessary for the attainment of intellectual virtue cannot unaided put flesh upon virtue's dry bones. For intellectual virtue to become active virtue—whether after the fashion of Washington or the fashion of Robespierre—favorable circumstances must occur. In the Thirteen Colonies, the altered relationships between Britain's Crown-in-Parliament and the dominant classes in America provided opportunity for the Americans schooled in virtue—particularly, though by no means exclusively, the men of actual virtue—to take power into their hands. And by 1832, the last survivors from America's intellectual-virtue school of earlier decades (John Quincy Adams, in particular) were being thrust aside by men of another pattern.

It is possible for schools of intellectual virtue to endure a great while, and to exert a very strong practical influence. In essence, the famous public schools (together with many good "private" boarding schools) of England have been for centuries centers for imparting intellectual virtue to boys who presumably have obtained (most of them, anyway) a good deal of moral virtue within their own families. Such, at least, has been the aspiration of the British public schools, represented at their best by the ideas and methods of Dr. Thomas Arnold. Probably the days of the public schools and the boarding schools generally are numbered in Britain now. But the long history of those schools suggests that intellectual virtue was better imparted in England than in Greece. At the English schools, until recent decades, the core of the discipline of intellectual virtue was the study of Cicero, Vergil, Plutarch, and classical literature generally.

In these United States, scarcely a school remains, I suppose, where the notion of intellectual virtue still is entertained. A fair amount of the content of such studies, nevertheless, used to be conveyed by literary and historical courses in American intermediate and secondary schooling. That remnant has been trickling away—and not in America only. C. S. Lewis, four decades ago, assailed the corruption of school courses in humane letters in England; he found the new textbooks sneering at virtue of any sort. Great literature used to train the emotions, Lewis wrote:

Without the aid of trained emotions the intellect is powerless against the animal organism. I had sooner play cards against a man who was quite skeptical about ethics, but bred to believe that 'a gentleman does not cheat,' than against an irreproachable moral philosopher who had been brought up among sharpers. In battle it is not syllogisms that will keep the reluctant nerves and muscles to their post in the third hour of the bombardment.... And all this time—such is the tragicomedy of our situation—we continue to clamour for those very qualities we are rendering impossible. You can hardly open a periodical without coming across the statement that what our civilization needs is more 'drive,' or dynamics, or self-sacrifice, or 'creativity.' In a sort of ghastly simplicity we remove the organ and demand the function. We make men without chests and expect of them virtue and enterprise. We laugh at honour and are shocked to find traitors in our midst. We castrate and bid the geldings be fruitful.

We are worse off still, in the 'Nineties. So far, what attempts we have made in America to impart virtue once more have been confined principally to "research projects" (usually with plenty of public funds behind them) in that hideous sham called "values clarification." But I am descending into bathos.

Can virtue be taught? Why, it can be learnt, though more through a kind of illative process than as a formal program of study. Surely it cannot be taught by those incompetent and chameleon-like intellectuals whom Solzhenitsyn calls "the Smatterers." Few seem competent to teach virtue in our Republic nowadays; and relatively few hungry sheep look up to be fed.

Yet adversity, which we Americans seem liable to experience sharply and suddenly in this present decade, frequently opens the way for the impulse toward virtue. The terrible adversity endured by decent folk in Soviet Russia forged the virtue of Solzhenitsyn, a hero for our age. Only rags and tatters of the old moral virtue survived in Russia after the triumphs of Lenin and of Stalin; Solzhenitsyn and some other Russians of moral vision found it necessary to raise up intellectual virtue from the ashes of revolution. They have succeeded, in the sense that Socrates and Plato succeeded; whether their reconstruction of virtue will take on flesh more swiftly than did the Greek reconstitution, we do not yet know.

"Feed men, and then ask them of virtue" is the slogan upon the banners of the Anti-Christ, in Solovyov's romance. We have done just that in this Republic, since the Second World War. We Americans have grown very well fed, very much starved for virtue. Nowhere is this more amply illustrated than in Washington. Whether or not virtue can be taught, we have not troubled our heads with it, nor our hearts. When the Rough Beast slouches upon us, what Theseus or Perseus, incandescent with the energy of virtue, will draw his sword?

VI

The Perversity of Recent Fiction: Reflections on the Moral Imagination

Not many of us, I trust, greatly esteem most recent fiction in the English language—or, for that matter, the French or the German or the Italian language. About all that can be said for printed fiction, in these closing years of the twentieth century, is that it seems somewhat less loathsome than the dramatic fiction of television.

Most fiction nowadays appears to be written for dirty-minded and naive adolescents, although perhaps most of it is read by middle-aged housewives. Even the fiction intended for "young adults" and commended by the American Library Association now begins to take on a salacious cast—and not merely in the works of Judy Blume. Not long ago I picked up a romance by a woman writer whom I often have praised, one whose writings have displayed a high if melancholy fancy; she writes fantasies, often set in imaginary worlds, of considerable power. But in this most recent book of hers occurred one scene of fornication and another of peculiarly disgusting violence, neither essential to plot or character: it was as if (what often occurs) the editors of the firm publishing her books had told her that such episodes are now *de rigueur,* if a book is to sell tolerably well. For boys and girls fourteen years of age? Oh, quite.

Or take the *genre* in which your servant looms a lonely colossus—the tale of the preternatural and the occult. Some three years ago I happened to receive the award for the best short fiction in this mode, from the Third World Fantasy Convention—which title may conjure up images of African fanatics and Arab terrorists, but actually was an assemblage of *aficionados* of the fantastic tale. I now find that I am virtually the only remaining writer of this sort of fiction who does not condescend to introduce a rather nasty and perverse eroticism into his stories. Indeed, the company in such writing has grown so lascivious that I have resolved not to contribute any more of my stories to anthologies of the fantastic and supernatural. Clearly the public's appetite in every field of fiction grows yet more ardent for ghastly violence and impossible sexuality—or at least so the publishers believe. In the franchise bookshops, the shelves are crowded with the prickly pears and Dead Sea fruit of literary decadence.

Yet no civilization rests forever content with literary boredom and literary violence. Once again, a conscience may speak to a conscience in the pages of books, and the parched rising generation may grope their way toward the springs of the moral imagination. Literature, after all, is an endeavor to attain that high power of perception which has been called "the moral imagination," and to relate that imagination to the human condition in the writer's time. What once has been, may be again.

So I offer you some reflections upon the perversity of the sort of imagination displayed by our profiteering "best-seller" authors, and the moral imagination that those writers deny or degrade. I will not tire you with a roster of such writers; anyone who strolls through a bookshop or troubles to read the shallow reviews in the

New York Times Book Review, say, knows that their name is legion.

*   *   *

Well, what is this "moral imagination" I mentioned a moment ago? The phrase is Edmund Burke's. It occurs in his *Reflections on the Revolution in France*. Burke is describing the destruction of civilizing manners by the revolutionaries. I quote him:

> All the decent drapery of life is to be rudely torn off. All the superadded ideas, furnished from the wardrobe of a moral imagination, which the heart owns, and the understanding ratifies, as necessary to cover the defects of our naked shivering nature, and to raise it to dignity in our own estimation, are to be exploded as a ridiculous, absurd, and antiquated fashion.
> On this scheme of things, a king is but a man; a queen is but a woman; a woman is but an animal; and an animal not of the highest order. All homage paid to the sex in general as such, and without distinct views, is to be regarded as romance and folly.... On the scheme of this barbarous philosophy, which is the offspring of cold hearts and muddy understandings, and which is as void of solid wisdom, as it is destitute of all taste and elegance, laws are to be supported only by their own terrors, and by the concern which each individual may find in them from his own private speculations, or can spare to them from his own private interests. In the groves of *their* academy, at the end of every vista, you see nothing but the gallows.... Nothing is more certain, than that our manners, our civilization, and all the good things which are connected

with manners, and with civilization, have, in this European world of ours, depended for ages upon two principles; I mean the spirit of a gentleman, and the spirit of religion.

By this "moral imagination," Burke signifies that power of ethical perception which strides beyond the barriers of private experience and momentary events—"especially," as the dictionary has it, "the higher form of this power exercised in poetry and art." The moral imagination aspires to the apprehending of right order in the soul and right order in the commonwealth. This moral imagination was the gift and the obsession of Plato and Vergil and Dante. Drawn from centuries of human consciousness, these concepts of the moral imagination—so powerfully if briefly put by Burke—are expressed afresh from age to age. So it is that the men of humane letters in our century whose work seems most likely to endure have not been neoterists, but rather bearers of an old standard, tossed by our modern winds of doctrine: the names of Eliot, Frost, Faulkner, Waugh, and Yeats may suffice to suggest the variety of this moral imagination in the twentieth century.

It is the moral imagination which informs us concerning the dignity of human nature; which instructs us that we are more than naked apes. As Burke suggested in 1790, letters and learning are hollow, if deprived of the moral imagination. And as Burke said, the spirit of religion long sustained this moral imagination, along with a whole system of manners. Such imagination lacking, to quote another passage from Burke, we are cast forth "from this world of reason, and order, and peace, and virtue, and fruitful pentinence, into the antagonist world of madness, discord, vice, confusion, and unavailing sorrow."

*   *   *

Burke implies that there exist other forms of imagination than the moral imagination. He was well aware of the power of imagination of Jean Jacques Rousseau, "the insane Socrates of the National Assembly." With Irving Babbitt, we may call the mode of imagination represented by Rousseau "the idyllic imagination"—that is, the imagination which, rejecting old dogmas and old manners, rejoices in the notion of emancipation from duty and convention. We saw this "idyllic imagination" intoxicate a great many young people in America during the 1960s and the 1970s—even though most of those devotees never read Rousseau. The idyllic imagination ordinarily terminates in disillusion and boredom.

When that occurs, too often a third form of imagination obtains ascendancy. In his lectures entitled *After Strange Gods,* T.S. Eliot touches upon the diabolic imagination: that kind of imagination which delights in the perverse and subhuman. The name of Sade comes to mind at once; but Eliot finds "the fruitful operations of the Evil Spirit" in the writings of Thomas Hardy and D.H. Lawrence, as well. Anyone interested in the moral imagination and in the anti-moral imagination should read carefully *After Strange Gods.* "The number of people in possession of any criteria for discriminating between good and evil is very small," Eliot concludes; "the number of the half-alive hungry for any form of spiritual experience, or what offers itself as spiritual experience, high or low, good or bad, is considerable. My own generation has not served them very well. Never has the printing press been so busy, and never have such varieties of buncombe and false doctrine come from it. *Woe unto the foolish prophets, that follow their own spirit, and have seen nothing!*"

This "diabolic imagination" dominates most popular fiction today—and on television and in the theaters, too, the diabolic imagination struts and postures. I once lodged at a fashionable new hotel; my single room cost about eighty dollars. One could tune the room's television set to certain movies, for an extra five dollars. After ten o'clock, *all* the films offered were nastily pornographic.

But even the "early" films, before ten, without exception were products of the diabolic imagination, in that they pandered to the lust for violence, destruction, cruelty, and sensational disorder. Apparently it never occurred to the managers of this fashionable hotel that any of their affluent patrons, of whatever age and whichever sex, might desire decent films. Since Eliot spoke at the University of Virginia in 1933, we have come a great way farther down the road to Avernus. And as literature sinks into the perverse, so modern civilization falls to its ruin: "The blood-dimmed tide is loosed, and everywhere/The ceremony of innocence is drowned."

So, having remarked the existence of the moral imagination, the idyllic imagination, and the diabolic imagination, I venture to remind you of the true purpose of humane letters. As C.E.M. Joad points out in his book *Decadence: a Philosophical Inquiry*, what we call "decadence" amounts to the loss of an end, an object. When literature has lost sight of its real object or purpose, literature is decadent.

*   *   *

What then is the end, object, or purpose of humane letters? Why, the expression of the moral imagination; or, to put this truth in a more familiar phrase, the end of great books is ethical—to teach us what it means to be genuinely human.

Every major form of literary art has taken for its deeper themes the norms of human nature. What Eliot calls "the permanent things"—the norms, the standards—have been the concern of the poet ever since the time of Job; or ever since Homer, "the blind man who sees," sang of the ways of the gods with men. Until very recent years, men took it for granted that literature exists to form the normative consciousness—that is, to teach human beings their true nature, their dignity, and their place in the scheme of things. Such was the endeavor of Sophocles and Aristophanes, of Thucydides and Tacitus, of Plato and Cicero, of Hesiod and Vergil, of Dante and Shakespeare, of Dryden and Pope.

The very phrase "humane letters" implies that great literature is meant to teach us what it is to be fully human. As Irving Babbitt observes in his slim book *Literature and the American College,* humanism (derived from the Latin *humanitas)* is an ethical discipline, intended to develop the truly human person, the qualities of manliness, through the study of great books. The literature of nihilism, of pornography and of sensationalism, as Albert Salomon suggests in *The Tyranny of Progress,* is a recent development, arising in the eighteenth century—though reaching its height in our time—with the decay of the religious view of life and with the decline of what has been called "The Great Tradition" in philosophy.

This normative purpose of letters is especially powerful in English literature, which never succumbed to the egoism that came to dominate French letters at the end of the eighteenth century. The names of Milton, Bunyan, and Johnson—or, in America, of Emerson, Hawthorne, and Melville—may be sufficient illustrations of the point. The great popular novelists of the nineteenth century—Scott, Dickens, Thackeray, Trollope—all assumed that the writer is under a moral obligation to normality: that is, explicitly or implicitly, to certain enduring standards of private and public conduct.

Now I do not mean that the great writer incessantly utters homilies. With Ben Jonson, he may "scourge the follies of the time," but he does not often murmur, "Be good, fair maid, and let who will be clever." Rather, the man of letters teaches the norms of our existence through allegory, analogy, and holding up the mirror to nature. The writer may, like William Faulkner, write much more of what is evil than of what is good; and yet, exhibiting the depravity of human nature, he establishes in his reader's mind the awareness that there exist enduring standards from which we fall away; and that fallen human nature is an ugly sight.

Or the writer may deal, as did J.P. Marquand, chiefly with the triviality and emptiness of a society that has forgotten standards. Often, in his appeal of a conscience to a conscience, he may row with muffled oars; sometimes he may be aware only dimly of his normative function. The better the artist, one almost may say, the more subtle the preacher. Imaginative persuasion, not blunt exhortation, commonly is the method of the literary champion of norms.

It is worth remarking that the most influential poet of our age, Eliot, endeavored to restore to modern poetry, drama, and criticism their traditional normative functions. In this he saw himself as the heir of Vergil and Dante. The poet seeks not to force his ego upon the public; rather, the poet's mission is to transcend the personal and the particular. As Eliot wrote in "Tradition and the Individual Talent":

> It is not in his personal emotions, the emotions provoked by particular events in his life, that the poet is in any way remarkable or interesting. His particular emotions may be simple, or crude, or flat. The emotion in his poetry will be a very complex thing, but not with the complexity of the emotions of people who have very complex or unusual emotions in life. One error, in fact, of eccentricity in poetry is to seek for new human emotions to express; and in this search for novelty in the wrong place it discovers the perverse. The business of the poet is not to find new emotions, but to use the ordinary ones and, in working them up into poetry, to express feelings which are not in actual emotions at all.

So pure poetry, and the other forms of great literature, search the human heart, to find in it the laws of moral existence, distinguishing man from beast. Or so it was until almost the end of the eighteenth century. Since then, the egoism of one school of the Romantics has obscured the primary purpose of humane letters. And many of the Realists have written of man as if he were brutal only—or brutalized by institutions, at best. (So arose Ambrose Bierce's definition in *The Devil's Dictionary:* "Naturalism, *n.* An accurate representation of human nature, as seen by toads.") In our own time, and particularly in America, we have seen the rise to popularity of a school of writers more nihilistic than ever were the Russian nihilists: the literature of disgust and denunciation, sufficiently described in Edmund Fuller's book *Man in Modern Fiction.* To the members of this school, the writer is no defender or expositor of standards, for there are no values to explain or defend; a writer merely registers, unreservedly, his disgust with humanity and himself. (This is a world away from Dean Swift—who, despite his loathing of most human beings, detested them only because they fell short of what they were meant to be.)

Yet the names of our twentieth-century nihilistic authors will be forgotten in less than a generation, I suspect, while there will endure from our age the works of a few men of letters whose appeal is to the enduring things, and therefore to posterity. I think, for instance, of Gironella's novel *The Cypresses Believe in God.* The gentle novice who trims the hair and washes the bodies of the poorest of the poor in old Gerona, though he dies by Communist bullets, will live a long span in the realm of letters; while the scantily-disguised personalities of our nihilistic authors, swaggering nastily as characters in best sellers, will be extinguished the moment the public's fancy veers to some newer sensation. For as the normative consciousness breathes life into the soul and the social order, so the normative understanding gives an author lasting fame.

Malcolm Cowley, writing two decades ago in *Horizon* about the then recent crop of first-novelists, observed that the several writers he discussed scarcely had heard of the Seven Cardinal Virtues or of the Seven Deadly Sins. Crimes and sins are mischances merely, to these young novelists; real love and real hatred are absent from their pages. To this rising generation of writers, the world seems purposeless, and human actions seem meaningless. They seek to express only a vagrant ego. And Cowley then suggested that these young men and women, introduced to no moral or literary norms in childhood and youth, except the vague attitude that one is entitled to do as one likes, so long as it doesn't injure someone else, are devoid of spiritual and intellectual discipline—empty, indeed, of real desire for anything.

This sort of aimless and unhappy writer is the product of a time in which the normative function of letters has been greatly neglected. Ignorant of his own mission, such a writer tends to think of his occupation as a mere skill, possibly lucrative, sometimes satisfying to one's vanity, but dedicated to no end. Even the "proletarian" writing of the 1920s and 1930s acknowledged some end; but that has died of disillusion and inanition. If writers are in this plight, in consequence of the prevailing "permissive" climate of opinion, what of their readers? Comparatively few book-readers nowadays, I suspect, seek normative knowledge. They are after amusement, sometimes of a vicariously gross character, or else pursue a vague "awareness" of current affairs and intellectual currents, suitable for cocktail-party conversation.

The young novelists described by Mr. Cowley are of the number of Eliot's "Hollow Men." Nature abhors a vacuum; into minds that are vacant of norms must come some new force; and often that new force has a diabolical character. *   *

A perceptive critic, Albert Fowler, writing in *Modern Age* two decades ago, put the question, "Can Literature Corrupt?"— and replied in the affirmative. So literature can; and also it is possible to be corrupted by an ignorance of humane letters, much of our normative knowledge necessarily being derived from our reading. The person who reads bad books instead of good may be subtly corrupted; the person who reads nothing at all may be forever adrift in life, unless he lives in a community still powerfully influenced by what Gustave Thibon calls "moral habits" and by oral tradition. And absolute abstinence from printed matter has become rare. If a small boy does not read *Treasure Island,* the odds are that he will read *Mad Ghoul Comics.*

So I think it worthwhile to suggest the outlines of the literary discipline which induces some understanding of enduring values. For centuries, such a program of reading—though never called a program—existed in Western nations. It powerfully influenced the minds and actions of the leaders of the infant American Republic, for instance. If one pokes into what books were read by the leaders of the Revolution, the Framers of the Constitution, and the principal men of America before 1800, one finds that nearly all of them were acquainted with a few important books: the King James version of the Bible, Plutarch's *Lives,* Shakespeare, something of Cicero, something of Vergil. This was a body of literature highly normative. The founders of the Republic thought of their new commonwealth as a blending of the Roman Republic with pre-scriptive English institutions; and they took for their models in leadership the prophets and kings and apostles of the Bible, and the noble Greeks and Romans of Plutarch. Cato's stubborn virtue, Demosthenes' eloquent vaticinations, Cleomenes' rash reforming impulse—these were in their minds' eyes; and they tempered their conduct accordingly. "But nowadays," as Chateaubriand wrote more than a century ago, "statesmen understand only the stock market—and that badly."

Of course it was not by books alone that the normative understanding of the Framers of the Constitution, for instance, was formed. Their apprehension of norms was acquired also in family, church, and school, and in the business of ordinary life. But that portion of their normative understanding which was got from books did loom large. For we cannot attain very well to enduring standards if we rely simply on actual personal experience as a normative mentor. Sheer experience, as Franklin suggested, is the teacher of born fools. Our lives are too brief and confused for most men to develop any normative pattern from their private experience; and, as Newman wrote, "Life is for action." Therefore we turn to the bank and capital of the ages, the normative knowledge found in revelation, authority, and historical experience, if we seek guidance in morals, taste, and politics. Ever since the invention of printing, this normative understanding has been expressed, increasingly, in books, so that nowadays most people form their opinions, in considerable part, from the printed page. This may be regrettable sometimes; it may be what D.H. Lawrence called "chewing the newspapers"; but it is a fact. Deny a fact, and that fact will be your master.

*   *   *

Another fact is that for some fifty years we have been failing, here in America, to develop a normative consciousness in young people through a careful program of reading great literature. We have talked about "education for life" and "training for life adjustment"; but many of us seem to have forgotten that literary disciplines are a principal means for learning to adjust to the necessities of life. Moreover, unless the life to which we are urged to adjust ourselves is governed by norms, it may be a very bad life for everyone.

One of the faults of the typical "life adjustment" or "permissive" curriculum in the schools—paralleled, commonly, by similarly indulgent attitudes in the family—has been the substitution of "real-life situation" reading for the study of truly imaginative literature. This tendency has been especially noticeable in the lower grades of school, but it extends upward in some degree through high school. The "Dick and Jane" and "run, Spot, run" school of letters does not stir the imagination; and it imparts small apprehension of norms. Apologists for this aspect of life-adjustment schooling believe that they are inculcating respect for values by prescribing simple readings that commend tolerant, kindly, cooperative behavior. Yet this is no effective way to impart a knowledge of norms: direct moral didacticism, whether of the Victorian or the twentieth-century variety, usually awakens resistance in the recipient, particularly if he has some natural intellectual power.

The fulsome praise of goodness can alienate; it can whet the appetite for the cookie-jar on the top shelf. In Saki's "The Story-Teller," a mischievous bachelor tells three children on a train the tale of a wondrously good little girl, awarded medals for her propriety. But she met a wolf in the park; and though she ran, the dangling of her medals led the wolf straight to her, so that she was devoured utterly. Though the children are delighted with this unconventional narrative, their aunt protests, "A most improper story to tell to young children!" "Unhappy woman!" the departing bachelor murmurs. "For the next six months or so those children will assail her in public with demands for an improper story!"

Well, Greek and Norse myths, for instance, sometimes are not very proper; yet, stirring the imagination, they do more to bring about an early apprehension of norms than do any number of the dull and interminable doings of Dick and Jane. The story of Pandora, or of Thor's adventure with the old woman and her cat, gives any child an insight into the conditions of existence—dimly grasped at the moment, perhaps, but gaining in power as the years pass—that no utilitarian "real-life situation" fiction can match.

Because they are eternally valid, Hesiod and the saga-singers are modern. And the versions of Hawthorne or of Andrew Lang are far better prose than the quasi-basic English thrust upon young people in many recent textbooks.

If we starve young people for imagination, adventure, and some sort of heroism—to turn now to a later level of learning—they are not likely to embrace Good Approved Real-Life Tales for Good Approved Real Life Boys and Girls; on the contrary, they may resort to the dregs of letters, rather than be bored altogether. If they are not introduced to Stevenson and Conrad, say—and that fairly early—they will find the nearest and newest Grub Street pornographers. And the consequences will be felt not merely in their failure of taste, but in their misapprehension of human nature, lifelong; and eventually, in the whole tone of a nation. "On this scheme of things...a woman is but an animal; and an animal not of the highest order." The Naked Ape-theory of human nature, the "reductionist" notion of man as a breathing automaton, is reinforced by ignorance of literature's moral imagination.

In one of his Causeries, Sainte-Beuve tells of a playwright, standing at a friend's window to watch a frantic Parisian mob pouring through the street: "See my pageant passing!" the author complacently murmurs. Art is man's nature; and it is true enough, as Oscar Wilde said whimsically, that nature imitates art. Our private and public actions, in mature years, have been determined by the opinions and tastes we acquired in youth. Great books do influence societies for the better; and bad books do drag down the general level of personal and social conduct. Having seen the pageant, the mob proceeds to behave as a playwright thinks it should. We become what others, in a voice of authority, tell us we are or ought to be.

*   *   *

So I think that in the teaching of literature, some of the theories of
the life-adjustment and permissive schools have done considerable
mischief. Nowadays the advocates of life-adjustment education are
giving ground, sullenly, before their critics. The intellectual ances-
tor of their doctrines is Rousseau. Though I am no warm admirer
of the ideas of Rousseau, I like still less the doctrines of Gradgrind,
in *Hard Times;* so I hope that life-adjustment methods of teaching
literature will not be supplanted by something yet worse conceived.
After all, *real* adjustment to the conditions of human existence is
adjustment to norms. Even an ineffectual endeavor to teach norms
is better than to ignore or deny all standards. A mistaken zeal for
utilitarian, vocational training in place of normative instruction; an
emphasis upon the physical and biological sciences that would push
literature into a dusty corner of the curriculum; an attempt to secure
spoken competency in foreign languages at the expense of the great
works of our own language—these might be changes in education
as hostile to the imparting of norms through literature as anything
which the life-adjustment and permissive people have done.

*　　　*　　　*

So I venture to suggest here, in scanty outline, how it is possible to
form a normative consciousness through the study of humane
letters. What I have to say ought to be commonplace; but these
ideas seem to have been forgotten in many quarters. This normative
endeavor ought to be the joint work of family and school. As the art
of reading often is better taught by parents than it can be taught in
a large class in school, so a knowledge of good books comes at least
as frequently from the home as from the school. My own taste for
books grew from both sources: my grandfather's and my mother's
bookshelves, and from a very good little grade-school library. And
if a school is failing to impart a taste for good books, this often can
be remedied by interested attention in the family.

Tentatively, I distinguish four levels of literature by which a normative consciousness is developed. The upper levels do not supplant the earlier, but rather supplement and blend with them; and the process of becoming familiar with these four levels or bodies or normative knowledge extends from the age of three or four to the studies of college and university. We may call these levels fantasy; narrative history and biography; reflective prose and poetic fiction; and philosophy and theology.

1) Fantasy. The fantastic and the fey, far from being unhealthy for small children, are precisely what a healthy child needs; under such stimulus a child's moral imagination quickens. Out of the early tales of wonder comes a sense of awe—and the beginning of philosophy. All things begin and end in mystery. For that matter, a normative consciousness may be aroused by themes less striking than the Arthurian legends or the Norse tales. The second book I had read to me was *Little Black Sambo*. Learning it by heart then, I can recite it still. (One symptom of the growing silliness of our time was the demand, a few years ago, that *Little Black Sambo* be banned as "racist.") Though I risk falling into bathos, I cannot resist remarking that even *Little Black Sambo* touches upon norms. What child fails to reflect upon the *hubris* of the tigers, or the prudence of Sambo?

If children are to begin to understand themselves, and other people, and the laws that govern our nature, they ought to be encouraged to read Lang's collections of fairy tales, and the brothers Grimm (even at their grimmest), and Andersen, and the Arabian Nights, and all the rest; and presently the better romancers for young people, like Blackmore and Howard Pyle. Even the Bible, in the beginning, is fantasy for the young. The allegory of Jonah and the whale is accepted, initially, as a tale of the marvelous, and so sticks in the memory. Only in later years does one recognize the story as the symbol of the Jews' exile in Babylon, and of how faith may preserve men and nations through the most terrible of trials.

2) Narrative history and biography. My grandfather and I, during the long walks that we used to take when I was six or seven

years old, would talk of the character of Richard II, and of Puritan domestic life, and of the ferocity of Assyrians. The intellectual partnership of an imaginative man of sixty and an inquisitive boy of seven is an edifying thing. My preparation for these conversations came from books in my grandfather's library: Dickens' *Child's History of England,* Hawthorne's *Grandfather's Chair,* Ridpath's four-volume illustrated *History of the World.* Later my grandfather gave me H. G. Wells's *Outline of History.* In the fullness of time, I came to disagree with Dickens' and Wells's interpretations of history; but that was all to the good, for it stimulated my critical faculties and led me to the proper study of mankind—and to the great historians, Herodotus, Thucydides, Xenophon, Polybius, Livy, Tacitus, and all the rest; to the great biographies, also, like Plutarch's, and Boswell's *Johnson,* and Lockhart's *Scott.* Reading of great lives does something to make decent lives.

3) Reflective prose and poetic fiction. When I was seven, my mother gave me a set of Fenimore Cooper's novels; and about the same time I inherited from a great-uncle my set of Hawthorne. That launched me upon novel-reading, so that by the time I was ten I had read all of Hugo, Dickens, and Mark Twain. Fiction is truer than fact: I mean that in great fiction we obtain the distilled wisdom of men of genius, understandings of human nature which we could attain—if at all—unaided by books, only at the end of life, after numberless painful experiences. I began to read Sir Walter Scott when I was twelve or thirteen; and I think I learnt from the Waverley novels, and from Shakespeare, more of the varieties of character than ever I have got since from the manuals of psychology.

Such miscellaneous browsing in the realm of fiction rarely does mischief. When I was eleven or twelve, I was much influenced by Twain's *Mysterious Stranger,* an atheist tract disguised as a romance of mediaeval Austria. It did not turn me into a juvenile atheist; but it set me to inquiring after first causes—and in time, paradoxically, it led me to Dante, my mainstay ever since. In certain ways, the great novel and the great poem can teach more of norms than can philosophy and theology.

4) Philosophy and theology. For the crown of normative literary studies, we turn, about the age of nineteen or twenty, to abstraction and generalization, chastened by logic. It simply is not true that

> *One impulse from a vernal wood*
> *May teach you more of man,*
> *Of moral evil and of good,*
> *Than all the sages can.*

It is not from vegetal nature that one acquires some knowledge of human passions and longings. There exist, rather, in Emerson's phrase, law for man and law for thing. The law for man we learn from Plato, Aristotle, Seneca, Marcus Aurelius; from the Hebrew prophets, Saint Paul, Saint Augustine, and so many other Christian writers. Our petty private rationality is founded upon the wisdom of the men of dead ages; and if we endeavor to guide ourselves solely by our limited private insights, we tumble down into the ditch of unreason.

"Scientific" truth, or what is popularly taken to be scientific truth, alters from year to year—with accelerating speed in our day. But poetic and moral truth change little with the elapse of the centuries. To the unalterable in human existence, humane literature is a trustworthy guide.

But enough! I try your patience. What I have been trying to describe in the preceding summary analysis is that body of literature which helps to form the normative consciousness: that is, to enliven the moral imagination. Here I have been historian and diagnostician; I have not endeavored to offer you facile remedies for our present bent condition. We hope for some remedies from the better minds and hearts among the American rising generation.

If a public will not have the moral imagination, I have been saying, then it will fall first into the idyllic imagination; and presently into the diabolic imagination—this last becoming a state of narcosis, figuratively and literally. For we are created moral beings; and when we deny our nature, in letters as in action, the gods of the copybook headings with fire and slaughter return.

I attest the moral vision of men like Aleksandr Solzhenitsyn; some have begun to make a stand, in the republic of letters, against the diabolic imagination and the diabolic regime. A human body that cannot react is a corpse; and a body of letters that cannot react against narcotic illusions might better be buried. Up the literary reactionaries! The theological virtues may find hardy champions in these closing years of the twentieth century: men and women of letters who remember that in the beginning was the Word.

VII

The Architecture of Servitude and Boredom

Britain's urban riots of July, 1981, came to Edinburgh somewhat tardily, but they arrived. Being there at the time, I asked a knowledgeable Scottish engineer, who builds roads but is an architect too, what had caused the Edinburgh troubles.

"Bad architecture," he told me. He meant that the Edinburgh riot arose in one of the ugliest and most boring of the county-council public housing schemes, afflicted by a ghastly monotony. He did not suggest that the rioters were endowed with good architectural taste; it was rather that the people who dwell in this Edinburgh housing-scheme are perpetually discontented, without quite knowing why—and spoiling for a fight.

It would not be difficult to show that the dreariness of life in "working-class" quarters of English and Scottish towns was a principal cause of the burning and the looting and the stoning of police which came to pass in Liverpool and London and other places. It was not that the districts where the riots occurred were architectural survivals from the Bleak Age: no, those quarters were built or rebuilt after the Second World War. But everything in them, including the police stations, was shoddy and badly designed. It has been said that mankind can endure anything except boredom. With great buildings or with small, the architecture of our mass-age, in this latter half of the twentieth century, has been wondrously boring. Also it has been an architecture of sham: the outward symbol of a society which, despite all its protestations of being "free" and "democratic," rapidly sinks into servility.

What Sir Osbert Sitwell has called "the modern proletarian cosmopolis" has been sliding, politically and architecturally, toward general boredom and general servitude. Talking vaguely of egali-tarianism and an "international style," the "renewers" of our cities have been creating vistas of boredom. Amidst this monotony, the natives are restless. With every month that passes, the rate of serious crimes increases. And what is done to alleviate such discontents? Why, not infrequently the public authorities are moved to relieve the barrenness of their urban landscapes by commissioning some-body to design (for a delightful fee) another piece of "junk" sculpture, product of the blow-torch, to be erected in some place of public assembly. Public funds have been made available lavishly to encourage such artistic frauds. Yet somehow these contributions to a city's amenities do not restore civic virtue: the rates of murder, rape, and arson continue to rise.

*   *   *

Two decades ago, when Jane Jacobs published her detailed and convincing study *The Life and Death of Great American Cities*, I naively assumed that the tide had turned; that our hideous blunders in urban planning were repented by the leaders of business and industry; that we might discern the beginnings of a recovery of the humane scale in our urban life and conceivably in our architecture.

Seventeen years ago, when I addressed at St. Louis (then the most decayed city in America) the National Conference of the American Institute of Planners, I fancied that I discerned among some urban planners glimmerings of sense and taste. But I was mistaken.

For the policies of the Johnson administration, in the name of urban "renewal," created urban deserts and jungles on a scale previously unparalleled in time of peace. George Romney, in his last address as governor of Michigan, declared that the great Detroit riots had been provoked by "urban renewal and federal highway building." He was accurate; and nobody paid any attention.

Dr. Martin Anderson's book *The Federal Bulldozer* described the Johnsonian folly, and suggested remedies; but only some minor checks upon the process were effected. We continued to dehumanize our cities; if the pace of destruction is somewhat slowed nowadays, that is chiefly for lack of funds. Quite literally, as T. S. Eliot observed concerning education in his *Notes Towards the Definition of Culture,* we are "destroying our ancient edifices to make ready the ground upon which the barbarian nomads of the future will encamp in their mechanized caravans."

*   *   *

As I endeavored to remind the American Institute of Planners, successful planning must be concerned primarily with the person, and how he thrives under a large plan; with the republic (or the public interest), and what sort of society arises from grand designs. I quote Eliot once more: "One thing to avoid is a *universalized* planning; one thing to ascertain is the limits of the plannable."

Assuming, however, that urban planning has no limits, the breed of urban planners have given us the architecture of servitude and boredom. Over the past quarter of a century and more, anarchy and desolation have been the consequences of grandiose pseudo-planning. One is a good deal safer in Palermo, or Tunis, or Fez, than in

New York, or Chicago, or Los Angeles. For those ancient towns, whatever their difficulties and their poverty, remain genuine communities, in which the townsman still is a person, not wholly lost in the faceless crowd; and in which, whatever the degree of civic corruption, still the public authority can maintain a tolerable order. Our urban planners have lost those civic advantages.

Some years ago I received a letter from a young man in Oklahoma, conservatively inclined, who had dropped out of college because his university, like the American urban behemoth, possessed neither imagination nor humane apprehension. I offer you some of his observations on urban planning and architecture.

> First, the quality of the architecture. Organic architecture is being ignored, for the most part, because of its personal and individual quality. Planning for the individual must entail an individual architecture, not international style *à la* the current mode of Paul Rudolph, Louis I. Kahn, Gordon Bunshaft, and the Eastern boys.
>
> Second, the sheer size of our cities will kill humane culture. You are acquainted with the Brave New Worlds that our latest periodicals display, such as Paulo Soleri's 'City on the Mesa.' Frightful, but it is coming—the mob loves it; togetherness.
>
> Third, the automobile is obsolete. It is time we recognized this before the auto makes civilization obsolete.... The Highway Commissioner must be stopped—or, better, overruled.
>
> Fourth, the land speculators are the great makers of slumurbia, responsible for the concentration of skyscrapers. All too often they are defended as part of a free economy.
>
> ...It seems to me that we can plan the functional requirements of a city, but the more we plan the *culture* of cities, meaning especially the

architecture of cities, the worse it will get. In other
words, plan part of the city, and include as part of the plan
a great deal that is unplanned.

Just so; this seeming paradox is what Eliot meant in his remarks
on the limits of planning. In American society, urban planning has
tended to reflect the talent of Americans for technological success,
but also to reflect their frequent deficiency in the realm of imagination, remarked by Tocqueville a century and a half ago. So we find
ourselves in our air-conditioned urban jungle.

*　　　*　　　*

I venture to suggest just now some general principles of urban
restoration which might help to redeem this country from boredom
and servitude.

First, the architecture of a city and a countryside ought to be
adapted to the humane scale. A city is not simply a collectivity; it is
a vital continuity, composed of a great many distinct individuals,
most of whom have no desire to be precisely like everybody else.
Society is not a machine: on the contrary, it is a kind of spiritual
corporation; and if treated as a machine, people rebel, politically or
personally.

Second, the community called a city must nurture roots, not hack
through them. Neighborhoods, voluntary associations, old land-
marks, historic monuments—such elements make men and women
feel at home. They bind together a community with what Gabriel
Marcel calls "diffused gratitude." Restoration and rehabilitation
almost always are preferable to grand reconstitution—even when
more expensive, which repair rarely is.

Third, the measure of urban planning should be not commercial
gain primarily, but the common good. In miscalled "urban renewal," the Johnson administration's "war on poverty" actually was

war against the poor, for the advantage of the speculator and the contractor. Once I spoke to an association of Jewish charities in a large meeting-room at the top of Boston's museum of science. From the windows, we looked across the bay to a district covered by immense high-rise and high-rent apartments, or even more costly condominiums. Only three years earlier, I was told by the rabbi who chaired our meeting, this had been a low-rent district inhabited by poor Jews. The area had not been a slum, he said; and he mused, looking out the window. "Where are they now?" he murmured. "Why, dead, or swept under the rug." Those words would have been as true in a hundred other American cities.

Fourth, civic restoration must be founded upon the long-established customs, habits, and political institutions of a community. Most convictions and institutions are products of a long historical process of winnowing and filtering. No planner, however ingenious, can make humanity happy by being stretched upon a Procrustean bed of social innovation. And among the deepest longings of humankind is the desire for permanence and security of territory, "a place of one's own."

These four very general principles, generally disregarded by the typical planner of the twentieth century, slowly obtain a hearing once more. We may see them at work practically in the successful restoration, for instance, of an eighteenth-century city of high interest—Savannah. But these beneficent concepts have not yet entered the heads of the run-of the-mill city politician and urban administrator.

*   *   *

Consider Detroit, the city I used to know best. Nobody can take pleasure in knowing Detroit well nowadays. That city's publicists boast of the Renaissance Center, a group of glittering colossal towers near the river, including a hotel, offices, and a shopping complex—the whole constructed very like a fortress, with re-doubts, doubtless in anticipation of a storm by the nearby prole-tariat, one of these days. From the restaurant at the summit of the Detroit Plaza Hotel, one can behold mile upon mile of decay and obliteration of a city founded at the beginning of the eighteenth century. Nearly all the old neighborhoods and districts of Detroit that I used to explore during my college days have been effaced. Even the old high-domed City Hall has vanished without trace. The central block of the Wayne County Courthouse, with its quadriga and elaborate baroque decoration, still stands—over-shadowed by the Renaissance Center; but those in Detroit's seats of the mighty mean to pull it down, another job for the wrecking contractors.

From the Renaissance Center, one may stroll in relative safety to the cafes of Greektown, less than a hundred yards distant. Beyond that little old quarter only the unwary venture: a glance at a map showing the incidence of violent crimes in Detroit will explain why.

Greektown is safe because the streets are thronged with people day and night; because its two- or three-story buildings are fully inhabited, with old women watching the streets from upper windows; because it is not much afflicted by vacant lots where predators lurk; because a social (and ethnic) community survives there. The humane scale has not been wiped out of existence by civic "planners."

But the boasted Renaissance Center, externally and internally a triumph of extravagantly bad taste, is a besieged island amidst the swamps of urban savagery. It is designed vertically, not horizontally: so its tenants meet chiefly in elevators, not knowing one another. Certain happy persons, true, have been mightily enriched by this Detroit development—persons with large political influence, which obtained abundant federal funds for the project. One wonders whether, twenty years from now, the Renaissance

Center will not have been demolished in its turn.

A few miles north of the Renaissance Center—on a clear day, one can see the district with the naked eye from the top of the Renaissance Center's towers—there used to lay the old district of Poletown, inhabited by people of eastern European stock. That whole neighorhood was pulled down, every brick, stone, and stick of it, to supply a site (mostly parking lots) for a General Motors plant. Thousands of people, many of them elderly, nearly all of them in narrow circumstances, were abruptly uprooted. They protested vehemently, to no avail. Where did they go? Some doubled up in slums—though they were not slum-folk before. Others presumably settled in new low-income housing developments, commonly uglier and more dangerous than the older slums. Two Catholic churches were demolished, despite the resistance of pastors and congregations. One protesting pastor died, a few months later, of a broken heart; newspapers and their writers to the editor praised him—after his funeral.

This scandalous "clearance," widely and unfavorably publicized, was made possible by an unholy alliance. The chief powers in this league were former Detroit Mayor Coleman Young; General Motors planners, said to have been bullied by Mayor Young; and the late Cardinal Dearden, archbishop of Detroit, who was given to much talk about injustice toward the poor (that is, the abstract poor at large, not the poor of Poletown), and all that. When General Motors tardily offered to move one of Poletown's churches to a new site, the Cardinal rejected the offer and insisted upon demolition—to the astonishment and rage of pastor and parishioners.

It is rather a nasty story, deserving of a short sardonic book. So Poletown is gone; and the decent folk of small means who lived there were shuffled off to the architecture of boredom and servitude. We may be sure they'll not spend their declining years in any Renaissance Center. Again, the power of eminent domain and plenty of public money were employed in this successful assault on community and the humane scale of living. Are people treated more arbitrarily, with greater disregard of their rights in property, in a socialist dictatorship?

After this fashion, even in these United States, there takes form the future collectivism, like one of H.G. Wells's utopias or Aldous Huxley's dystopia: the countryside almost wholly depopulated; the great bulk of the population packed into smart, shoddy, comfortless, impersonal "housing developments"; and looming above this land-scape and manscape, the blank-walled towers of the administrative class. The architecture of this future domination—or, rather, this emerging domination—retains nothing whatsoever that wakes the imagination or satisfies the memory. One may predict that in this domination of utilitarianism, life will be unsafe increasingly, as well as unsatisfying; and that despite an outward appearance of material accomplishment, real incomes will diminish steadily: architectural impoverishment and general impoverishment are joined histori-cally. Jacquetta Hawkes's fable "The Unites" represents the final degradation of such a collectivism.

In that tale, Miss Hawkes (Mrs. J.B. Priestley) describes a future society from which all privacy, all art (except degraded vestiges), all beauty of architecture, and all symbols have been stripped away, together with all belief in the divine. Production and consump-tion—though reduced to bare subsistence levels—are the obses-sions of the folk who call themselves the Unites. I quote a passage from this fable:

> Perhaps it was this utilitarianism more than anything else which made Unite existence fall so far below the worst of human life in former days. Peasants of old had lived from birth to death almost as helplessly, with almost as little hope of escape, but their life's course had been decked with fantasy and symbol, with simple art and ritual, with

very many things that were of no use in daily life except to make it human and significant. Now utilitarianism itself was at its most base, for needs and expectations had been so much reduced that all were perfectly satisfied. To have no desire is far more dreadful than for desire to remain unfulfilled.

The population of our cities is not very far from that condition. When all interesting architecture has fallen into the limbo of lost things, presumably the rising generation will raise no objection to the architecture of servility and boredom, because they will know no alternative. Desire will have starved to death. As Jacquetta Hawkes implies, architecture, like all art and all science, arises originally out of the religious impulse; and when a culture's religious quest and yearning have expired, then architecture, like all the other aspects of a culture, falls into decadence. Thus the total condition of our urban life and the dreariness of our architecture are not separate phenomena.

*   *   *

But I must permit some cheerfulness to break in, at this point. Here and there in this land, effective resistance is offered to the evangels of architectural boredom. Two decades ago, it was proposed to sweep away the old streets of Galena, Illinois—one of our surviving historic towns with a good deal of interesting architecture—in order to build supermarkets and "modernize" generally. After a hard fight, in which I took some hand, the "developers" were defeated.

Through years of protest and litigation, we succeeded in one major contest against utilitarian city planners, in a really big city: the defeat of the Riverfront Expressway at New Orleans, which would have blighted the French Quarter and done other mischief. You can read about that fight in a book by Richard Baumbach and William Borah, *The Second Battle of New Orleans* (University of Alabama Press). The advocates of preservation of our architectural patrimony do obtain some hearing today—after most of that patrimony has been flattened.

Preservation of good buildings, good streets, and good districts is only one aspect of our struggle against the architecture of servility and boredom. New construction, whether downtown or in the suburbs, looms larger. High costs of all building unite with the sorry limitations of most architects to produce barren public buildings, office towers, and "motor hotels"; while the condominiums and the tract-houses employ third-rate materials and fourth-rate interior decoration. Ever since the Second World War, the old arts of building have lain in the sere and yellow leaf. Facile apologies for shoddy and dreary work are offered—as, in Waugh's novel *Helena,* the architects and sculptors of the Emperor Constantine offer him excuses for not building a triumphal arch in the old grand style: "That is not the function of the feature, sire," and similar jargon. At length Constantine demands of them, *"Can* you do it?" And those architects are compelled to answer, "No." So it is in our age: a principal reason why our buildings are ugly is that our architects and craftsmen have quite forgotten how to construct handsome buildings. Incidentally, I commend to everyone interested in the relationships between social decay and the decline of architecture and the arts a slim book published in 1952 by Bernard Berenson: *The Arch of Constantine, or The Decline of Form.*

About all that can be said of most recent building, on every scale, in this country is this: American building is not quite so wretched as building today in most of the rest of the world. Recently I spent a few hours—as much time as I could endure— in the City of London, once dominated by St. Paul's and the

Tower. Here Julius Caesar built his fortress on the Thames, and the hideous new museum of the City of London is full of Roman artifacts. The City, for centuries past the financial center of British Empire and Commonwealth, was badly smashed by German bombs; strange to say, some of the damage still has not been cleared up. But the City has been rebuilt, of really nasty gray concrete, already badly streaked, obscuring the great dome of Wren's cathedral, elbowing aside the Tower, supplanting the old picturesque confusion of the streets by a new ugly confusion worse confounded. This "Barbican Scheme" betrays the failure of intellect and imagination throughout Britain since the Second World War. What has been done in the neighborhood of the Barbican is a disgrace to England so embarrassing that few people mention it. Even in a Communist state, such an architectural atrocity would not be permitted, and the engulfing of a famous cathedral by dismal office-buildings would be rejected. Surely it is not from Britain today that a revival of architectural imagination can be expected. Nor do we encounter imaginative building in Germany, France, Italy, or Scandinavia. Everywhere it is the architecture of the mass-age, so far as "lodging" goes; and the architecture of the Bureaucrat's Epoch, so far as public buildings are in question.

Well, do I give you naught for your comfort? Do we descend steadily, and now somewhat speedily, toward a colossal architecture of unparalleled dreariness, and a colossal state of unparalleled uniformity—at best Tocqueville's "democratic despotism"? Will all of us labor under a profound depression of spirits (in part conscious, in part below the level of consciousness) because of the boring and servile architecture about us? And will the society now taking form in America resign itself to a parallel barrenness of soul and mind, under a political domination of unimaginative and complacent bureaucrats and managers?

No, not necessarily. Let us leave historical determinism to the Marxists and other ideologues. The courses of nations depend upon the energy and the talents of particular individuals—and upon Providence, always inscrutable. It remains true even in this mass-age of ours that individual genius and courage—or, at least, the imagination and boldness of a handful of men and women—may leaven the lump of dullness and apathy, all across the land. In practical politics, something of that sort has begun to occur among us.

From causes which at present no one guesses, conceivably there may come about a reinvigoration of urban planning and of architecture and of the humane scale. Rather as the current discoveries about the Shroud of Turin conceivably may work a widespread renewal of belief in the literal resurrection of the body, so people at the end of the twentieth century may discover afresh old truths about form, symbol, and pattern in architecture and in urban living.

The architectural and artistic charlatan, leagued with the spoils-man and the bureaucrat, may be thrust aside, abruptly, by a new breed of architects and artists endowed with the moral imagination. There have occurred ages when an architecture of vigor and freedom flourished, nurtured by myth and symbol and human confidence. Given faith and hope, it is yet imaginable that we may draw upon the architectural well of the past to bring into being an architecture (in the larger sense of that word) strong and humane. I have endeavored to diagnose the architectural malady; others must prescribe the remedies.

VIII

Regaining Historical Consciousness

The middle decades of our twentieth century have been marked intellectually by the publication of historical writings of the first importance—even though simultaneously there has occurred a decline in the teaching of history to the rising generation. I have in mind such historians of a philosophical cast as Arnold Toynbee, Eric Voegelin, Christopher Dawson, Herbert Butterfield, John Lukacs, and Friedrich Herr. The scope of their work is so vast I confine myself to one strong theme which runs through the books of many of our major recent historians: the meaning of historical consciousness. This subject is best examined by particular attention to the writings of John Lukacs.

Permit me to commence with certain lines from "Gerontion":

> *After such knowledge, what forgiveness? Think now*
> *History has many cunning passages, contrived corridors*
> *And issues, deceives with whispering ambitions,*

Guides us by vanities. Think now
She gives when our attention is distracted
And what she gives, gives with such supple confusions
That the giving famishes the craving.

Here Eliot's gypsy witch called history may be understood in two senses. In the one sense, Eliot means the word "history" as we understand that word ordinarily: the record of a nation's or a civilization's past. In the second sense, Eliot's meaning is best defined by Elizabeth Drew: "'History' is human experience lived without the framework of a Logos; lived by the 'knowledge' supplied by empirical science. It is man relying on his own desires and 'whispers,' believing that he can control his own fate; directed only by arbitrary expediency...." Yet in both of Eliot's meanings, through the dying lips of Gerontion we touch upon the urgent concern of our chief twentieth-century historians with the meaning of historical consciousness. Is history no better than *el amor bruja*, ensnaring us in contrived corridors? Or was Gerontion mistaken? May there exist great truths to be perceived through historical learning? Perhaps, after all, the framework of a Logos may be discerned, however dimly, by the historian possessed of a philosophic habit of mind.

Before we stumble into Gerontion's cunning passages and issues, permit me to make it clear that when I refer to possible great truths to be perceived through historical study, I do not have in mind any nineteenth-century notion of Progress, nor yet any ideological infatuation. Instead, I am acutely aware of Gabriel Marcel's warning against "that armed ghost, the 'meaning' of history." We know the past only fragmentarily and imperfectly: it is fatuous to suppose that our scant knowledge of the past might enable us to foretell the future. Yet that fatuity has afflicted men of learning, Hegel among them, and many of the great movers and shakers of our century. On this subject, Raymond Aron, in his book *The Opium of the Intellectuals,* is quotable:

Those who aspire to command history seem to dream
either of eliminating the intervention of accidents, of
great men and chance encounters, or of rebuilding society according to a global plan and discarding the heritage
of unjustifiable traditions, or of putting an end to the
conflicts which divide humanity and deliver it up to the
tragic irony of war. Reason teaches us precisely the
opposite—that politics will always remain the art of the
irrevocable choice by fallible men in unforeseen circumstances and semi-ignorance.

Amen to that. So I, like the living historians I am about to
discuss, do not follow the armed ghost. To seek for truths in history,
for these philosophical inquirers, distinctly is not to indulge in
dreamy visions of unborn ages, or to predict the inevitability of
some political domination. Rather, the truths of history, the real
meanings, are to be discovered in what history can teach us about
the framework of the Logos, if you will: about the significance of
human existence: about the splendor and the misery of our condition. In this inquiry, there must be joined with the historical
discipline certain insights of philosophy and psychology. For
historical consciousness necessarily is entwined with the mystery of
personal consciousness. For elucidation of this declaration, we turn
to the writings of John Lukacs.

*   *   *

Applying a philosophical intellect to the study of history, Lukacs
believes that historical studies may become the principal literary
form and way to wisdom in the dawning age. This does not mean
that he endeavors to present a "philosophy of history"—on the

contrary, he agrees with Burckhardt that the notion of a philosophy of history is "a centaur, a contradiction in terms; for history coordinates, and hence is unphilosophical, while philosophy subordinates, and hence is unhistorical."

A bold scholar, Lukacs stands in the line of Tocqueville and Burckhardt; also he has read Samuel Johnson through and through. His own specialty is contemporary history, and he is the author of a well-known short history of the Cold War, and of a lengthy study of eastern Europe during and since the Second World War. His *Decline and Rise of Europe* (1967) was in part a prolegomenon to *Historical Consciousness.* He is a master of the neglected art of annotation—footnotes and appended notes, witty and illuminating. In humane letters, he has read widely in several languages, and deeply. Here is a thesis of his:

> I believe that the future of Western thought will be historical; but, I repeat, this does not mean a philosophy of history but a chastened historical philosophy, concentrating on the historicity of problems and of events, assuming the uniqueness of human nature anew, presenting no new definitions, no freshly jigsawed categories, emphasizing the existential—and not merely philosophical—primacy of truth: a more mature achievement of the human mind than even the mastering of certain forces of nature through the scientific method, and certainly more mature than the simplistic conception of causalties.

Although lucid, *Historical Consciousness* and Lukacs' other books are complex and never doctrinaire or ideological—which naturally diminishes attention to them in the quasi-literary mass media. Lukacs' candid convictions, never shrouded, tempt the critic to digress at length on Lukacs' distinction between "the public" and "the people" (for, like Plato, Lukacs is a lover of distinctions); upon his mordant criticisms of positivistic historians; upon his remarks about national character; or his discussions of objectivity and subjectivity; or his doubts about Darwin; or his appreciation of Heisenberg. This historian casts his net wide. But I must endeavor to take up Lukacs on his central theme of historical consciousness.

"We are outgrowing some of our standard intellectual 'problems,' at least in the West, where the conflict between science and religion has become outdated," Lukacs writes; "and it is at least possible that history and religion, and history and science, may be brought together, but on a higher level." We live today in an intellectual interregnum. "It is, for example, historical thinking that provides us with the best explanation of the chaotic development of scientific thinking during its last phase," Lukacs continues; "and it is not impossible that as we struggle through a tremendous jungle of dying concepts and half-truths, many convergent paths in science, history, and religion may emerge before us: there are certain discernible symptoms that point in these directions."

Historical studies conceivably may lead us out of the jungle, but this is not certain: excessive specialization, positivistic prejudices, shallow scientism, and the thinness of culture in the mass age afflict the historical discipline, as they afflict every other field of study today. Lukacs' book *Historical Consciousness* is intended to help in effecting a grand reform of historical writing and teaching.

Lukacs readily confesses that often historical thinking has been disorganized and weak, and that historical consciousness may be employed to deceive. A reformed history, he declares, must be imaginative and humane; like poetry, like the great novel, it must be personal rather than abstract, ethical rather than ideological. Like the poet, the historian must understand that devotion to truth is not identical with the cult of facts.

It is easier to write a mediocre history than a mediocre novel. It is more difficult to write a great history than a great novel. Certainly this is the reason why, in the last two hundred years, there have been more great novels than great histories. Probably this is why the Western world is yet to see the appearance of a truly classic historian, a historian Dante, a historian Shakespeare.

In the modern age we have known no Thucydides, no Polybius, no Livy, no Plutarch. Obsessed by the Fact, a nineteenth-century idol, most modern historians have forgotten that facts, too, are constructions—and meaningful only in association. It is the *event*, rather than the isolated *fact*, which is the proper concern of historians. In the commendable sense, the genuine historian must be at home with fiction.

If the historian is to supplant the novelist as culture's guardian, he must learn to write more nobly and more philosophically than he does today. "In the beginning was the Word, not the Fact; history is thought and spoken and written with words; and the historian must be master of his words as much as of his 'facts,' whatever those might mean." Lukacs is appealing here not to linguistic analysis, not to semantics, but to rhetoric in its original signification.

Popular interest in good historical writing increases nowadays. Yet this may work mischief if the writing of history is dominated by "professional intellectuals"—that is, by positivists, ideologues, Benda's treasonous clerks. Meritocracy among historians would be as dismal as meritocracy in the state, "a poisonous development." Increasingly, guardianship of traditional common sense and of the language has been abandoned by most intellectuals for "more advantageous occupations... Yet these melancholy developments have not weakened my belief that among all kinds of people, in these very times, and even in the United States, appetite for all kinds of historical knowledge, and their historical consciousness in many different ways, is growing."

A restored historical consciousness must rest upon certain very old insights. The most important of these insights, Lukacs implies, is the power of religious understanding—lacking which, there can exist no order in the soul and no order in the state; indeed, no history which can be recorded without a shudder. Here Lukacs stands with Johann Huizinga, Christopher Dawson, and Herbert Butterfield, whom he quotes frequently. Cartesian objectivity is a limited thing, and dying; our situation is post-scientific, rather than post-Christian; the new physics undoes the smug pseudo-certitudes of the mechanists. Human nature is central once more, and it may fall to the historian to renew our apprehension of that nature.

> In this sense a Christian and a historical understanding of human nature may very well complement each other—especially now when our world is suffering from a decay of love, a condition which is obscured by the grim preoccupation with sex, and obfuscated by an increase of bureaucratic welfare and of legalistic tolerance, with the corresponding decline in human sensitivities. In this sense we are already living in a world where unassuming love, again, becomes curiously and existentially practical.

There is no man but historic man. Forgetting this truth, we justify Hegel's observation that we learn from the study of history how mankind has learned nothing from the study of history. The Darwinians "fantastically elongated the history of man on this earth," mistaking the Java or Peking or Rhodesian anthropoids for humanity at one end of the scale, and projecting man into an unprovable Progressive future—"Ye unborn ages, crowd not on my soul." But abruptly we have become aware that through the progress of technology it now lies in our power to terminate human history some two thousand years after the birth of Christ: man working upon himself retributive providential judgment, as man has done so often in the past. The Last Judgment once more can be reasonably postulated as the terminal event in history.

If all history is a drama, the time cries out for a new Thucydides. More and more, the people of our era become conscious that, as Santayana expressed it, those who ignore the past are condemned to repeat it; and, one may add, to repeat it without pleasure or hope. When the moral imagination is starved, when generation cannot link with generation, Kipling's fable of the Hive is realized; and the fire awaits. Like his mentor Tocqueville, John Lukacs seeks historical understanding that we may prophesy in our time.

*   *   *

To prophesy is not the same as to predict. Lukacs does not believe that scientific knowledge of history can enable people to predict tomorrow's events or the next century's events. Yet a knowledge of human nature derived from historical thinking may enable a talented historian, or indeed any person well schooled historically, to foresee with reasonable prospect of fulfillment the consequences of certain tendencies or courses of action—supposing, always, that such tendencies or courses are not interrupted or diverted by other influences (whether contrived or seemingly happenstance). What most of the Hebrew prophets did was to foretell the coming of divine wrath, should not Israel mend her ways. Rather in that sense, Lukacs and certain others prophesy as historians.

For John Lukacs, like T. S. Eliot, foresees the coming wrath. Here the titles of certain chapters in his book *The Passing of the*

Modern Age must suffice to suggest his disgust with our time: the monstrosity of government; the impotence of powers; the separation of races; the conformity of nations; the purposelessness of society; the fiction of prosperity; the dissolution of learning; the meaninglessness of letters; the senselessness of the arts; the destruction of nature; the decay of science; the faithlessness of religion; the mutation of morality.

Because of the disintegrating of our moral order, Lukacs argues, we stand now upon the forbidding threshold of the new Dark Age. The nineteenth-century notion of ineluctable Progress is undone altogether. Our ancestors of the last century expected our present technological developments.

> What they did not see was the state of the mind and hearts of millions of well-fed and well-clothed men and women in these airheated and air-cooled rooms. They could not imagine how in the greatest city of the Western world millions would be living next to each other as entire strangers, that millions of the better off would flee the city at night, abandoning entire portions of it to hostile people of various races; that in the richest and largest of buildings robberies would occur at any hour of the day; that no one would dare to cross the city parks and few would dare to walk midtown streets at night; that an enormous body of policemen, large enough for the armed forces of a Middle European republic, would be distrusted and feared and yet unable to insure order and safety; that many of the schools of the city would fulfill only a desperate and necessary function of daytime custodial prisons, with police patrolling their corridors, where teachers and overgrown boys and girls would confront one another with screaming hatred and con-

cealed weapons; that hundreds of thousands of people, including children, would be dependent on narcotics; that thousands of well-to-do people would implore their psychiatric doctors to place them in certain hospitals where, injected with soporific drugs, they could be put into a state of cold sleep for months.

*   *   *

Thus we arrive at the end of the Modern Age. What will succeed? Anarchic poverty of body and mind, perhaps, with great slaughter, smiting and sparing not? Perhaps; but also, as even the melancholy Hungarian Lukacs reminds us, perhaps not.

Among living historians, Lukacs is the chief champion of the doctrine of free will. Nevertheless, in *The Passing of the Modern Age*, he took a dim view of the prospects for our civilization; but he rejected historical determinism and all forms of materialism and mechanism as applied to the study of human beings. He found correspondences to his historical thought in the quantum physics of Werner Heisenberg, particularly in Heisenberg's Gifford Lectures at St. Andrews. Lukacs makes ten points about the discoveries of Heisenberg. First, no longer does any scientific certitude exist. Second, the ideal of objectivity is illusory. Third, by nature, definitions are illusory. Fourth, there is no absolute truthfulness of mathematics. Fifth, "factual" truth is an illusion. Sixth, the mechanical concept of causality has broken down. Seventh, potentialities return to scientific speculation. Eighth, not the essence of "factors," but their relationship, counts. Ninth, the principles of "classical" logic are no longer unconditional: new concepts of truth are recognized. Tenth, at the end of the Modern Age the Cartesian partition falls away.

For the fashion in which Lukacs finds corresponding developments in historical thinking, I must refer you to his *Historical
Consciousness,* a new edition of which was recently included in my
Library of Conservative Thought series published by Transaction.
In substance, Lukacs tells us that the will is free; we enter once more
upon the mystery and wonder of human existence, redeemed from
"reductionism"; and for those willing to learn, the historical consciousness may be fuller than ever it was before. I offer a passage
from Arthur Koestler (at the end of his slim *Roots of Coincidence)*
which summarizes Lukacs' point better than Lukacs puts it himself:

> We have heard a whole chorus of Nobel Laureates in
> physics informing us that matter is dead, causality is
> dead, determinism is dead. If that is so, let us give them
> a decent burial, with a requiem of electronic music. It is
> time for us to draw the lessons from twentieth-century
> post-mechanistic science, and to get out of the strait-
> jacket which nineteenth-century materialism imposed
> on our philosophical outlook. Paradoxically, had that
> outlook kept abreast with modern science itself, instead
> of lagging a century behind it, we would have been
> liberated from that straitjacket long ago.

In large part, Lukacs says, our bent world at the end of the
twentieth century has been deformed by false understandings of the
human condition. We are beginning to free ourselves from those
delusions, and to learn afresh that human beings do possess free
will. But news of renewed concepts of the human condition
penetrates only very slowly to the mass of people—by reflections
and refractions, Coleridge said—and so possibly the social and
intellectual age we have known may perish even while people of

imagination (always a tiny minority) are at work endeavoring to restore a moral order.

A fuller and more acute historical consciousness is one important instrument for our regeneration. This must commence with self-consciousness, Lukacs reasons: "For self-consciousness and self-knowledge are marks of the historical evolution of the Western mind in the twentieth century: man turning inward rather than outward, the recognition that he is facing himself, alone." We begin the study of mankind with the study of ourselves. Lukacs says that he is a darkroom, not a camera: that is, far from being some "objective" detached observer, the human being is the active developer of impressions—in historical consciousness especially.

Indeed, this power of fuller perception by our historical consciousness may be the chief advantage of man at the end of the twentieth century over his predecessors. "There are two ways in which we can speak of progress in history," Lukacs writes.

> In the Christian sense history is a teleological process, moving toward the end of mankind, the Day of Judgment. This may or may not be complemented by another recognition, which is that there is such a thing as human evolution, but perhaps only in the sense of the evolution of our consciousness—an evolution which, if determined at all, is determined from the inside. Since history is a kind of philosophy made by examples, and since every one of these examples has actually taken place, every generation is *potentially* richer in its consciousness; it has more examples to draw upon, it knows more varieties of human behavior, ever different incarnations of human problems, more evidences about the complexities of human acts and about the divagations of human hearts. I wrote *potentially* because...the increase of the historical

information available to us does not necessarily mean a corresponding increase of historical understanding.

*   *   *

In speaking here of history as "a kind of philosophy," Lukacs does not embrace the notion of a philosophy of history. The search for that, he remarks, was a certain phase in the development of modern historical consciousness. "The greatest Western historians have always understood that a sane understanding of human nature literally preempts the need for a philosophy of history. Therefore, they knew, too, that—save for certain specialized branches of research—there is, strictly speaking, no such thing as a historical *method*, even though history has become a principal, perhaps the principal, Western *form* of thought."

What we find in Lukacs, then, is not some new philosophy of history, but instead a fresh approach to the character of historical consciousness, illuminated by humane letters, psychology, and natural science. I have not done John Lukacs justice here: in this brief compass I am able only to suggest the individuality and quick penetration of his thought—frequently digressive and deliberately personal in approach.

I conclude our present examination of Lukacs by quoting two of his asides which may seem sufficiently laconic, not to say sibylline. These observations have a bearing upon the nature of personal and historical consciousness.

The first passage concerns imagination and perception.

Self-knowledge, and the existing potentiality of past-knowledge, are involved intimately with imagination— a word which suggests a colorful mental construction on the one hand, and an inward tendency on the other....

The part played by the imagination, as Collingwood rightly puts it, 'is properly not ornamental but structural'; and the meaning of this truth goes beyond our interest in history. If, for example, imagination is more than a superstructure of perception, the term 'extrasensory perception' is, strictly speaking, misleading, for all human perception is, to some extent, extrasensory.

The second Lukacs passage which I submit for your meditation refers to the notion of "absolute time" typical of the Bourgeois Age. Then John Lukacs continues,

Now we have to learn something about the relativity of our notion of time, that what we had been thinking of as absolute 'time,' too, is but a concept of the human mind, a fiction, that mathematical time and living duration are two different things.... There is no human being who has not experienced the relativity of time (though he may not have recognized its meaning): that there is a sense of time which resides within ourselves, whose dimensions may on occasion stretch to impossible lengths or contract within an instant to the standing stillness of death, and that this personal sense of time does not always correspond to the mechanical and mathematically progressing—and therefore man-made—categories of clock and calendar.

You will have perceived that John Lukacs has been doing his best to exorcise the armed ghost we call historical determinism. His weapons against ideology are the arts of humane philosophy. Though he is an enemy to arid unnecessary abstraction in historical writing, and an able practitioner of the art of concrete representation, still he must employ to some extent the vocabularies and the concepts of metaphysics and theology. If some people find Lukacs—like his exemplar Tocqueville—too ready with large generalization, let me remind them of Coleridge's admonition regarding the invisible power of ideas, in his *Essays on His Own Times:*

> In every state, not wholly barbarous, a philosophy, good or bad, there must be. However slightingly it may be the fashion to talk of speculation and theory, as opposed (sillily and nonsensically opposed) to practice, it would not be difficult to prove, that such as is the existing spirit of speculation, during any given period, such will be the spirit and tone of the religion, legislation, and morals, nay, even of the fine arts, the manners, and the fashions. Nor is the less true, because the great majority of men live like bats, but in twilight, and know and feel the philosophy of their age only by its reflections and refractions.

Aye, just so: even more true now than in the day of Samuel Taylor Coleridge, perhaps. Concepts of history may be prophecies which work their own grim fulfillment—if we accept the postulates of determinism. Other concepts of history, waking personal and historical consciousness, may redeem the character of a century. For good or ill, ideas about history and its lessons probably will be powerful in the dawning era—even though the average member of the rising generation has studied not history, but "social stew." If ignorant of history, that rising generation may wander bewildered in cunning passages, contrived corridors and issues. And at the heart of such a labyrinth, we are told, there has lurked for ages the Minotaur.

IX

Humane Learning in the Age of the Computer

Permit me to offer you some desultory reflections concerning the effect of the electronic computer upon the reason and the imagination. We are told by many voices that the computer will work a revolution in learning. So it may; but that accomplishment would not be salutary.

As I stated earlier in this book, the primary end of the higher learning, in all lands and all times, has been what John Henry Newman called the training of the intellect to form a philosophical habit of mind. University and college were founded to develop right reason and imagination, for the sake of the person and the sake of the republic. The higher education, by its nature, is concerned with abstractions—rather difficult abstractions, both in the sciences and in humane studies. Most people, in any age, are not fond of abstractions. Therefore, in this democratic time, higher education stands in danger everywhere from leveling pressures.

In Britain, a few years ago, the member of the opposition who
had been designated minister of education in a prospective Labour
government denounced Oxford and Cambridge universities as
"cancers." Presumably he would have converted those ancient
institutions, had it been in his power, into something like the
Swedish "people's universities"—that is, institutions at which everybody could succeed, because all standards would be swept away
for entrance or for graduation. Every man and woman an intellectual king or queen, with an Oxbridge degree! The trouble with this
aspiration is that those kings and queens would be impoverished
intellectually—and presumably Britain in general would be impoverished in more ways than one.

Recently we have heard similar voices in the graduate schools of
Harvard. Why discriminate against indolence and stupidity? Why
not let everybody graduate, regardless of performance in studies?
Wouldn't that be the democratic way? If young people don't care for
abstractions, and manifest a positive aversion to developing a
philosophical habit of mind, why not give them what they think
they would like: that is, the superficial counter-culture?

Such educational degradation of the democratic dogma already
has prevailed throughout the Western world; it has gone farthest in
France and Italy. At the University of Paris, several years ago, mobs
of students rioted fiercely because the Socialist government had
proposed a very modest restoration of intellectual standards at the
end of the second year of university studies.

In the United States, ever since the Second World War and
especially during the past three decades, the lowering of standards
for admission and graduation, the notorious disgrace of "grade
inflation," and the loss of order and integration in curricula, are too
widely known and regretted for me to need to labor these afflictions
here. Some cold comfort may be found in the fact that we have not
sinned more greatly than have other nations of the West—somewhat less, indeed.

Here and there, some signs of renewal in higher education may be discerned; certainly there occurs a great deal of bother about it. But it remains to be seen whether it is possible to restore or improve the true higher learning, what with the powerful political and economic pressures against improvement. Being somewhat gloomy by conviction, yet sanguine by temperament, I mutter to myself, "Say not the struggle naught availeth!"

Why are this lowering of standards and this loss of intellectual coherence ruinous to higher education? Because the higher learning is intended to develop, primarily, a philosophical habit of mind. The genuine higher education is not meant, really, to "create jobs" or to train technicians. Incidentally, the higher education does tend to have such results, too; but merely as by-products. We stand in danger of forgetting the fundamental aim in the pursuit of the incidentals.

Why were universities established, and what remain their more valuable functions? To discipline the mind; to give men and women long views, and to instill in them the virtue of prudence; to present a coherent body of knowledge for its own sake; to help the rising generation to make its way toward wisdom and virtue. The university is an instrument to teach that truth is better than falsehood, and wisdom better than ignorance. Of course the university has done other things as well, some of them mildly baneful—such as serving as a form of social snobbery. But I am speaking still of the higher learning's fundamental mission.

Now a higher schooling merely technological and skill-oriented—what once would have been called a mechanical education, as opposed to a liberal education—can neither impart wisdom to the person nor supply intellectual and moral leadership to the republic. I do not object to learning a trade—far from it. But a trade is best learned, ordinarily, through apprenticeship, internship, on-the-job training, or technical schools. Except for the learned professions, learning a trade is ill-suited to a university

campus. The university has other responsibilities. For if the philosophical habit of mind is developed nowhere, "the centre cannot
hold; / Mere anarchy is loosed upon the world."

*   *   *

Let me descend to particulars. The biggest fad in education
today is the movement styled the Information Revolution. An
extensive jargon is developing to serve this revolution's uses.
The revolution is supposed to result in an Informational Society;
we are even instructed that this Informational Society will
supplant the Knowledge Society. Practically speaking, all this
jargon means that in the highly-developed industrial countries,
a much more extensive employment of computing machines and
robots is occurring.

One of the grave failings of American schooling, at every level,
is the eagerness to embrace the newest gadget (mechanical or
intellectual) at the expense of the tested tools of learning. Some
readers will remember how, during the 1950s and 1960s, we were
told that audio-visual aids would supplant the teacher for most
purposes. At gigantic public expense, film-projectors, sound
systems, and other impedimenta were thrust upon virtually every
school. Most of this hardware soon was locked away in closets,
where it reposed until obsolete. Some firms made a great deal of
money from selling it. Effective teaching still is done by effective
live teachers, not by television sets, tapes, recordings, or projec-
tors. "Programmed learning" was another step toward the vaunted
Information Revolution. By and large, programmed learning did
not work well. A human being talking with other human beings,
and that antiquated tool called a book, have had more satisfactory
results so far as genuine development of young intellects is
concerned. Television certainly worked a revolution. But does
anyone still maintain that the boob-tube has improved the minds

of the young? Certainly television opened the way for an even fuller Information Revolution. The apologists for television used to tell us that their darling had molded the minds of "the best-informed generation in the history of America." Also it had molded the minds of the most ignorant generation in the history of America. As a witty friend of mine says, "This is the bird-brained genera-tion." He does not mean that young people have brains the size of birds'; instead, that like birds, boys and girls flit from flower to flower, watching the flickering screen, never settling long enough to learn anything important.

For information is not knowledge; and knowledge is not wis-dom. This is movingly expressed by Eliot in some lines of his choruses for *The Rock*:

> *Where is the Life we have lost in living?*
> *Where is the wisdom we have lost in knowledge?*
> *Where is the knowledge we have lost in information?*
> *The cycles of Heaven in twenty centuries*
> *Bring us farther from God and nearer to the Dust.*

Aye, where is the knowledge we have lost in information—not to mention the wisdom? What humane learning used to impart was not miscellaneous information, a random accumulation of facts, but instead an integrated and ordered body of knowledge that would develop the philosophical habit of mind—from which cast of mind one might find the way to wisdom of many sorts.

Doubtless the development of computers will confer various material benefits upon us. But so far as genuine education goes, the computer and its Informational Society may amount to a blight. They seem calculated to enfeeble the individual reason and to make most of us dependent upon an elite of computer programmers (at the higher level of the Informational Society, I mean). They may develop into vigorous enemies of the philosophical habit of mind.

Let me offer a very simple example of what I mean. At one time I was an electronic typist in the Ford Motor Company, working in conjunction with comptometer operators. Now and again the comptometer-men would fancy that something might be wrong with their computations; and they would appeal to me, for I had memorized the multiplication table at an early age. "What's seven times nine?" they would inquire. "Sixty-three," I would reply promptly. "Let's check that out," they would murmur doubtfully. They never came to apprehend how I could be trusted more than their machines.

Everything depends on how the computers are programmed, and on who programs them, and with what intent. The man or woman who receives his Information from on high, as gospel, tends to become servile—a mechanical.

Books and lectures about the Information Revolution have become numerous and profitable. One lady goes about to major cities lecturing on "information as a commodity." (At the devil's booth, wisdom is one commodity not in stock.) This lady stands ready to restructure the whole educational system, through the information supplied by an organization for which she works. She is even ready to tackle World Peace.

"We continue to make decisions based almost on a nineteenth-century sense of isolationism," she told an interviewer. "How many Americans understand what's going on in Central and South America or even have any concepts of what those cultures are about? Or how many Americans understand the Soviet Union or China or Africa? Just as citizens we're going to have to dramatically speed up the amount of information we have about the rest of the world."

Now doubtless it always has been desirable for more Americans to know more about affairs abroad; it is particularly desirable today. But information scarcely is lacking already. Are there no newspapers, popular magazines, serious periodicals, television sets, radios, teachers? The mass of miscellaneous information thrust upon us already is overwhelming and dismaying. What we need is not more information; what we require, as a public, is the ability to discriminate and integrate that mass of information, and to reflect upon it. For thirteen years I was a syndicated newspaper columnist. I found it quite impossible, though I was paid for the work, to gather and integrate all the information about everything that happened everywhere. I did not even learn to "understand Africa," although I traveled there and read many serious books and articles about that continent.

Mere "speeding up" of the deluge of information cannot help us: for already information rushes upon us daily with a terrible velocity that the average man and woman, or even skilled journalists, cannot endure. How many newspapers are we to read, how many books on current affairs are we to absorb, how many lectures are we to hear?

But possibly what the evangels of the Informational Society have in mind is this: so to select and pre-digest information that the public will receive such facts and opinions as the elite of the Informational Society think it well they should receive. Already we are subjected to a mild dose of this treatment by the pundits of television. It would be an exaggeration, and impolite, to call such arrangement and distribution of information "brainwashing." Yet this facile delivery of allegedly accurate information may be ominous for the American democracy. Big Brother will inform us.

Undoubtedly commercial benefits result from increased use of computers, especially to the purveyors of hardware and software. We are told, too, that computers assist in diminishing certain types of learning-disability. And as Craig Brod observes in his book *Technostress: the Human Cost of the Computer Revolution,* "In the schools, districts vie to be the first to make computer courses compulsory or to find funding for kindergarten computers." Enthusiasts for the Informational Society may be found everywhere. Members of the staff of the National Institute of Education inserted praise of "computer science" in the report of the Commission on Excellence in Education; they even made that alleged science one of their Five New Basics, commended to every school, along with English, mathematics, science, and social studies.

Now there is no more reason to object to learning how to use a computer in school, or at home, than there is to object to learning how to use a typewriter in school, or at home. But who speaks of Typewriter Science for grade schools? Are we to elevate computer operation and apprehension to a level equivalent to all the genuine sciences, which the Commission's report lumps together as Basic 3?

The development of electronic computers results from the genuine sciences of physics and mathematics. If we are to be masters of the computer, rather than its subjects, we need to understand physics and mathematics. Otherwise we are passive vessels, at best skilled operatives. And if facility in operating computers tends to be emphasized at the expense of serious study of physics and mathematics, the springs of the scientific imagination may dry up. This zeal for making "computer science" compulsory for practically everybody is rather as if, when Morse invented the telegraph, every school had been urged to devote a large proportion of its time and funds to teaching young people to be telegraphers. Is not the computer business, like industry generally, capable of instructing its own technicians?

Nevertheless, various institutions allegedly of higher learning already have proclaimed their fealty to Holy Computer. Some have made the completion of a course in computer science a requirement for graduation. "Relevance" is all—even when it is irrelevant to a philosophical habit of mind.

Dr. Joseph Weizenbaum, in 1984, was interviewed by a French magazine. Professor Weizenbaum has been a pioneer in the invention of the computer, devising the Eliza computer program, by which a computer "converses" with human beings. Weizenbaum is not pleased by the widespread enthusiasm for computerized schooling.

"The fad for home and school computers," he says, "that is creating such a furor in the United States, as well as in Great Britain and France," does mischief. "A new human malady has been invented, just as the makers of patent medicines in the past invented illnesses such as 'tired blood.' Now it's computer illiteracy. The future, we are told, will belong to those familiar with the computer. What a joke this would be if only it didn't victimize so many innocent bystanders. It reminds me of the old encyclopedia fad: 'If you buy one,' proclaimed the salesman, 'your child will do better in school and succeed in life.' And parents complied. But the encyclopedia was rarely consulted and was soon retired to the shelves."

The computer itself inhibits children's creativity, Weizenbaum goes on to say; nor do computers reinforce a child's problem-solving ability. The more one really knows about education by computer, apparently, the less one thinks of its possibilities.

Craig Brod, a psychotherapist, points out that computer advocates have for their goal the teaching of formal, mathematical logic, early in life. But as Saint Ambrose remarked, it has not pleased God that men should be saved by logic. Brod mentions that formal logic is only one of nine cognitive styles that children develop; and to emphasize one style unduly may diminish the other styles. "Once they stray outside the computer's world," Brod writes of children thrust into this mindset, "they find their technical mastery irrelevant and their ability to communicate with others weakened. No one has proved that learning to write a good computer program helps a person behave with greater wisdom or reason in the real world. In fact, what is rational in a computer program—such as efficiency and brevity—can appear irrational when it guides one's relationships with others."

Such are the limits and perils of computer-schooling at the lower levels. What of humane learning at the level of the university?

Already, at some colleges, more than a third of the undergraduates are majors, or intending majors, in computer science—although the drop-out rate among this body of young persons is remarkably high. They are attracted by the glowing promise of lucrative employment in the booming computer industries, and perhaps by their addiction to video games. And they fancy, many of them, that computer-mastery is power.

This computer-fascination grows at the expense of humane learning; and if carried far enough, it works its own destruction. For the ingenious men of science who have given us the computer are not themselves the product of computerized schooling. Their powers of reason and imagination were developed out of old disciplines unrelated to electronic mechanical devices. They were not restricted, in school and college and university, to a single mode of cognition. But if the theories of the enthusiastic behaviorists and cognitive psychologists triumph, the computer-mentality will become virtually universal among the rising generation. Then we will have no more creative scientists, and no more humane scholars and men of letters. Then indeed a revolution will have occurred—that is, we will have come full cycle, and the revolution will have devoured its children, as revolutions have a way of doing.

Brod makes this point succinctly: "Underlying the race to computerize the educational process is a deeper trend. An information-processing model of learning is gaining acceptance as the new educational norm. This model holds that the brain is essentially a data-processing computer. Knowledge and learning can be reduced to 'effective procedures,' much like a computer program. Children's brains should thus accept any data that are 'formatted correctly.' Schools have been on the defensive lately due to dropping student test scores and suspect teaching standards, and the information-processing model offers those institutions a way back to respectability."

The creators of the computers, however, did not themselves suffer from pedagogical methods of this sort; they were not "formatted correctly." Their insights came from different sources—highly mysterious sources, connected with what John Henry Newman called the illative sense. Their minds were not computerized, praise be.

"The cognitive psychologists, in promoting this brain-as-computer model, stress the advantages of speed, reliability, uniformity, and efficiency," Brod continues. "Teachers and students can interact in specific predictable ways. Poor teaching can be controlled more easily because the teachers must no longer meet the demands of the humanist model, serving as a combination role model, entertainer, surrogate parent, psychologist, friend, and master of educational technique. Instead, the job of teaching can be, in effect, de-professionalized; one doesn't have to have years of experience or limitless insight in order to teach when one is following a comprehensive, step-by-step lesson plan."

Aye, computerization might eliminate much teaching; also it might eliminate much thinking and imagining. Its aim is to produce "logical" intellects efficient for operating computers and obeying computers. Such an intellect is a servile intellect.

The triumph of the computer-theory of education also might bring about what Robert Graves prophetically denominates the Logicalist Society. In that romance of the future which I commended at length in chapter one entitled *Seven Days in New Crete,* Graves pictures a future domination, after the post-Christian era, "called Logicalism—pantisocratic economics divorced from any religious or nationalistic theory."

> Logicalism, hinged on international science, ushered in a gloomy and anti-poetic age. It lasted only a generation or two and ended with a grand defeatism, a sense of perfect futility, that slowly crept over the directors and managers of the regime. The common man had triumphed over his betters at last, but what was to follow?

To what could he look forward with either hope or fear? By the abolition of sovereign states and the disarming of even the police forces, war had become impossible. No one who cherished any religious beliefs whatever, or was interested in sport, poetry, or the arts, was allowed to hold a position of public responsibility; 'icecold logic' was the most valued civic quality, and those who could not pretend to it were held of no account. Science continued laboriously to expand its over-large corpus of information, and the subjects of research grew more and more beautifully remote and abstract; yet the scientific obsession, so strong at the beginning of the third millennium A.D., was on the wane.

Before long, most of the Logicalist directors and managers go mad, suffering from delusions. "No cure could be found by the psychiatrists, who were themselves peculiarly subject to this new form of insanity: all who caught it had to be 'lethalized.'" The Logicalist regime collapses; and so, in time, does the civilization—devoid of imagination and hope—that had produced Logicalism. For man does not live by ice-cold logic of the computerized variety.

A society dominated by the computer-mentality could be directed only by an elite of computer geniuses far wiser than Aristotle, Aquinas, or Bacon. But where are such wondrous programmers to come from? The minds of the men who offer us the computer theory of the human intellect—men like B. F. Skinner—are not imperial intellects; rather, they are afflicted by what Burke called "cold hearts and muddy understandings." (It will be understood that I distinguish radically here between the zealots for computerized education and the imaginative scientists, Weizenbaum eminent among them, who have given us the perilous computer. As Weizenbaum says of attempts to apply the computer to automatic psychotherapy, "There's a whole world of real problems, of human problems, which is essentially being ignored.") Indeed, a computerized people would be a race from among whom imperial intellects had been extirpated, as under Graves's Logicalism.

So let us drop some grains of salt into the Informational Society stew. It is *humanitas,* as the Romans called it, that rouses reason and imagination—including the scientific imagination. In particular, great humane literature, joined to the religious impulse, has brought about what Pico della Mirandola called "the dignity of man," so that it is possible for human beings to be only a little lower than the angels. Infatuation with computerized minds and a computerized society can dehumanize.

Waves of technological innovation commonly carry in a mass of flotsam and jetsam. A disagreeable heap of such rubbish was flung upon the beaches of Academe by the ideological tempests of the 1960s and 1970s; we are only beginning to recover from the damage done to the philosophical habit of mind by that storm. The gentlefolk and scholars of the Academy would be highly imprudent if they should assist in fresh devastation by setting gadgetry above humane learning.

What we ought to resist is a schooling that turns out young people who know the price of everything and the value of nothing: people replete with information and unable to digest it. If we restore the dignity of humane learning, we may transcend the Informational Society; we may even achieve a Tolerable Society.

X

The Age of Sentiments

Our civilized world is passing out of one age and into another epoch. The age that is passing has been called the Age of Discussion. The age that we are entering I call the Age of Sentiments. Most people are aware of this change only vaguely, if at all. As Disraeli put it, "Prevailing opinions generally are the opinions of the generation that is passing."

This profound alteration of the climate of opinion is not merely related to changes in the mass media; it is *caused*, in considerable part, by such changes in the mass media; and particularly by the triumph of television.

The phrase "the age of Discussion" I take from Walter Bagehot's chapter by that title, in his book *Physics and Politics*—published in 1869, two years after passage of Britain's Reform Bill. The genial and perceptive Bagehot, the best critic of his own time, understood well that during the nineteenth century the old order of things was being effaced—swept away by the nineteenth-century triumph of what Bagehot called Discussion. In effect, the Age of Discussion was the Age of Liberalism, which nowadays is fallen into the sere and yellow leaf. It was not so much democracy that undid the old social and moral order, Bagehot argued, as it was Discussion. Democracy itself, for that matter, was a product of Discussion, in ancient times and in modern: democracy arose first in towns of Greece and Italy where Discussion prevailed. Near the close of the eighteenth century, Discussion began to work as a tremendous social force, converting modern nations into states close-knit and sensitive to novelty, as Athens and Florence had been.

Discussion it was that broke the cake of custom in Christendom, that engulfed what Burke called prejudice and prescription, that subverted men's ancient aversion to relinquishing the ways of their ancestors. Modern democracy was the fruit, rather than the seed, of this eighteenth-century and nineteenth-century Discussion; so was that view of the civil social order called Liberalism. As Bagehot put it, "Since Luther's time there has been a conviction more or less rooted, that a man may by an intellectual process think out a religion for himself, and that, as the highest of all duties, he ought to do so. The influence of the political discussion, and the influence of the religious discussion, have so long and so firmly combined, and have so effectually enforced one another, that the old notions of loyalty, and fealty, and authority, as they existed in the Middle Ages, have now over the best minds almost no effect."

This is the Private Judgment against which John Henry Newman inveighed in Bagehot's time. Bulwer-Lytton, in that era, had exclaimed, "Democracy is like the grave—it perpetually cries, 'give, give,' and, like the grave, it never returns what it has once taken." Walter Bagehot, referring to Bulwer-Lytton's analogy, remarks that this simile is equally apt for Discussion. "Once effectually submit a subject to that ordeal," in Bagehot's words, "and you can never withdraw it again; you can never again clothe it with mystery, or fence it by consecration; it remains for ever open to free choice, and exposed to profane deliberation."

Just so. Now private judgment and free discussion, the indispensable postulates and chief supports of nineteenth-century democracy and liberalism (not that those two are identical), were made possible in the nineteenth and twentieth centuries by a cheap press, speedy communication, popular access to firearms (a subject deserving of a lecture by itself), and urban concentrations of population; thus the chief European nations, and America, too, obtained the advantages of the ancient city-states, but also were exposed to the dangers of public opinion as it had been known in ancient Greece and Italy.

Discussion and private judgment, rather than the physical suffering that Karl Marx predicted, have goaded modern people to experiment and alteration during the past two centuries. Marxism has won its zealots not so much because of positive suffering—after all, suffering has been the lot of the majority of mankind ever since Adam and Eve—but because Marxism has been a new mode for protest and private judgment. Is the voracity of Discussion indeed insatiable as the appetite of the grave? If so, then are permanence and continuity impossible for modern society?

In our latter days of the Age of Discussion, much of the world has fallen to crushing tyranny, with almost no discussion permitted; or into anarchy and endless civil war, in which all discussion seems fruitless. Discussion appears to have swung full cycle: commencing in one authoritarian domination, and ending in an authoritarian domination far more merciless. It has not come to that in these United States—not yet; but though we may be spared tyranny and anarchy, it does not follow that somehow we can prolong greatly in America that Age of Discussion which has vanished or is now vanishing, from the rest of the world.

*   *   *

Presently I shall return to some analysis of the symptoms of dissolution of the Age of Discussion. Permit me to explain, just now, what I mean by my other phrase "the Age of Sentiments."

Words are tools that break in the hand; and this word "sentiments" is employed loosely in a variety of ways. I use it in the signification attached to it by those friends David Hume and Adam Smith, about the commencement of the Age of Discussion. That is, the word "sentiment" implies "higher feeling" or "emotion"; psychologically, an emotional judgment. Think of Pascal's famous phrase "The heart has reasons which the reason cannot know": there's the gist of it.

In the definition of the old *Century Dictionary,* "*Sentiment* has a peculiar place between *thought* and *feeling,* in which it also approaches the meaning of *principle.* It is more than that *feeling* which is sensation or emotion, by containing more of *thought* and by being more lofty; while it contains too much *feeling* to be merely thought, and it has large influence over the will: for example, the *sentiment* of patriotism; the *sentiment* of honor; the world is ruled by *sentiment.* The *thought* in a *sentiment* is often that of duty, and is penetrated and exalted by *feeling.*"

For David Hume and Adam Smith, sentiments exerted greater power, and indeed were better guides, than reason—though Hume remarks in his *Principles of Morals* that sentiment and reason usually coincide. I suppose we may say that for Hume and Smith a sound sentiment is a moving conviction; but a conviction derived from some other source than pure reason. You will note that I employ sentiment not as a term of derision, but as a term of description.

I have digressed at this length in order to define my terms—being of a philosophical habit of mind—so that we may try to understand the large transition of society, conducted by mass media, which we are experiencing in this present decade. When I say that we are passing from the Age of Discussion to the Age of Sentiments, I am not preaching a comminatory sermon: I am doing no more than describing a process, probably ineluctable. A good deal has been written on this subject, but not precisely in the fashion I am about to present to you. Just now I offer you two vignettes that may clarify my meaning.

Four decades ago I first saw the ancient city of Verona, where Catullus was born. Having settled at my hotel, I made my way afoot to the Piazza delle Erbe, which in Catullus' time was the Roman forum, and is still the busiest place in Verona. It was Saturday evening. For some two thousand, five hundred years, I reflected, the people of Verona have gathered in this square, talking endlessly at its cafes while the centuries crept past: one of the world's venerable centers of Discussion. In the Piazza delle Erbe I would be part of the great continuity of talk.

But I was astonished to find the Piazza delle Erbe utterly dark, that Saturday night. I had read somewhere that Verona was rather a melancholy place—so Chateaubriand described the city at the time of the Congress of Verona, I believe—but this total silence and emptiness of the great square was overwhelming. Many cafes lined the piazza; the doors of all were shut; and no Romeo, no Juliet, nor any other native of Verona was to be seen. Could any place in Italy have sunk into such apathy on a Saturday evening?

I walked slowly round the Piazza. As I proceeded, I found that a little light escaped from behind the shutters of the cafes. I peered in: every cafe was crowded with people sitting at little round tables and sipping drinks; but nobody was uttering a word. One and all, they were watching television sets—which miracle, I learned next day, had come to Verona not long before. A week of television had put an end to twenty-five centuries of civilized conversation in Verona.

Demon TV's empire is universal. Some years after my experience in the Piazza delle Erbe, I was exploring the Orkneys, in company with a friend. Not long after docking at Kirkwall, we took dinner in the best hotel of that quaint city, in the midst of which stands the Norman cathedral built in this remote northern fastness about the year 1137. When we had finished our dinner, the headwaiter told us, "Gentlemen, I know ye're not staying in the hotel; but if ye wish, ye'll be welcome to watch television in the writing-room."

Tony and I were no enthusiasts for television; but somewhat puzzled at this civil gesture, we entered the writing-room. Formerly there must have been a score of desks here, and corresponding chairs, intended for the diligent use of commercial travelers—a dying breed. But that old furniture had been thrust out, perhaps into the wild seas; and the desks were supplanted by uncomfortable little metal folding chairs, crowded close together. Every chair in that long darkened room was occupied by an Orkneyman—staring, one and all, at a television set. Television had arrived in Orkney only that week. Of the long, long winter nights at Kirkwall, since the cathedral was consecrated by the murdered Saint Magnus, men had gathered by Kirkwall firesides for telling of tales and much argumentation—so developing the Scottish intellect. For all those centuries, Kirkwall had talked; hereafter, Kirkwall would *view*. The Age of Discussion had given way to the Age of Sentiments, even in the Orkneys.

Sentiments are feelings; hereafter the folk of Verona and the folk of Kirkwall will feel more, perhaps; certainly many of them will think less. I confess to being by education, at least, more a man of thought than of *feeling*. I may be regarded as a survivor—perhaps a captain in the rear guard—of the Age of Discussion. Like the Celts of the twilight, we survivors of the Age of Discussion go forth to battle often, but to victory never. The rising generation say unto us, "We *feel* that human rights are being violated in Cloudcuckooland"—not knowing it, not thinking it, but feeling. Policy becomes the art of applying institutions. Soon the rising generation will murmur, very possibly, "We *feel* that two and two make four"—not knowing it, not thinking it, but *feeling* that mathematical truth. It may be said that this is harmless. Aye; but what if they come to feel that two and two do *not* make four? Are all sentiments infallible?

We veterans of Discussion's rear guard are beaten down, horse, foot, and dragoons. Serious periodicals, weekly, fortnightly, monthly, and quarterly, were the meat and the drink of the Age of Discussion, beginning (in Britain) with *The Edinburgh Review* and *The Quarterly Review*. I began writing for such serious periodicals—*The South Atlantic Quarterly* and *The English Journal*, first of all—when I was a sophomore in college; I have grown gray in their service. On either side of the Atlantic, those magazines have fallen dead even as I have served them. *Requiescat in pace, Dublin Review, Fortnightly Review, World Review, Pacific Spectator, Church Quarterly Review, Measure, New English Review*, and many more that printed my lucubrations; some of you were very old when you were slain, and some quite young; but young or old, there was no room for you in the dawning age that prefers effusions to lucubrations.

Into the Age of Sentiments there will survive some serious periodicals, and some decent books, and here and there obscure corners where a few people earnestly discuss some matters that cannot well be swept into oblivion. Yet this remnant of genuine thinkers and readers and talkers may be very small. The immense majority of human beings will *feel* with the projected images they behold upon the television screen; and in those viewers that screen will rouse *sentiments* rather than reflections. Waves of emotion will sweep back and forth, so long as the Age of Sentiments endures. And whether those emotions are low or high must depend upon the folk who determine the tone and temper of television programming.

Such are my general sentiments about television as evocative of sentiments. In my own household, I pursue a policy of war to the knife—or rather, war to the wire-cutter—against the television set.

When some people learn that no television is tolerated in our tall Italianate house, they inquire, wondering, "But what do you do about your daughters?" And we reply, "We give them tools." "What kind of tools?" "Why, tools called books."

Occasionally TV has reared its hideous head at Piety Hill. Clinton Wallace, our hobo butler, was permitted to keep a well-worn portable TV in his bedroom. This I thrust into the cellar the day we buried Clinton.

Some months thereafter, on returning home late at night, I saw lights burning in every room of our house, but encountered no living soul. It was very like the mystery of the derelict *Marie Celeste*. At length I penetrated to a remote quarter of the cellar, and there I found my spouse and all our household huddled round the forbidden TV, watching the late news—or, more particularly, viewing a rather ordinary snowstorm in Manhattan. I dispersed them in wrath. Then, taking a pair of powerful wire-cutters, I did fierce things to the set, and flung portions of it into trash-cans.

In the fullness of time, nevertheless, one of the Ethiopians who dwelt with us, young Sahle Selassie Makonnen, secretly repaired the mutilated contraption, installing it in his room—which did not improve his collegiate studies. When I was about to confiscate this shabby article of contraband, it vanished again. Presently a secret agent of the gentler sex informed me that our eldest daughter, Monica, had contrived to transport the set somehow to the topmost room of the foretower of our archaic house, and there sometimes turned it on.

Monica being out of the house when I learned this, I climbed the ladder to the summit of the foretower, with some difficulty forced open a small octagonal window, and flung the accursed set to its destruction. To my chagrin, the confounded thing caught in a gutter, and there hung like Mahomet's coffin, invisible from most points of view.

Yet wondrous to relate, our housekeeper, Mrs. Cole, described the suspended television; and the strong-willed Annette, my wife, sent my stalwart assistant scrambling over the roofs to retrieve it. At my stern command, my assistant immured the set in the crawlspace under the front portion of his cottage; and there it may rest until the Last Trump. Monica thinks her parents odd, particularly in their attitude toward television. Once she inquired why I couldn't be like other dads, who "get a six-pack and sit down to watch the game on TV."

Perhaps our daughters will grow up amenable occasionally to Discussion; not wholly subservient to Sentiments. If so, they will be members of a band about so numerous as that which fled from the Cities of the Plain. Yet in the fullness of time they may inherit the earth: for intelligence and imagination will tell in the long run—even in a television studio, even in a university.

I suppose I have made it clear that I am dragged kicking and screaming into the Age of Sentiments. It is painful enough to be governed by other people's reasoning, without being governed by their sentiments. Yet it should not be thought that I bow down in worship before the late Age of Discussion. For the most part, the Age of Discussion was an age of shams and posturings. I promised earlier to say something about the dissolution of the Age of Discussion; to that I turn now.

That vaunted Age of Discussion has fallen apart because it never had much vitality in it. For most men and women are little interested in abstractions, and so grow bored speedily with discussions; their talk is of bullocks, or of Toyotas. There have existed, true enough, some periods in some regions when Discussion was fairly general, even to a fault—Scotland late in the eighteenth century (well, Edinburgh, anyway), or the seventeenth-century Massachusetts of my ancestors (among the godly there, at least). But these have been oases in a wasteland of complacency or of violence; and even in Scotland and New England during such periods, the serious talkers may not have been the more pleasant for their insistence that "Life is real! Life is earnest! And the grave is not its goal." It cannot be certified that their relish for Discussion made them into better people; or that it brought to pass a world of fuller freedom and justice and order.

In fine, there never was an age in which the majority of men and women participated actively in a public process of discussions—though occasionally the majority may have entertained the illusion that they so participated. Actually, in all ages public opinion is formed by those unknowable individuals whom Dicey calls the real molders of public opinion—those strong-willed persons, each with his little circle of friends and acquaintances round him, whose opinions prevail over the minds of his associates. At the very height of Bagehot's Age of Discussion, relatively few persons formed their own considered judgments. Rather, they were presented with wise or foolish opinions on many subjects, by clergymen, newspaper editors, eminent politicians (in a time when public addresses counted for far more than they do today); and they conformed to those quasi-authoritative opinions, especially if those particular opinions seemed to coincide with the private interest of those conforming. "Discussion," that is, always has amounted to discussions among a relatively few people; the rest conform to the doctrines of one faction or another.

In the twentieth century, first the cinema and then the radio began to compete with the old agencies for forming public opinion; and their appeal was to the Sentiments, not to Discussion. I can recall listening with a certain juvenile horror, during the early 'Thirties, to the strident voices of such radio commentators as Gabriel Heatter and Boake Carter, frantically defaming and misrepresenting everything and everybody; and I marvelled that the Republic could survive such lunatic or malign shapers of public opinion, until it occurred to my youthful reflective faculty that these radio zealots tended to cancel out one another, setting error against error; besides, the public soon learns not to act upon the admonitions of a person who daily cries "Wolf, wolf!"

In departing from the Age of Discussion, then—and the flight from Discussion grew rapid, once radio triumphed in every home—we have left behind much pretense and many Hollow Men. Also, it is sadly true, we have lost some promise and wisdom by our departure into Sentiments. One of the last noble endeavors to redeem the Age of Discussion was that of my old friend T. S. Eliot, in his quarterly magazine *The Criterion*. Aspiring to help to save the world from suicide, Eliot got up, at great expenditure of his own time and energy, this excellent review; and to it there contributed the more important serious men of letters and scholars of the 'Twenties and 'Thirties. The bound volumes of this magazine remain available in the better institutional libraries; and if you will take the trouble to browse through those volumes, you will find that the contents have lost little of their interest and pertinence with the passage of the decades. It was Eliot's fond hope that his journal would be read by public men of importance, whose policies might be affected thereby. But the circulation of *The Criterion* never exceeded a few hundred copies, despite the lip-service given to the magazine in many quarters; and I never have discovered evidence that "the Criterion Crowd" succeeded in influencing a single eminent politician—even though the journal was international in character and circulation. For Eliot made this gallant assault on public apathy at the tag-end of the Age of Discussion. Like Pompeius Magnus, T. S. Eliot stamped his foot—but no legions rose at his summons. Nobody worth mentioning, among public men and the masters of the mass media, remained much interested in Discussion, by the 'Forties. The Age of Sentiments already had won the field. In that Age of Sentiments, nevertheless, T. S. Eliot's name remains grand: for Eliot himself understood the Sentiments; and it is the Sentiments, including religious sentiments, that his poetry evokes.

Turn we at last, then, to some defense of the Age of Sentiments.

For, as Eliot put it, there are no lost causes because there are no gained causes; and perhaps we may do something in the cause of order, private and public, through the instruments of the Sentiments.

* * *

Just how despicable the general character of television programming is today, everybody already knows; I shall not labor the point. The sentiments imparted by the typical television station are sentiments of avarice, gluttony, sloth, anger, lust, pride, and envy. Most of the cable networks are worse than the commercial stations. The sentiments imparted by the educational or "public" television stations are more commendable; but often the introduction of sentiments by such media is dull and erroneous, vestiges of the methods of the Age of Discussion.

Is it conceivable that the medium of television might yet be employed to wake the sentiments associated with the Seven Gifts of the Holy Ghost: wisdom, understanding, counsel, fortitude, knowledge, righteousness, fear of the Lord? Does such an endeavor sound perfectly absurd, given the present abhorrent state of television programming and the appetites, natural and unnatural, of the average sensual man in these closing decades of the twentieth century?

Even through television, may emotions be evoked to help restore order in the soul and order in the commonwealth? My friend Malcolm Muggeridge, so successful in his television appearances, declares fervently that no good can come out of television. In our Age of Sentiments, how do we try to restore some order amidst what Eliot, in "Burnt Norton," calls "the general mess of imprecision of feeling?"

It will not do to use the deteriorated equipment of the Age of Discussion. I mean that the didacticism of the classroom lecturer is altogether unsuited for television. Every program must work upon the emotions, rather than upon the rational private judgment: the method must be that of drama, with the ethical end of Greek drama. The creator of the drama should appear little, if at all. What television does is to create impressions, not to engage in discussions; and to rouse sentiments, not to impart encyclopedic information.

In any age, unless we are to be vanquished utterly, we must take up the tools—the weapons, if you will—effective in that age. In the Age of Sentiments, television has become the great mover and shaker. I remind you that there persist in human nature both bad sentiments and good sentiments. Repairing once more to the *Century Dictionary,* we need to bear in mind that sentiment is more lofty than mere feeling; and that there exist such sentiments as patriotism, honor, and duty. Sentiments of that order may yet be raised up in the Waste Land—conceivably through the innovating weapon called television.

An age moved by high sentiments can be more admirable than an age mired in desiccated discussions. Those who fancy that the philosophical and political notions of John Stuart Mill can suffice to govern the pride, the passion, and the prejudice of man—why, they wander bewildered in the ghost-realm of yesteryear, and must perish. Is it a fantastic aspiration to endeavor to employ television as a means for our regeneration?

One may apply certain lines from "East Coker"—

> *There is only the fight to recover what has been lost*
> *And found and lost again and again: and now, under conditions*
> *That seem unpropitious. But perhaps neither gain nor loss.*
> *For us, there is only the trying. The rest is not our business.*

At any rate, as Henry Adams was given to saying, the fun is in the process. To the studios, men of high sentiments!

XI

Renewing a Shaken Culture

My wife, not long ago, fell into casual conversation with three medical men. All three of the doctors were dismayed at the present situation and future prospects of the American people, and, unsolicited, expressed at some length their vaticinations. A surgeon, after remarking that on the imminent breadlines people would be armed and fighting, claiming rights but denying duties, then groaned. "It's all over! I thought we had more time! We lasted only two hundred years!"

This mood of despondency is widespread today. "Shine, perishing Republic!" in the line of Robinson Jeffers. The parallel with Roman decay is sufficiently obvious. As the American economy staggers under a burden of taxation that soon, we are promised—under Clinton Caesar—will be increased, the federal government sends the Marines to Somalia to take two million Somalis under our spread-eagle wings. It was thus the Romans occupied Greece, for the sake of the wayward Greeks—and never left Greece until the

Greek cities were ruined in the collapse of the whole Empire. Whom the gods wish to destroy, they first make mad.

Yesteryear's great expectations are blasted. For the first time, a great many Americans suspect that America's culture is decadent. Some of them seem well content with the sickness of our old culture. "What do you mean by 'culture?'" the former governor of New York exclaimed a couple of years ago. "That's a word they used in Nazi Germany." This uncultured and unscrupulous demagogue is mentioned by President Clinton as a praiseworthy future associate justice of the Supreme Court of the United States. When such persons are elevated to great power in the Republic, indeed there exists reason to raise the question of social decadence.

*   *   *

There has appeared a spate of books about the present "Culture War." And much obloquy is cast upon the so-called "cultural elite" of the United States. Succinctly, how may we define this "culture" that has grown controversial? In my book *America's British Culture*, I examine at length such definitions; but for the present, let us take a definition by Christopher Dawson, the great historian of culture. Here, extracted from Dawson's first book, *The Age of the Gods* (1928), is that definition:

> A culture is a common way of life—a particular adjustment of man to his natural surroundings and his economic needs.... And just as every natural region tends to possess its characteristic forms of animal and vegetable life, so too will it possess its own type of human society.... The higher culture will express itself through its material circumstance, as masterfully and triumphantly as the artist through the medium of his material.

Just so. Our American culture, derived in large part from centuries of British culture, has grown in this continent to a tremendous civilization; President Bush took great pride in the fact that America is now the only superpower. Pride goeth before a fall. That is why I am writing on the subject of whether this civilization of ours may endure during the twenty-first century of the Christian era. What, if anything, may you and I do to renew this shaken culture of ours?

Well, before we endeavor to prescribe remedies, we need to ascertain the causes of our difficulties. We must remind ourselves, to begin, that culture arises from the cult: out of the religious bond and the sense of the sacred grow any civilization's agriculture, its common defense, its orderly towns, its ingenious architecture, its literature, its music, its visual arts, its law, its political structure, its educational apparatus, and its mores. Christopher Dawson, Eric Voegelin, and other historians of this century have made this historical truth clear.

*   *   *

Modern society's gravest afflictions, conversely, are caused by the decay of the cult upon which a society has been founded, or by the sharp separation of the trappings of a sophisticated civilization from the nurturing cult, with its glimpse of the transcendent. Alexander Solzhenitsyn, in his Templeton Address at London, put this plainly enough:

> Our life consists not in the pursuit of material success but in the quest of worthy spiritual growth.

> Our entire earthly existence is but a transition stage in the movement toward something higher, and we must not

stumble or fall, nor must we linger fruitlessly on one rung
of the ladder.... The laws of physics and physiology will
never reveal the indisputable manner in which The
Creator constantly, day in and day out, participates in the
life of each of us, unfailingly granting us the energy of
existence; when this assistance leaves us, we die. In the
life of our entire planet, the Divine Spirit moves with no
less force; this we must grasp in our dark and terrible
hour.

Thus it should be understood that the ideology of secular
humanism and the ideology of democratism that lies behind
professed "multiculturalism," all are assaults upon a common way
of life that has developed out of Christian insights—or, if you will,
Judeo-Christian insights—into the human condition. Ideology
always is the enemy of religion, and endeavors to supplant its
adversary among humankind. But ideology has been unable to
produce a counterculture that endures long—witness the collapse
of the Soviet Union after seven decades of power.

The relationship between religious faith and a high culture,
described here by Solzhenitsyn, has been denied or ignored by the
intellectuals, although not forgotten by the humble. At the
beginning of his Templeton Address, Solzhenitsyn made that
point. "Over half a century ago, while I was still a child,"
Solzhenitsyn said, "I recall hearing a number of older people offer
the following explanation for the great disasters that had befallen
Russia. 'Men have forgotten God; that's why all this has happened.'" They were right, and so are their counterparts in the
United States today.

About a decade ago, the Brookings Institution published a
careful study by James Reichley, entitled *Religion in American
Public Life*. In a chapter entitled "Religion, Politics, and Human

Values," Mr. Reichley examined eight value-systems, and found only one of those sufficient to balance individual rights against social authority, so bringing about harmony in a culture. That one value system he called "theist-humanism": most people recognize it as Christianity, in Reichley's description. It is only a renewed sense of the sacred, I am suggesting—by a return to Christian understanding of the human condition and its limitations, I am suggesting, that the American nation may withstand the designs of ideology and restore those common ways of life that we call America's culture.

*   *   *

The governor of Mississippi was reproached a few years back for declaring that America is a Christian nation. Despite objections, he was quite right; his opponents seem not to understand the meaning of the word "nation," except as it is incorrectly employed by the daily journalist. True, the United States of America is not a Christian *state*, for the country's Constitution forbids the establishment of a national church by Congress, and stands tolerant of all religions. But the words state and nation signify different concepts. "State" means the governmental organization of a country, political society with sovereign power; while "nation" means the people of the land, with their culture—and not merely the people who are living just now, but also their ancestors and those who will descend from them: that is, a nation is extended in time and shares a culture: those participants in a common culture who are living today, and the participants in that culture who have preceded them in time, and those participants in the common culture who are yet to be born. One might call a nation a community of souls.

In that proper understanding of what a nation amounts to, the American nation is Christian, although more Christian formerly, perhaps, than it is just now. For Christianity, if sometimes in a diluted form, is the religion of the majority of Americans nowadays; and beyond church communicants, there are millions of Americans who do not attend churches, but nevertheless are strongly influenced by Christian morals; moreover nearly everyone else who has lived long in the United States, though he be Jew or Moslem or agnostic, conforms in large degree to American folkways and customs and conventions that are Christian in origin: in short, the American culture, with its Christian roots, is everywhere dominant in these United States, among the larger "minorities" of the population as well as among Americans of European descent; that is, the Christian ethos is no less strong among blacks and persons of Latin-American descent than among Americans who can trace their descent in this country back to the seventeenth century.

So the Governor of Mississippi is quite right: America is a Christian nation; this is a matter of fact, not of opinion. Whether America will remain a Christian nation is matter for argument, perhaps: the creation of special rights for pathics, for instance, indicates that Christian morals are going by the board; and the prevalence of abortion, the deliberate destruction of one's offspring, is another suggestion that both Christian belief and Christian morals have begun to succumb to total religious indifference, if not yet to atheism. But if Christian faith and morals will be generally rejected in of the twenty-first century, then probably the whole culture will disintegrate, the material culture as well as the intellectual and moral culture; and human existence here will become poor, nasty, brutish, and short: unless some quite new culture, which as yet nobody can imagine, should rise up. Any such unnameable innovative culture, to endure, would require some transcendent sanction, perhaps some theophanic event—something more enduring than mere Marxist ideology, which was a violent attempt at a new faith and a new culture.

Why have an increasing number of Americans endeavored to break with our inherited culture and its religious roots? The reasons are diverse; but the fundamental impulse to reject a religious patrimony is expressed by T. S. Eliot in his choruses for *The Rock*, especially in the following lines:

> *Why should men love the Church? Why should they love her*
> *   laws?*
> *She tells them of Life and Death, and of all that they would*
> *   forget.*
> *She is tender where they would be hard, and hard where they*
> *   like to be soft.*
> *She tells them of Evil and Sin, and other unpleasant facts.*
> *They constantly try to escape*
> *From the darkness outside and within*
> *By dreaming of systems so perfect that no one will need to be*
> *   good.*

Religion restrains the passions and the appetites: and sensate natures flout restraints. The more perverse the pleasure, the more it is sought by some. So it is that public funds have been employed to subsidize obscene representations of Jesus of Nazareth; this seems to some titillatingly smart. I find it odd that, so far as I know, nobody has compared these "works of art" to the obscene representations of Jews in which Joseph Goebbels and his colleagues rejoiced during the regime of Hitler.

*   *   *

I have been suggesting that for our culture—our inherited ways of life that have nurtured our American society in the past—to be reinvigorated, a renewal of religious faith is required. So long as many of us deny the dignity of man and indulge what T. S. Eliot called "the diabolic imagination," our culture limps downward. Our public schools, almost totally secularized, starve the religious imagination; federal and state courts often tend to frown upon Christian morals and churches' claims to independence. Will a time arrive when religion is indulged by public authorities only on sufferance?

What can be done to restore the religious imagination within our common culture? One cannot look to many seminaries for such a vigorous work of renewal: most of those institutions are pursuing theological or quasi-theological novelties, and are caught up in the humanitarian spirit of the age. No one can sincerely embrace a religious creed merely because it might be socially beneficial to do so. Conceivably some great preacher or great novelist or great poet may move minds and hearts toward the transcendent again, opening eyes that had been sealed; there come to mind the examples of John Wesley in eighteenth-century England, Chateaubriand in France at the end of the French Revolution, T. S. Eliot in this century. Or possibly men of the natural sciences may come to perceive design in the universe, purpose in mutations. Or, as in ages past, we may be given a Sign.

Some people, after the fashion of T. S. Eliot, may turn toward Christianity once they have discovered how unendurable a place the twentieth- or twenty-first-century world would become were that faith altogether lacking. Others, myself among them, may come from much reading and meditation to conclude that Augustine of Hippo and Sir Thomas Browne and Samuel Johnson and Samuel Taylor Coleridge and John Henry Newman, professed Christians and apologists, too, were no fools. Whether enough such persons may take up the cause of Christian teaching to alter the spirit of the age—why, who can tell? C. S. Lewis and Malcolm Muggeridge succeeded in moving intellects and consciences, and a half-dozen American writers continue to do so among us today. By the way, I particularly commend to you a book by William Kirk Kilpatrick, *Why Johnny Can't Tell Right from Wrong: Moral Illiteracy and the Case for Character Education*. This earnest book very effectively exposes the mischief being done by those educators who in Britain are called "the crazies." At one American gathering of that educationist clan, hard haters of old moral principles, all the major religions of the world were dismissed as "male chauvinist murder cults."

Short of a mighty reinvigoration of the religious imagination, what may you and I do to redeem the time?

Confining ourselves to three causes of cultural decadence, I declare that we can do much, in a practical way.

With respect to multiculturalism, it is entirely possible to resist this silly, malign movement, despite its temporary successes, and to begin to restore a decent curriculum to schools, colleges, and universities; if we succeed, nine-tenths of the students will bless us. At the University of Texas the multicultural program was opposed by a majority of the faculty in a secret ballot; and the university's president resigned in consequence, praise be. A little more courage on the part of college administrators and professors would undo this anti-cultural tyranny. And yet the advantages still lie with the aggressors. At one Michigan college black militant students engaged in wild demonstrations. Far from disciplining the student offenders, the president of the college ordered two or three members of the faculty to undergo sensitivity training, so that they would learn to be sufficiently servile to militant students. A mad world, my masters! Let us prod some university presidents and trustees into defense of true academic freedom.

With respect to the assaults upon religious belief, which has been the source of all high culture over the ages, it is high time for us to oppose most strenuously those governmental policies which discriminate against religion and received morality. In New York City, Dr. Russell Hittinger, a redoubtable learned champion of the doctrines of natural law, issued from the platform a virtual call to arms against the enemies of moral order—some of them entrenched behind the federal bench. Let us remember that not even the Supreme Court of the United States is endowed with arbitrary and absolute power: Congress, if it so chooses, may remove from the Court's appellate jurisdiction certain categories of cases, and in other ways may remind the judiciary that it is not a constitutional archonocracy. But I leave to your ingenuity the devising of ways to resist and even to intimidate those zealots for the abolition of all restraint upon sensual impulse.

In connection with this possible restoration of the religious imagination, it is of the first importance to bring about more choice in education at every level—so that those parents and others who would have their children obtain religious knowledge may be enabled to do so. The national administration of President Bush gave at least lip-service to this cause: and more than ever before, there exists a possibility of persuading state legislators to pass such measures.

Third, I urge you to resist manfully and womanfully the thought-less centralization of political and economic power. Not content with having reduced the several American states, nominally sover-eign, to impotent provinces, America's centralizers, with their dream of a New World Order, have commenced to acquire prov-inces overseas—Somalia the first in this decade, perhaps. "Take up the white man's burden," certain liberal voices exhort us. One can imagine the nightmare of a universal domination of egalitarian "democratic capitalism" directed by the Washington bureaucracy— unimaginative, arrogant, everywhere resented in the twenty-first century—draining America's resources and energies as Rome was drained by her empire. The more centralization, the less freedom and the less energy.

Is this the manifest destiny of the United States to become the New Rome? Have you and I no choice about that? Nay, not so. I return here to old Edmund Burke's first *Letter on a Regicide Peace*, which I cited in the opening chapter, and which denied that great states have to obey some irresistible law of progress or decay; Burke set his face against the attitude now called "determinism." Permit me again to quote a key passage:

> It is often impossible, in these political inquiries, to find any proportion between the apparent causes we may assign, and their known operation. We are therefore obliged to deliver up that operation to mere chance; or, more piously (perhaps more rationally), to the occasional interposition and the irresistible hand of the Great Disposer. We have seen states of considerable duration, for which ages have remained nearly as they have begun, and could hardly be said to ebb or flow. The meridian of some has been most splendid. Others, and they the greatest number, have fluctuated, and experienced at different periods of their existence a great variety of fortune. At the very moment when some of them seem plunged in unfathomable abysses of disgrace and disaster, they have begun a new course, and opened a new reckoning, and even in the depths of their calamity, and on the very ruins of their country, have laid the foundations of a towering and durable greatness. All this happened without any apparent previous change in the general circumstances which had brought on their distress. The death of a man at a critical juncture, his retreat, have brought innumerable calamities on a whole nation. A common soldier, a child, a girl at the door of an inn, have changed the face of fortune, and almost of Nature.

In those two sentences, Burke may refer to the reverses of Pericles, to the death of the Constable of Bourbon and other startling historical instances of a country's fate hanging upon a single life. Providence, chance, or strong wills, Burke declares, abruptly may alter the whole apparent direction of "that armed ghost, the meaning of history" (Gabriel Marcel's phrase).

Even such as you and I, if we are resolute enough and sufficiently imaginative, may alter the present course of events. God, we have been told, helps those who help themselves. In the face of increasing tribulations, sometimes conservatives and liberals are making common cause in the defense of America's culture. Both Arthur M. Schlesinger, Jr., and your servant have written books in repudiation of multiculturalism. Once more, say not the struggle naught availeth. A great number of the American people already have taken alarm at the drift of policy and morality in this land. Reactions may be salutary: as the poet Roy Campbell used to say, a human body that cannot react is a corpse; and so it is with society. Up the reactionaries against decadence!

Permit me, in conclusion, to quote a heartening passage from a book, *Our Present Discontents*, published in 1919. The author was William Ralph Inge, then Dean of St. Paul's in London, commonly described by journalists as "the Gloomy Dean." The passage I offer you, however, is one of hope:

> There may be in progress a store of beneficent forces which we cannot see. There are ages of sowing and ages of reaping; the brilliant epochs may be those in which spiritual wealth is squandered; the epochs of apparent decline may be those in which the race is recuperating after an exhausting effort. To all appearances, man still has a great part of his long lease before him, and there is no reason to suppose that the future will be less productive of moral and spiritual triumphs than the past. The source of all good is like an inexhaustible river; the

Creator pours forth new treasures of goodness, truth, and beauty for all who will love them and take them, 'Nothing that truly *is* can ever perish,' as Plotinus says; whatever has value in God's sight is for evermore. Our half-real world is the factory of souls in which we are tried as in a furnace. We are not to set our hopes upon it, but learn such wisdom as it can teach us while we pass through it.

America has overcome the ideological culture of the Union of Socialist Soviet Republics. In the decade of this victory, are Americans to forswear the beneficent culture that they have inherited? For a civilization to arise and flower, centuries are required; but the indifference or the hostility of a single generation may suffice to work that civilization's ruin. We must confront the folk whom Arnold Toynbee called "the internal proletariat" as contrasted with the "external proletariat" from alien lands. Otherwise we may end, all of us, as fellow-proletarians, culturally deprived, in a nation that will permit no one to rise above mediocrity.

Section II

Reconsidering the Civil Social Order

XII

America's Augustan Age?

Two thousand years ago, Augustus Caesar restored order to the civilized world, which had been ravaged by civil and international wars for several decades. A "time of troubles" comparable to the grim disorders of the first century before Christ commenced about *anno domini* 1914. Today the American Republic is attempting a restoration analogous to the Roman reinvigoration by Augustus.

When we employ the word "augustan" we imply a grand maturity. In humane letters, the term signifies the best period of literary accomplishment; and so it is also with architecture and allied arts. In politics, "augustan" connotes a majestic even-handed justice, the restored rule of law. In morals, the word suggests the recovery of venerable standards. The Vergilian associations of the Augustan Age remind us of Vergil's *labor*, or purposeful restoring work; his *pietas*, or reverence for what has been; and his *fatum*, or civilizing mission. An augustan age, in short, is an era of successful renewal of ancient constitutions and neglected mores; also it is a time for erecting greater structures upon venerable foundations. The augustan architect finds a city brick, and leaves it marble.

Now may we justly draw a parallel between the Roman task toward the close of the first century before Christ, and the American task toward the close of the twentieth century after Christ? History does repeat itself—yet always with variations. We study history because much of it is relevant to our present difficulties and prospects. Of all periods in history, it seems to me, the one most nearly parallel with our own era is Rome's Augustan Age—little studied in our schools nowadays. Permit me first to suggest certain outward similarities of these Roman and American eras, and then to examine the prospects for American reinvigoration, two centuries after the founding of the American Republic.

There exist two fundamental ends of the state. One is the keeping of the peace; the other, the administration of justice. In a high degree, Augustus succeeded at both tasks. To the world he gave the Pax Romana—which, whatever its shortcomings, provided security of life and property for the peoples of the Roman system over several generations; hanging together, indeed, for four centuries and a half. And within the Roman structure, Augustus achieved a political reform which sustained law and order for a great while, and which in part has been passed down to modern civilization.

The immediate necessities of the American Republic in the closing years of the twentieth century after Christ resemble those of Rome after the triumph of Octavian, styled Augustus. For the keeping of peace in the world, America at the end of the Second World War was as strong as Rome had been after the defeat of Antony. We Americans let slip our supremacy during the Cold War, but it is not fantastic today to imagine a Pax Americana.

Within the United States, Americans have to confront the problem of reinvigorating the written constitution and the unwritten constitution, lest this country sink altogether into a centralized "plebiscitary democracy," a mockery of the original American pattern of politics. A principal intention of conservatives has been to resist the drift toward a condition called by Tocqueville "democratic despotism."

Those are conspicuous political questions common to the eras we are discussing. Other similarities must be noted. One, the especial concern of Augustus in his hour, is the decay of public and private morality—from the loss of virtue among men holding high office to the dismaying divorce-rate in Roman society and American. Yet another common difficulty, bound up with mores, is above politics: I mean the life of spirit, the religious understanding of existence, in a society that has sampled all fancied pleasures and experienced all forms of brutality. Finally, both the Roman and the American societies in question, after years of war and social confusion, found themselves distressed economically. (This last problem, though it might loom largest for the average Roman citizen or the average American citizen, actually could be dealt with more readily than could the difficulties of peace, political structure, morality, and the life of spirit.)

Now Augustus and the great Roman restorers of his time—poets and historians conspicuous among them—did succeed in their work of renewal. They did not succeed perfectly, for human institutions never achieve perfection. But they did revive, among the better Romans, hope and a sense of mission. They did preserve until the fifth century—or, in the East, until the fifteenth century—the general framework of the Roman order. They did confer upon Latin literature, upon Roman architecture, upon all those civilizing influences called *Romanitas,* an enduring majesty. They gave us the word "augustan" as the symbol of a nation's fullest achievement. Two thousand years later, can America know its own augustan age?

*   *   *

Some shrill liberal voices would persuade us that the American nation is descending into economic exhaustion, civil disorder, and ignominy among the powers of the earth. Something fatal indeed is occurring: but the disaster is befalling the shallow ideology called American liberalism, not the American nation.

In 1913, near the beginning of the world's present time of troubles, George Santayana wrote that the American liberals had subordinated quality to quantity—in economic life, as in much else. The liberal philanthropists, Santayana remarked, were then preparing "an absolute subjection of the individual, in soul and body, to the instincts of the majority—the most cruel and unprogressive of masters; and I am not sure that the liberal maxim 'the greatest happiness of the greatest number' has not lost whatever was just or generous in its intent and come to mean the greatest idleness of the largest possible population."

Aye, for most of this century the liberal philanthropists have been subjecting the individual and encouraging idleness; and now the nation begins to summon them to a reckoning. The prophets of despair wailing in our midst are the remaining ideologues of liberalism. They are fallible. A generation ago, they or their counterparts were informing us that the Terrestrial Paradise would be ours within a very few years, if only we would abide by their counsels. For the most part, persuaded, we did abide by their counsels—and so found ourselves defeated in Asia, saddled with an enormous bureaucracy at home, tormented by urban disorders, ruinously taxed, wretchedly schooled, subjected to inflation of the currency, infected by narcotics and promiscuity, stalled in industrial production, and generally exhibiting the symptoms of decadence.

Having flung wide the lid of this Pandora's box of troubles, the liberal prophets nowadays instruct us that these afflictions have been visited upon the American nation for not having been liberal enough; that all is lost, or virtually all; that we shall experience economic reverses greater far than those of the Depression of the

'Thirties; that we shall be rejected by the comity of nations as imperialistic warmongers; that we shall be even as Nineveh and Babylon. Many false spirits are gone forth into the world.

I do not mean to make light of our difficulties as a nation. Any Roman who made light of Rome's difficulties before the battle of Actium must have been wondrously complacent. Yet I venture to suggest that, most of our afflictions having resulted from intellectual fallacies and imprudent public policies, rather than from ineluctable decrees of Fate—why, it may be possible to undo folly by the employment of reason and imagination.

In the dawning years, quite possibly we Americans must come to know augustan ways—or else resign ourselves to some other Roman form of domination, much less exalted. So let us take stock of our American resources, visible and invisible. Do we as a people possess the talents and the means required for the making of a future more impressive than our past?

*   *   *

Turn we first to the material resources, which remain abundant. Given reform of public fiscal policy, the American economy can produce a prosperity that would make possible the restoration of our cities, the revival of our countryside, the satisfaction of every genuine public need, material comfort for the whole population. In such augustan material circumstances, the problems of too great an abundance of creature-comforts would become far graver than the problems of vestigial poverty, but that is a topic for another lecture. Here I am suggesting merely that it is not economic insufficiency which could deny America an augustan age.

Economic concerns, as I mentioned earlier, stand in the forefront of many American minds; nevertheless, if we would be augustans, economic difficulties are the least of our worries. I am painfully aware, for all that, how governmental mismanagement of the economy, or unsalutary neglect of the economy, can ruin a country's—nay, an empire's—prosperity permanently. For an examination of the mischief done to the ancient economy by the failure of the masters of the Roman Empire to apprehend prudent economic policies, I commend to you such books as Freya Stark's *Rome on the Euphrates,* M. I. Finley's *The Ancient Economy,* and H. P. L'Orange's *Art Forms and Civic Life in the Late Roman Empire.*

How the peaceful prosperity of Italy during the age of the Antonines (a very moderate and doubtful prosperity by our twentieth-century standards, of course) became the poverty of Italy during the age of Saint Augustine may be expressed by reference to a brief episode in the life of Augustine of Hippo. When Augustine and his mother Monica went down to the port of Ostia that Monica might return to Africa—their final parting—they lodged in a large building near the Tiber; archeologists believe they know where the building stood. The houses in that Ostian street formerly had been inhabited by wealthy merchants in the corn trade. By the time Augustine and Monica sojourned in Ostia, all those houses were the dwellings of tax-collectors, it is thought. Such glimpses of antiquity enable one to understand the Jewish prejudice against publicans. They also suggest, those glimpses, how economic mismanagement, in any age, may undo a high culture.

Nevertheless, the restoration of America's economic vigor is the simplest of the many labors required for the creating of an augustan age. No member of Congress, I suppose, desires to impede the recovery of the American economy. But whether most members of both houses of Congress possess the courage required for the adopting of measures, temporarily unpopular or opposed by strong lobbies, that will remedy inflationary deficits, the curse of governments in most centuries—why, that will depend upon how many representatives of the people of the several states can persuade themselves to take long views in an exigency. Taking long views, rather than short ones, is one mark of the augustan mind.

* * *

Goods and services aside, how well prepared are we Americans to enter upon augustan ways? What of the life of the mind? Have we developed, in this affluent democracy, a class of people endowed with the imperial intellect? In the United States we have spent more money upon formal schooling than has all the rest of the world in all ages, combined. Have we succeeded in preparing ourselves, as a people, for high augustan duties in a mature American civilization?

For thirty years I wrote in magazines and newspapers about American education at various levels; at the end of that time, I diminished my task in disgust, being convinced that I had accomplished next to nothing: schooling of every sort had grown steadily worse, as the decades passed.

Educational permissivism, television, the indulgence of an affluent society, domination of many schools by the anti-intellectual trade union called the National Education Association, and plain educational racketeering have brought about intellectual apathy among the rising generation. Every discipline of the mind has suffered from decay, at every level of American schooling—with the exception, of course, of this or that school, this or that department at one university or another, and this or that young person who acquires some measure of wisdom despite obstacles placed in his path.

The ends of education, Plato tells us, are wisdom and virtue. Certainly wisdom and virtue, as we find those ends expressed in Vergil and Horace and Livy, were the aims of schooling in the Age of Augustus. Those ends, and those authors, were at the heart of the European and the American school curricula until the later years of the nineteenth century—in some countries, much later than that. But it is a rare school nowadays that retains some snatches of Vergil, Horace, or Livy; and I know of no American public school which proclaims the imparting of wisdom and virtue as its purpose.

What the rising generation of Americans are subjected to is not an august schooling, but a frivolous schooling. One might think that boys and girls were being prepared for spending their lives at play. Most of the teachers, wretchedly schooled themselves and bored with the whole undertaking, have next to no notion of how an intellectual discipline may be imparted. The textbooks are wondrously superficial. Schools are large buildings in which boys and girls are kept off the streets and out of their parents' way for a portion of the day, five days a week—not much more than that, during recent decades, having been demanded of schools.

In our American democracy, the young people so reared soon must make decisions, as electors, that may decide the course of the Republic, and perhaps of the world. They have not been prepared intellectually or morally to make even decisions pertinent to neighborhood concerns; no, not even to make decisions about their family concerns. Such is our intellectual readiness for the opportunities and duties of an augustan age.

In his charge of October, 1981, to the new National Commission on Excellence in Education, President Reagan urged that Commission's members to be concerned with four fundamental principles. The first and most important of these, Mr. Reagan said, is that instruction begins at home, in the family; and that more formal educational institutions exist to assist families in their educational responsibilities. The second principle is that excellence demands competition. The third principle is the need for diversity and pluralism in schooling, with emphasis upon independent schools. The fourth principle is that schooling should teach the difference between right and wrong.

This little address clearly was of Mr. Reagan's own composition. How rarely one hears such sound sense from professors of education! President Reagan's remarks may foreshadow the development in this country of an augustan mode of education. But many professional educationists will fight hard—so far as there is any fortitude in them—to prevent such improvement.

* * *

Finally, what of the life of spirit necessary to an augustan era? A state may be majestic without what we call wealth: after all, Athenians in the "Great Age" of Greece were thought decadently luxurious if they ate fish more than once or twice a week (touching meat not at all). A state may maintain a high dignity and formidable power although its people's schooling is simple, the example of Sparta may suffice. But the term "august" cannot be applied to a society whose people are blind and deaf to the transcendent. Such a society, lacking the truth of myth which is life-giving, cannot long cohere, let alone display greatness.

Why, it can be said of the United States still that (as Burke said of England) "atheists are not our law-givers." Try though the American Civil Liberties Union may to drive out from schools and public places any reference to religious faith, nevertheless as a people American citizens—or the majority of them—remain attached to Christian morality, with its Hebraic roots. As Tocqueville wrote a century and a half ago, the American religion may not be imaginative, but its influence upon private life and public affairs is profoundly beneficent. The same cannot be said of any other power of the first rank in today's world.

Ideology—as we see it decayed today in Russia, shaken in Communist China, sodden and contemptible in "emergent" Africa, murderous in Cambodia and Vietnam, or a facade for banditry in Latin America—does not long endure, once its pretensions are exposed after its seizure of power. A close friend of mine, an exile from Poland, told me just prior to the fall of communism in his country that no Communists at all remained in Poland: merely the masters and agents of a police state, members of a power-bloc calling itself the Communist Party. So it was, too, in the other countries of eastern Europe. Even an enfeebled religious faith outlasted nineteenth-century ideology: that is clear in the examples of the ex-Communist Bloc countries.

That being so, America holds the possibility of attaining that life of spirit which is augustan. I do not mean that we can discern much augustan tone just now among American Protestants, Catholics, or Jews. Protestantism today is mostly what Will Herberg called "the ethos of sociability," mingled with vague humanitarian preachments. Catholicism is gone over to yesteryear's Protestant social gospel. American Judaism is not conspicuous for moral elevation or imagination in our time. But even so, these bodies of belief (however shallow at the moment) are not going to give way in this country to the pseudo-religion of ideology, which makes immanent the symbols of transcendence. American churches are engaged in a kind of unconscious holding-action, as if awaiting an event which lies concealed in the hand of God.

We Americans seem caught up in what my old friend Max Picard called "the world of the flight"—that is, the flight from God. We flee; God pursues. God may catch up; He can if He chooses. Then indeed American churches might be transfigured, and purged, and made worthy of an augustan age. I think I discern some portents of such an uprising in the American life of spirit.

However that may be, at the moment America lacks prophets, saints, and martyrs. America has no poet of the high dream on the model of Vergil; no historian like Livy who gives meaning to the obscurity of a people's past. We think of our comforts, and of what private advantages we may extract from our government.

To be called augustan, a nation must be courageous and swift in its own defense and its own interest. It must be strict and equitable in its administration of justice. It must be accustomed to moral restraints. It must seek wisdom and virtue through the education of the young. It must give approval to an ethical literature of high beauty, to architecture of an enduring dignity, to harmony and imagination in all the arts. It must uphold order in all of order's aspects—including that diversity which is natural within a healthy order.

Our country must go far before it takes on an augustan aspect. Yet the sands run swiftly through Fate's hourglass. Only augustan talents can suffice to quiet our time of troubles; only augustan *gravitas* can reprove our self-satisfied strutting and clowning.

Some members of the Congress, possessing historical knowledge, might do well to recollect the high dignity and remarkable foresight of leaders of the infant Republic of the United States, two centuries ago. That newborn Republic, to the historical imagination, seems to have been more august than is our present gigantic Union. By an effort of will and right reason, and with the models of earlier augustan times for guidance, America may yet—under the pressure and challenge of events—come to deserve the designation of augustan.

XIII

The American Mission

Does the nation called the United States of America possess a mission, providentially ordained? If so, does America have the ability and the courage to pursue that mission, at the close of the twentieth century?

Four decades ago, during the Eisenhower era, we heard much talk about the "American Century"; and there was printed much discussion—some of it superficial, and the rest not conspicuously imaginative—about American national goals. Since then, American expectations often have been chastened. If it remains possible that this still may become the American Century in the eyes of future historians, what is America's mission?

Let us repair, with this question in mind, to Orestes Brownson, who was born in 1805 and died in 1876. Lord Acton, possessed of one of the better intellects of the nineteenth century, believed that Orestes Brownson was the most penetrating thinker of his day. That was a high compliment indeed, for in the United States it was the day of Hawthorne, Melville, Emerson, and a half-dozen other men of the first rank—not to mention the great Victorians of Britain. Brownson was a considerable political philosopher, a seminal essayist on religion, a literary critic of discernment, a serious journalist with fighting vigor, and one of the shrewder observers of American character and institutions.

Although a radical in his youth, Brownson became after 1840 a formidable defender of the permanent things. He was the first writer to refute Marx's *Communist Manifesto*.

"In most cases," Brownson wrote in 1848, replying to Marx, "the sufferings of a people spring from moral causes beyond the reach of civil government, and they rarely are the best patriots who paint them in the most vivid colors, and rouse up popular indignation against the civil authorities. Much more effectual service could be rendered in a more quiet and peaceful way, by each one seeking, in his own immediate sphere, to remove the moral causes of the evils endured."

Without Authority vested somewhere, Brownson told the Americans of his age, without regular moral principles that may be consulted confidently, justice cannot long endure anywhere. Yet modern liberalism and democracy, he continued, are contemptuous of the whole concept of moral authority. If not checked in their assaults upon habitual reverence and prescriptive morality, the liberals will destroy justice not only for their enemies, but for themselves. *Under God,* Brownson emphasized, the will of the people ought to prevail; but many liberals and democrats ignore that prefatory clause.

Brownson was an outspoken champion of the American Republic. His book entitled *The American Republic* was published the year after the end of the Civil War; it contains his most systematic exposition of the idea of the American Mission.

Every living nation, Brownson wrote in that book, "has an idea given it by Providence to realize, and whose realization is its special work, mission, or destiny." The Jews were chosen to preserve traditions, and that the Messiah might arise. The Greeks were chosen for the realizing of art, science, and philosophy. The Romans were chosen for the developing of the state, law, and jurisprudence. And the Americans, too, have been appointed to a providential mission, Brownson declared. America is meant to continue the works of the Greeks and the Romans, but to accomplish yet more. The American Republic has the mission of reconciling liberty with law.

Brownson was a champion of ordered freedom. Yet America's mission, he added in 1866, "is not so much the realization of liberty as the realization of the true idea of the state, which secures at once the authority of the public and the freedom of the individual—the sovereignty of the people without social despotism, and individual freedom without anarchy. In other words, its mission is to bring out in its life the dialectical union of authority and liberty, of the natural rights of man and those of society. The Greek and Roman republics asserted the state to the detriment of individual freedom; modern republics either do the same, or assert individual freedom to the detriment of the state. The American republic has been instituted by Providence to realize the freedom of each with advantage to the other."

So America's mission, as Brownson discerned it, was to present to mankind a political model: a commonwealth in which order and freedom exist in a healthy balance or tension—in which the citizen is at once secure and free. This reconciling of authority and liberty is the central problem of politics. As the German scholar Hans Barth points out, Edmund Burke is the most important political thinker of modern times precisely because Burke understood the necessary tension between the claims of order and the claims of freedom. In America, Orestes Brownson discerned this cardinal problem of politics better than did anyone else.

The reconciling of authority and liberty, so that justice might be realized in the good state: that mission for America is not yet accomplished, a century and a quarter after Brownson wrote; but neither is that mission altogether forgotten. *Under God*, said Brownson in his emphatic way, the American Republic may grow in virtue and justice. A century later, the word "under God" would be added to the American pledge of allegiance.

Yet also, during the past three decades, the influence has grown of those Americans who would prefer to stride along without any divinely-ordained mission—who believe, indeed, that the American Republic could do famously without bothering about God. The Supreme Court of the United States has tended to side with these militant secularists, correctly styled "humanitarians" by Brownson. Humanitarian liberals, Brownson wrote in his *American Republic*, are the enemies—if sometimes the unwitting enemies—of true freedom and true order.

"The humanitarian democracy," Brownson said, "which scorns all geographical lines, effaces all individualities, and professes to plant itself on humanity alone, has acquired by the [Civil] war new strength, and is not without menace to our future." Brownson declares that the humanitarian presently will attack distinctions between the sexes; he will assail private property, as unequally distributed. "Nor can our humanitarian stop there. Individuals are, and as long as there are individuals will be, unequal: some are handsomer and some are uglier, some wiser or sillier, more or less gifted, stronger or weaker, taller or shorter, stouter or thinner than others, and therefore some have natural advantages which others have not. There is inequality, therefore injustice, which can be remedied only by the abolition of all individualities, and the reduction of all individuals to the race, or humanity, man in general. He [the humanitarian] can find no limit to his agitation this side of vague generality, which is no reality, but a pure nullity, for he respects no territorial or individual circumscriptions, and must regard creation itself as a blunder."

This humanitarian, or social democrat (here Brownson uses these terms almost interchangeably), is by definition a person who denies that any divine order exists. Having rejected the supernatural order and the possibility of a Justice that is more than human, the humanitarian tends to erect Envy into a pseudo-moral principle. It leads him, this principle of Envy, straight toward a dreary tableland of featureless social equality—toward Tocqueville's "democratic despotism," from which not only God seems to have disappeared, but even oldfangled individual human beings are lacking.

A truly just society is not a democracy of degradation, Brownson argues. The just society does not reduce human beings to the condition of identical units on the dismal plain of absolute equality. The just society will not speak in the accents of envy, but will talk of order, duty, and honor.

In any particular country, Brownson maintains, the form of government must be suited to the traditions and the organic experience of the people. In some lands, therefore, the form of government will be monarchy; in others, aristocracy; in America, republicanism or democracy *under God*. America must not contest the sovereignty of God, which is absolute over all of us. The American government must secure to every citizen his freedom. And from such freedom comes the justice of which Plato wrote in his *Republic*, and Cicero in his *Offices:* the right of every person to do his own work, free of the meddling of others.

Such is the character of true social justice, Brownson tells us: a liberation of every person, under God, to do the best that is in him. Poverty is no evil, in itself; obscurity is no evil; labor is no evil; even physical pain may be no evil, as it was none to the martyrs. This world is a place of trial and struggle, so that we may find our higher nature in our response to challenges.

It is America's mission, Brownson told his age, to offer to the world the example of such a state and such a society, at once orderly and free. A year after Brownson published *The American Republic,* Marx published *Das Kapital.* Among the more interesting concepts in that latter work I find this confession by Marx: "In order to establish equality, we must first establish inequality." Marx means that to make all men equal, we must first break the strong, the energetic, the imaginative, the learned, the thrifty; they must be broken, indeed, by the dictatorship of the proletariat. Then, having established by force a universal mediocrity, we may enjoy the delights of total equality of condition.

The American mission, Brownson knew so early as 1848, is to show all nations an alternative to the dreary socialist sea-level egalitarian society of equal misery. To that high duty, Brownson earnestly believed, the American nation has been appointed by divine providence.

Do Brownson's phrases ring strange in our ears? Yes, they do, in some degree. And why? Because the humanitarians—that is, the folk who take it for granted that human nature and society may be perfected through means purely human—have come to dominate our universities, our schools, our serious press, most of our newspapers, our television and our radio. The thought, and the very vocabulary, of this Republic have fallen under the domination of humanitarian ideology. Why, the churches themselves, or many of them, have been converted into redoubts of humanitarianism, issuing humanitarian fulminations or comminations against such public men as still stubbornly maintain that politics is the art of the possible.

Some popular revolt against humanitarian dogmas is obvious enough today. As George Santayana put it, it will not be easy to hammer a coddling socialism into America. It is still less easy to eradicate altogether the influence of religious belief in the United States—hard though the humanitarian zealots have been laboring at that task. Yet whether traditional Americans retain coherence and intellectual vigor sufficient to undo humanitarian notions and policies—why, that hangs in the balance nowadays. The tone and temper of American thought and public policy have drifted, for the last three decades at least, toward the humanitarian goal of a materialistic egalitarianism, toward what Robert Graves calls the ideology of Logicalism: that is, a social Dead Sea without imagination, diversity—or hope. It is not that the humanitarians have been especially numerous: rather, their work has been accomplished by small circles of intellectuals, centered chiefly in New York City. Yet ideas do have consequences. America's media of opinion increasingly have reflected the assumptions of that humanitarianism which Brownson denounced in his day.

Some of the unpleasant consequences of humanitarian intellectuality having become apparent to a large part of the American public, that public has begun to react at the polling-booths. (A human body that cannot react, I venture to remind you, is a corpse.) Also there has occurred some healthy reaction intellectually against humanitarian ideology. Yet this reaction comes late, and is relatively feeble as yet: consider, for instance, the continued domination of book-publishing by humanitarian liberals; or the prejudices of most professors; or the fewness in numbers of those theologians and church leaders of intellectual powers who boldly assert that Christianity and Judaism are transcendent religions, not instruments for the destruction of society's cake of custom.

How does this contest between the American humanitarians and the American traditionalists affect the question of the American mission? Why, part of this struggle is a competition between two very different concepts of what the American mission ought to be. I have outlined already the traditionalists' understanding of the American mission: that is, to maintain and improve a Republic in which the claims of freedom and the claims of order are balanced and reconciled—a Republic of liberty under law, endowed with diversity and opportunity, an example to the world. There exists also a humanitarian, or social-democratic, understanding of the

American mission, which already has brought upon us disastrous consequences, in domestic policy and in foreign policy. Permit me to suggest the character of this humanitarian notion of America's mission, with a few illustrations of its practical effect.

*   *   *

The words "humane" and "humanitarian" mean quite different things. The humanitarian believes in brotherhood: that is, "Be my brother," he says, "or I'll kill you." He aspires to assimilate others to his mode and substance.

The humanitarian, whose roots are in the French Enlightenment (full of enlighteners, but singularly lacking in light, Coleridge says), suffers from the itch for perpetual change. Change in what direction? Why, change away from superstition (by which he means religion), from old customs, from established constitutions, from anything that is private (property especially), from local and national affections, from the little platoon that we belong to in society. And change toward an arid rationalism, toward emancipation from old moral obligations and limits, toward a classless "people's democracy," toward collectivism and total equality of condition, toward a sentimental internationalism (a world without diversity), toward concentration of power. The aim of humanitarianism—that is, the ideology which denies the divine and declares the omnicompetence of human planners—is singularly inhumane. Were it possible for the humanitarians to accomplish their design altogether, humankind would be reduced to the inane and impoverished state foretold by Jacquetta Hawkes in her fable "The Unites."

To understand the humanitarian mentality, American variety, to which I refer, we may turn to Santayana's novel *The Last Puritan*. In that shrewd and moving book, we encounter a minor character, Cyrus P. Whittle, a Yankee schoolmaster, a "sarcastic wizened little man who taught American history and literature in a high quavering voice, with a bitter incisive emphasis on one or two words in every sentence as if he were driving a long hard nail into the coffin of some detested fallacy.... His joy, so far as he dared, was to vilify all distinguished men. Franklin had written indecent verses; Washington—who had enormous hands and feet—had married Dame Martha for her money; Emerson served up Goethe's philosophy in ice-water. Not that Mr. Cyrus P. Whittle was without enthusiasm and a secret religious zeal. Not only was America the biggest thing on earth, but it was soon going to wipe out everything else: and in the delirious dazzling joy of that consummation, he forgot to ask what would happen afterwards. He gloried in the momentum of sheer process, in the mounting wave of events; but minds and their purposes were only the foam of the breaking crest; and he took an ironical pleasure in showing how all that happened, and was credited to the efforts of great and good men, really happened against their will and expectation."

Here we have the American humanitarian in a nutshell. For the humanitarian, America's mission is "to wipe out everything else"— to destroy the old order in all the rest of the world, the old faiths, the old governments, the old economies, the old buildings, the old loves and loyalties. And in the delirious dazzling joy of that consummation, the American humanitarian forgets to ask what would happen afterwards.

The influence of this evangelical humanitarianism, this very odd passion for doing good to other people by virtually or literally effacing them, is not confined to one American party or one American class. One thinks of President Wilson, sure that he could make the world safe for democracy by resort to arms—and succeeding, as he saw himself toward the end, merely in delivering eastern Europe into the hands of the Bolsheviki. One thinks, too, of the designs for Americanizing Africa that Colonel House put into Wilson's head—but which never came to pass.

Or one thinks of President Franklin Roosevelt's privately-expressed detestation of the French and British systems, and of his intention (frustrated by events) to make all of Africa (after an expected victory at Dakar) into an American sphere of influence. One thinks, too, of the courses of Presidents Kennedy and Johnson in Indo-China, and of their illusion that American-style democracy, middle-of-the-road parties and all, could be established instantly in Vietnam and neighboring states—if only persons like President Diem were swept away, by such means as might be thought necessary.

I have heard this humanitarian doctrine about America's mission expressed from a Washington platform (which I shared) some four decades ago by the president of the Chamber of Commerce of the United States. If only all the peoples of the world, he said in substance, could be induced or compelled to abolish their old ways of life and become good Americans, emancipated from their ancient creeds and habits, buying American products—why, how happy they all would become!

And these humanitarian doctrines were preached forty years ago by an eminent official of the American labor movement—who confessed indeed that this humanitarian Americanizing might take a century or more of turmoil, and must include the destruction of all existing ruling classes, the driving of handicraft producers to the wall, and the overwhelming of all old religions. But (borrowing a phrase from Robespierre) you can't make an omelet without breaking eggs, you know, he reminded his readers. And think of how happy everybody everywhere will be when everything but an amorphous Americanism is wiped out!

Such is America's mission as perceived by the humanitarian. Yet there remains that very different kind of American mission for which Brownson hoped. Probably Brownson's concept of a national mission was derived in part from Vergil's idea of *fatum*—that is, fate, destiny, mission.

In the age of Augustus, the poet Vergil aspired to consecrate anew the mission of Rome. He did not prevail altogether against the pride, the passion, and the concupiscence of his time: no poet can do that. Yet had there been no Vergil, rousing the consciences of some men of the Empire, the imperial system would have been far grosser and more ruthless than it was. Had it not been for Vergil, the society of the early Empire might have been consumed by its own materialism and egoism. Vergil perceived at work in Roman civilization a divine mission—a purpose for which the Christian adjective is "providential." Communicating that insight to the better minds of his age and of succeeding generations, Vergil made of *Romanitas*, the Roman culture, an ideal which in part fulfilled his prophecy of Rome's mission.

By *fatum*, Vergil meant the Roman imperial destiny—Rome's duty, imposed by unknowable powers, to bring peace to the world, to maintain the cause of order and justice and freedom, to withstand barbarism. For Vergil, this mission was the true significance of Rome's history.

So it was with Brownson's idea of the American mission. The achieving of that mission seemed remote about the time when Brownson described his principle of "the dialectical union of authority and liberty." We have not yet achieved that mission. But today, America has arrived, probably, at its maximum territorial extent, its maximum population (or nearly that), and its height of political, military, and economic power. We Americans, like the Romans of the age of Augustus, must make irrevocable choices. At that time, Rome had either to renew the idea and the reality offiatum, or else to sink prematurely into private and public corruption, internal violence, and disaster on the frontiers. Just so is it with us now.

Then what is America's mission in our age? It remains, as Brownson put it, to reconcile liberty with law. The great grim tendency of our world is otherwise: sometimes toward anarchy, but more commonly toward the total state, whose alleged benefits delude. This is no easy mission, even at home: consider how many people who demand an enlargement of civil liberties at the same time vote for vast increase of the functions and powers of the general government.

And this mission is more difficult still in the example the United States sets for the world. If we are to experience a Pax Americana, it will not be the sort of American hegemony that was attempted by Presidents Truman and Eisenhower and Kennedy and Johnson: not a patronizing endeavor, through gifts of money and of arms, to cajole or intimidate all the nations of the earth into submitting themselves to a vast overwhelming Americanization, wiping out other cultures and political patterns.

An enduring Pax Americana would be produced not by bribing and boasting, but by quiet strength—and especially by setting an example of ordered freedom that might be emulated. Tacitus said that the Romans created a wilderness, and called it peace. We may aspire to bring peace by encouraging other nations to cultivate their own gardens: in that respect, to better the Augustan example.

So much for the precepts of Vergil and Brownson. Either, in the dawning years, we Americans will know Augustan ways—or else we may find ourselves in a different Roman era resurrected. It might be the era of the merciless old Emperor Septimius Severus. As Septimius lay dying at York, after his last campaign, there came to his bedside his two brutal sons, Geta and Caracalla, asking their father how they should rule the Empire once he had gone. "Pay the soldiers," Septimius told them, in his laconic fashion. "The rest do not matter."

In such servitude, lacking both order and freedom, end nations whose mission has been false, or who have known no mission at all. To borrow phrases again from *The Last Puritan*, Americans always were consecrated to great expectations. Adherents to the old traditions of America know that we are not addressed to vanity, to some gorgeous universal domination of our name or manners. Nor are we intended to play the role of the humanitarians with the guillotine. The American mission, I maintain with Brownson, is to reconcile the claims of order and the claims of freedom: to maintain in an age of ferocious ideologies and fantastic schemes a model of justice.

XIV

The Meaning of "Justice"

The word "justice" is on everyone's lips nowadays, and may signify almost anything. We hear the cry "Peace and Justice!" from folk who would destroy existing societies with fire and sword. Other folk fancy that *perfect* justice might readily be obtained by certain financial rearrangements—as if anything in this world ever could be perfected. One thinks of the observation of William James: "So long as one poor cockroach suffers the pangs of unrequited love, this world will not be a moral world." At the end of the twentieth century, the liberal mentality demands justice for roaches, too.

All confusion about the meaning of the word "justice" notwithstanding, the latest edition of the *Encyclopedia Britannica* contains no article under the heading "Justice." Yet there is a succinct article about justices of the peace, of whose number I once was one, before the state of Michigan swept away that high office. This essay may be regarded as the attempt of a fool, rushing in where the angelic Britannica fears to tread. Yet possibly the nature of justice may be apprehended by a mere quondam justice of the peace: for the fundamental purpose of law is to keep the peace. "Justice is the ligament which holds civilized beings and civilized nations together," said Daniel Webster at the funeral of Justice Joseph Story, in 1845; and so say I today.

Nowadays, near the close of the twentieth century, moral and political disorders bring grave confusion about the meanings of old words. As T. S. Eliot wrote in "Burnt Norton"—

> *Words strain,*
> *Crack and sometimes break, under the burden,*
> *Under the tension, slip, slide, perish,*
> *Decay with imprecision, will not stay in place,*
> *Will not stay still. Shrieking voices*
> *Scolding, mocking, or merely chattering,*
> *Always assail them.*

Conspicuous among such venerable words, in our era often abused and misrepresented, is this necessary word *justice*. I attempt here to purify the dialect of the tribe—to borrow another phrase from my old friend Eliot, who endeavored lifelong to rescue words from the clutch of the vulgarizer or of the ideologue.

Permit me first to offer preliminary descriptions or definitions of this word *justice*. Jeremy Taylor, in the middle of the seventeenth century, wrote that there exist two kinds of justice. The one is commutative justice, or reciprocal justice, expressed in Scripture thus: "Whatsoever ye would that men should do to you, even so do to them." In Taylor's words, "This is the measure...of that justice which supposes exchange of things profitable for things profitable, that as I supply your need, you may supply mine; as I do a benefit to you, I may receive one by you...."

The other kind is distributive justice, expressed in this passage from Romans: "Render to all their dues; tribute to whom tribute is due, custom to whom custom, fear to whom fear, honor to whom honor; owe no man anything but to love one another." Upon this Taylor comments, "This justice is distinguished from the first, because the obligation depends not upon contract or express bargain, but passes upon us by some command of God, or of our superior, by nature or by grace, by piety or religion, by trust or by office, according to that commandment, 'As every man hath received the gift, so let him minister the same one to another, as good stewards of the manifold grace of God.'"

But perhaps I proceed too fast; I shall have more to say a little later about the Christian concept of justice. Just now a little about the classical idea of justice. The classical definition, which comes to us through Plato, Aristotle, Saint Ambrose, and Saint Augustine of Hippo, is expressed in a single phrase: *suum cuique,* or "to each his own." As this is put in Justinian's *Corpus Juris Civilis,* "Justice is a habit whereby a man renders to each one his due with constant and perpetual will." Aristotle instructs us that the prevalence of injustice makes clear the meaning of justice. Also Aristotle remarks that it is unjust to treat unequal things equally. Of the *virtue* called justice, Saint Augustine declares, "Justice is that ordering of the soul by virtue of which it comes to pass that we are no man's servant, but servants of God alone."

Upon such ancient postulates, classical or Christian, rests our whole elaborate edifice of law here in these United States—even though few Americans know anything about the science of jurisprudence. For public order is founded upon moral order, and moral order arises from religion—a point upon which I mean to touch later. If these venerable postulates are flouted or denied—as they have been denied by the Marxists in the present century, and were denied by sophists in Plato's time—then arbitrary power thrusts justice aside, and "they shall take who have the power, and they shall keep who can."

*   *   *

All these brief definitions require explanation. But for the moment I pass on to the common understanding, the common sense, of the meaning of *justice*. All of us entertain some notion of what justice signifies. From what source do we obtain such a concept? Why, very commonly, from observation of a just man or a just woman. We begin by admiring someone—he may be some famous judge, or he may be an obscure neighbor—who accords to every person he encounters that person's due. Just men, in short, establish the norm of justice. When I began to write my book *The Conservative Mind*, I discovered that the abstraction "conservatism" amounts to a general term descriptive of the beliefs and actions of certain eminent men and women whom we call "conservative" because they have endeavored to protect and nurture the Permanent Things in human existence. So it is with justice: in large part, we learn the meaning of justice by acquaintance with just persons.

In the ancient world, the most just of men was Solon, Athens' lawgiver, poet, and hero. As Solon wrote of his reform of the Athenian constitution—

> Such power I gave the people as might do,
> Abridged not what they had, nor lavished new;
>   Those that were great in wealth and high in place
> My counsel likewise kept from all disgrace.
> Before them both I kept my shield of might,
> And let not either touch the other's right.

To each class, that is, Solon gave its due, and so preserved the peace: that is social justice.

But we need not turn to the pages of Plutarch to discover just men: they are not an extinct species, though perhaps an endangered one. As I did in my essay *Can Virtue Be Taught?*, I think of my grandfather, Frank Pierce, a bank-manager in Plymouth, twenty miles north of Detroit. He was the leading man of Lower Town (now called Old Town), near the railroad yards—not because he was either rich or charismatic, but because he was just. Justice, of course, is one of the cardinal virtues; and like the other virtues, justice is said to be its own reward—which is well, the virtue of justice seldom earning material rewards. When a member of the town council, my grandfather refused to supply water free of charge to the town's principal industrial plant, on the grounds that if the factory couldn't pay water bills, who could? For that offense, the firm's president swore he would have Pierce discharged by the bank; but the bank's president happening also to be a just man, my grandfather's livelihood was not swept away. My grandfather's counsel was sought by everyone in the Lower Town who needed advice; and his kindliness even moved him, on occasion, to extend interest-free personal loans, from his own pocket, to young married couples who could not meet the requirements for loans from the bank. (His salary was two hundred dollars a month.) I do not mean that he was indiscriminately sentimental; not at all. On the several occasions when robbers invaded his branch bank, he successfully repelled them, at great risk: for the just man defends vigorously whatever is entrusted to his charge, and sets his face against the lawless. He was just to children, too: taking me on long walks, during which we talked of everything under the sun, but rapping sharply on the dining-room table when I waxed impudent at meals—I immediately abashed and repentant. By watching this kindly paterfamilias, and listening to what he said, I came to apprehend justice quite early. For Frank Pierce gave every man his due, without fear or favor.

In every society, from the most primitive to the most decadent, there are found some persons, like my grandfather, whom everyone recognizes as just. (Even bank-robbers and kidnappers—for he was kidnapped once by desperadoes—remarked that Frank Pierce was a just man.) From what source do such just men and women derive their habits or principles of justice?

Are they familiar with jurisprudential theories? Only rarely: even most judges on the bench nowadays are not well grounded in the philosophy of law. My grandfather, who possessed a substantial library—perhaps the only library in Plymouth's Lower Town—read history, but not philosophy or law.

Are their concepts of justice learnt in church? Not so, ordinarily. My grandfather never attended church: he came from a family that began as Pilgrims to Massachusetts and gradually moved through all the American stages of the dissidence of dissent. He never read the Bible at home. He inherited Christian morals, but not Christian faith in the transcendent.

Do they create for themselves a rough-and-ready utilitarian scheme for the administering of justice, founded principally upon their private experience of the human condition? Only infrequently, I think; for most of them would subscribe to the maxim of Benjamin Franklin, "Experience is a hard master, but fools will have no other."

Well, then, how *do* just men and women apprehend the meaning of justice? From tradition, I maintain: from habits and beliefs that have long persisted within family and within local community. As pointed out earlier in this book, Aristophanes, contradicting Socrates, argued that virtue cannot be taught in schools or by tutors: rather, virtue inheres in old families. I believe that to be especially true of the cardinal virtue called justice. Or this tradition of justice, families and communities aside, may become known through private reading, perhaps: anyone who attentively reads the great Victorian novelists, say, cannot well escape absorbing, even if unaware of his acquisition, principles of personal and social justice. More obvious, if more rare nowadays, is the influence of the Greek and Roman classics toward forming an affection for justice. Until well into the nineteenth century, Cicero was studied in every decent school; and this passage from that statesman-philosopher implanted an apprehension of the nature of justice:

> Law is the highest reason, implanted in nature, which commands what ought to be done and forbids the opposite. This reason, when firmly fixed and fully developed in the human mind, is law. And so they believe that law is intelligence, whose natural function it is to command right conduct and forbid wrongdoing. They think that this quality has derived its name in Greek from the idea of granting to every man his own, and in our language I believe it has been named from the idea of choosing.

*　　　*　　　*

In short, there exists a literary tradition expounding the idea of justice. The most recent popular example of this tradition is to be found in an appendix to C. S. Lewis's little book *The Abolition of Man*. Therein Lewis sets side by side, drawn from various cultures, illustrations of the Tao, or Natural Law. He groups these precepts or injunctions under eight headings: the law of general beneficence; the law of special beneficence; duties to parents, elders, ancestors; duties to children and posterity; the law of justice; the law of good faith and veracity; the law of mercy; the law of magnanimity. Everywhere in the world, in every age, Lewis is saying, wise men and women have perceived the nature of justice and expressed that nature in proverb, maxim, and injunction.

At this point one may inquire, "Are you implying that just men and women find in religious doctrines—Hebraic, Christian, Moslem, Hindu, Buddhist—the fountains of justice?" Yes, I am so reasoning. The sanction for justice will be found, ultimately, in religious insights as to the human condition, and particularly in Revelation. Our so-called "Western" concepts of justice are derived from the Decalogue, Platonic religious philosophy, and the teachings of the Christ. Somewhere there must exist an authority for beliefs about justice; and the authority of merely human, and therefore fallible, courts of law is insufficient to command popular assent and obedience.

It does not follow, however, that all just men and women recognize the ultimate source of ideas about justice, or appeal to that ultimate source. My grandfather never read a line that Saint Thomas Aquinas wrote, though his understanding of justice accorded well enough with what Aquinas expresses so convincingly in the *Summa*. To my grandfather the justice-concepts of the Hebraic and classical and medieval cultures were transmitted through British and American moral, legal, and literary traditions, and through long custom and habit within his family and within the small-town American communities where he had lived. If pressed as to why he held a certain understanding of the word "justice"— indeed, he once compulsorily engaged in a dialogue on that subject with a rather Nietzschean desperado intent on persuading my grandfather to open his bank's safe—I suppose that Frank Pierce would have replied, "Because good men always have so believed." *Securus judicat orbis terrarum, bonos non esse qui se dividunt ab orbe terrarum in quacunque parte terrarum,* Saint Augustine of Hippo instructs us—"The calm judgment of the world is that those men cannot be good who, in any part of the world, cut themselves off from the rest of the world." The word justice implies obligation to others, or to an Other.

Thus far I have been describing the concept of justice that prevailed in the Western world down to the closing years of the eighteenth century. Behind the phrase "to each his own" lay the beliefs that divine wisdom has conferred upon man a distinct nature; that human nature is constant; that the idea of justice is implanted in the human consciousness by a transcendent power; and that the general rule by which we endeavor to do justice is this: "to each man, the things that are his own."

What is meant by this famous phrase? To put the matter very succinctly, the doctrine of *suum cuique* affirms that every man, minding his own business, should receive the rewards which are appropriate to his work and duties. It takes for granted a society of diversity, with various classes and interests. It implies both responsibility toward others and personal freedom. It has been a strong protection for private property, on a small scale or a great; and a reinforcement, for Jews and Christians, of the Tenth Commandment. Through the Roman law, this doctrine of justice passed into the legal codes of the European continent, and even into English and American law.

Injustice, according to this doctrine, occurs when men try to undertake things for which they are not fitted, and to claim rewards to which they are not entitled, and to deny to other men what really belongs to those other men. As Plato puts it, in *The Republic,* quite as an unjust man is a being whose reason, will, and appetite are at war one with another, so an unjust society is a state afflicted by "meddlesomeness, and interference, and the rising up of a part of the soul against the whole, an assertion of unlawful authority, which is made by a rebellious subject against a true prince, of whom he is the natural vassal—what is all this confusion and delusion but injustice, and intemperance and cowardice and ignorance, and every form of vice?"

Edmund Burke re-expressed this doctrine of "to each his own" when, in his *Reflections on the Revolution in France,* he wrote of *true* natural rights: "Men have a right to the fruits of their industry, and to the means of making their industry fruitful. They have a right to the acquisitions of their parents, to the nourishment and improvement of their offspring, to instruction in life, and to consolation in death. Whatever each man can separately do, without trespassing upon others, he has a right to do for himself; and he has a right to all which society, with all its combinations of skill and force, can do in his favor."

And yet in Burke's own time, there arose a very different idea of justice, the Utilitarian concept, expounded by Jeremy Bentham. From Bentham's jurisprudence there is descended the powerful present-day school of legal thought that we call legal positivism or legal realism. Positivistic jurisprudence arose in alliance with nineteenth-century nationalism and with scientific mechanism and materialism. To the legal positivist or realist, laws are the commands of human beings merely. There exists, for the positivist, no necessary connections between law and morals, or between law as it is and law as it ought to be. The positivists' legal system is a closed, logical system without need for referring to social aims, policies, or moral standards. So-called "moral judgments," to the positivists, are "value judgments" merely: and value judgments cannot be established or defended by rational argument. This positivistic understanding of justice and law looms large in American courts today.

But I do not here have space to analyze the strengths and weaknesses of legal positivism. For the present, I do no more than to point out that nineteenth- and twentieth-century positivism stands in harsh opposition to both the classical and the Christian understanding of justice and law. In Catholic universities, at least, some defense still is offered of the Augustinian virtue of justice and the venerable theory of natural law.

It is my purpose here to state the classical and the Christian concept of justice, as opposed to the positivists' denial of any source for justice except the commands of the sovereign state. And I will touch glancingly upon the connections among religion, justice, and law. (Justice and law are not identical, though they may be closely related: in a good commonwealth, law is an attempt to maintain standards of justice, so far as that may be achieved in a bent world.)

All law is derived from the religious understanding—that is, all law in the traditional societies of the West; law in totalist states is another matter entirely. Moses came down from Horeb and did justice upon criminous Israelites: the prophet as lawgiver. Solon reformed the laws of Draco: the religious poet as lawgiver. When law is divorced from the moral sanction of religious convictions, presently the law is corrupted by passion, prejudice, private interest, and misguided sentimentality.

*   *   *

The church is concerned with the inner order: the order of the soul. The state is concerned with the outer order: the order of the commonwealth. Between state and church, nevertheless, relationships are ineluctable. Among these relationships is an understanding of justice.

Such relationships took shape in the West so early as the fifth century of the Christian era. We perceive them in the connections between Augustine, Bishop of Hippo, and his friend Boniface, Count of Africa. In theory, all Christians of the West believe in separation of church and state—though sometimes that principle has been more honored in the breach than in the observance.

The church recognizes the necessary end of the state, and so submits to the state's laws. Because of human sinfulness, the Fathers of the Church taught, the state is ordained of God. As best it can, the state restrains the three chief forms of lust: cupidity, the lust for possessions; the *libido dominandi*, the lust for power; and sexual lust, the abuse of the gift of procreation. When the state is enfeebled, these lusts work the ruin of the person and the republic.

So it is that the church, even in Roman imperial times, has taught obedience to civil magistrates. Saint Augustine reasoned that the good citizen, the believing Christian, should obey every command of the state, save one: an order to worship false gods and to serve Satan.

Yet church and state have different ends, though both uphold justice. There runs through the history of Christianity the doctrine of the two swords: the church's sword of faith, the state's sword of secular justice.

Knowing that this earthly existence is not the be-all and end-all, the church holds that perfect justice is in the power of God alone, beyond the confines of time and space. In this world here below, we mete out justice as best we may. Sometimes we err in our administering of justice; it cannot well be otherwise; we are not perfect or perfectible creatures.

To apprehend the church's stand on mundane justice, it is desirable to make distinctions between crime and sin. A crime is an act or omission which the law punishes on behalf of the state, whether because that act or omission is expressly forbidden by statute, or because it is so injurious to the public as to require punishment on the ground of public policy.

A sin is a transgression against moral law, with that law's divine sanctions. It is God, not the State, who punishes or forgives sins.

Not all sins are crimes. We have it on the authority of Saint Paul that the greatest of the theological virtues is charity. Therefore uncharitableness is a great sin; yet lack of charity is not an offense at law. A man may be all his life snarling, sneering, contemptuous, envious, abominable in his language toward his wife, his children, and others to whom he owes obligations—that is, perfectly uncharitable; yet he will run no risk of being haled before the bar of criminal justice. The uncharitable may be dealt with at the Last Judgment. But mundane courts of law do not touch the sinner unless his sins result in violence or fraud or substantial damage to others. The state is unconcerned with sins unless they lead to breaches of the peace, or menace the social order. This separation of function accords with the doctrine of the two swords.

Quite as the state—that is, the constitutional state—does not lay down religious dogmata in recent times, so the church does not decree the laws of mundane justice, as expressed through courts of law. When the church has endeavored to impose its doctrines through the operation of the state's criminal law, the church has erred.

I have been speaking of orthodox Christian doctrine, interwoven with principles of law in America, Britain, and many other countries—interwoven, that is, until recent decades. But great confusion has fallen upon us in these years near the end of the century. Increasingly, the state—aye, the democratic state, too—separates itself from the religious understanding of the human condition. And a good many churchmen abandon Christian realism for a sentimental humanitarianism.

Let me remind you of the true signification of this word "humanitarianism." Properly defined—and this is the definition one still finds in the Oxford English Dictionary—humanitarianism is the doctrine that Jesus of Nazareth possessed a human nature merely, not being divine; and, by extension, the doctrine that mankind may become perfect without divine aid. A humanitarian is a person totally secularized in his convictions. Yet erroneously many people use "humanitarian" as a term of commendation. "He was a great humanitarian," they say of Albert Schweitzer. That charitable and heroic man, a professing Christian, would have rejected indignantly that label.

Now what has this distinction between humanitarianism and charity to do with justice? The point is this: the humanitarian denies the existence of sin, declaring that what we call "sins" are not moral matters at all, resulting instead from circumstance, faulty rearing, or social oppression. In the view of the humanitarian, sins—and crimes, too—are the work of "society"; and sinners and criminals are victims, rather than unjust offenders. Such reasoning is the consequence of holding that man and society may be perfected through mere alteration of social conditions, without the intervention of divine grace.

The humanitarian frequently proclaims his abhorrence of severe punishments—perhaps of any punishments. Why? First, because of his illusion that no human being possesses the ability to make moral choices. Second, because of his horror of inflicting pain. He leaves no ultimate justice to God, because he fancies that no God exists. The mere preservation of one's comfortable earthly life is his obsession, he fancying that man is not made for eternity.

On the other hand, the humanitarian fulminates against those who disagree with his principles. Thus there occurs the phenomenon called "the humanitarian with the guillotine." (The recent French film called *Danton* sufficiently illustrates this ferocious love of all humankind.) As Edmund Burke put it, speaking of the humanitarian Jacobins, men who today snatch the worst criminals from the hands of justice tomorrow may approve the slaughter of whole classes. Humanitarian apologies in our own time for butchery by Communist revolutionaries sufficiently suggest the persistence of this curious intolerant humanitarianism. The ideologue need merely proclaim that his object is universal happiness here below, and he is approved uncritically by the humanitarian.

In this disordered age, when it seems as if the fountains of the great deep had been broken up, our urgent need is to restore a general understanding of the classical and Christian teaching about justice. Without just men and women, egoism and appetite bring down a civilization. Without strong administration of Justice by the state, we all become so many Cains, every man's hand against every other man's. The humanitarian fancies himself zealous for the life impulse; in reality, he would surrender us to the death impulse. The humanitarian's visions issue from between the delusory gates of ivory; justice issues from between the gates of horn.

Public instruction that ignores both our classical patrimony and our religious patrimony may fail to rear up just men and women. Positivist jurisprudence that denies any moral order and any religious sanction for justice may end in a general flouting of all law. We prate of "peace and justice" in a dissolving culture, without apprehending tolerably the words we employ. "Shrieking voices/ Scolding, mocking, or merely chattering,/ Always assail them." These are the voices of the ideologue, the neurotic, and the nihilist, pulling down the old understanding of Justice, "to each his own."

"Justice is a certain rectitude of mind, whereby a man does what he ought to do in the circumstances confronting him." So Thomas Aquinas instructs us. At every college and university, the doctors of the schools ought to inquire of themselves, "Do we impart such rectitude of mind? And if we do not, will there be tolerable private or public order in the twenty-first century?"

XV

---

*The Case For and Against
Natural Law*

The literature of natural law is complex, copious, and monthly growing vaster. All I aspire to accomplish in this brief overview is to offer some general introduction to the subject, together with reflections on the protections and dangers of natural-law doctrines, and observations concerning natural law and constitutional government.

A great deal of loose talk about natural law has occurred in very recent years. It was objected to Judge Bork's nomination to the Supreme Court that Bork did not believe in natural law; and when Judge Thomas was interrogated for that bench, the objection was raised that he *did* believe in natural law. These protestations came mostly from the same group of senators. Clearly a good many public men and women nowadays have only vague notions of what is signified by this term *natural law.*

Objectively speaking, *natural law,* as a term of politics and jurisprudence, may be defined as a loosely knit body of rules of action prescribed by an authority superior to the state. These rules variously (according to the several differing schools of natural-law and natural-rights speculation) are derived from divine commandment; from the nature of humankind; from abstract Reason; or from long experience of mankind in community.

But natural law does not appertain to states and courts merely. For primarily it is a body of ethical perceptions or rules governing the life of the individual person, quite aside from politics and jurisprudence. When many persons ignore or flout the natural law for human beings, the consequences presently are ruinous—as with the unnatural vices that result in the disease of AIDS, or with the ideological passions, defying the norm of justice, that have ravaged most nations since the First World War.

The natural law should not be taken for graven Tables of Governance, to be followed to jot and tittle; appealed to in varying circumstances, the law of nature must be applied with high prudence. As Alessandro d'Entrèves writes, "The lesson of natural law is in fact nothing but an assertion that law is a part of ethics." And, he concludes "The lesson of natural law [is] simply to remind the jurist of his own limitations.... This point where values and norms coincide, which is the ultimate origin of law and at the same time the beginning of moral life proper, is, I believe, what men for over two thousand years have indicated by the name of natural law."

On the one hand, natural law must be distinguished from positive or statutory law, decreed by the state; on the other, from the "laws of nature" in a scientific sense—that is, from propositions expressing the regular order of certain natural phenomena. Also natural law sometimes is confounded with assertions of "natural rights," which may or may not be founded upon classical and medieval concepts of natural law.

The most important early treatise on natural law is Cicero's *De Re Publica*. The Ciceronian understanding of natural law, which still exercises strong influence, was well expressed in the nineteenth century by Froude: "Our human laws are but the copies, more or less imperfect, of the eternal laws so far as we can read them, and either succeed and promote our welfare, or fail and bring confusion and disaster, according as the legislator's insight has detected the true principle, or has been distorted by ignorance or selfishness."

As interpreted by the Roman jurisconsult, and later by the medieval Schoolmen and Canonists—Thomas Aquinas especially—the legacy of the classical *jus naturale* endured with little challenge until the seventeenth century. In England during the sixteenth century it was powerfully upheld by Richard Hooker in his *Laws of Ecclesiastical Polity*. In the Christian world the natural law was received as a body of unwritten rules depending upon universal conscience and common sense, ascertainable by right reason. But with the stirrings of secularism and rationalism during the seventeenth century, a new interpretation of "natural law" began to develop, conspicuous (near the end of the century) in the works of Hugo Grotius and Baron Samuel von Pufendorf. This latter secularized concept of natural law was held by many of the *philosophes* of the eighteenth century, and took on flesh during the French Revolution, when it was vulgarized by Thomas Paine.

Nevertheless, the older understanding of natural law was not extinguished. It was ringingly reasserted by Edmund Burke, in his distinction between the "real" and the "pretended" rights of men. Through the disciples of Burke, and through the influence of the Catholic Church, the classical and Christian natural law has experienced a revival in the latter half of the twentieth century.

During the nineteenth century, natural-law concepts were overshadowed by the powerful Utilitarian system of Jeremy Bentham; by the theories of John Austin and the Analytical Jurists; by legal positivism; and later—particularly in the United States—by legal pragmatism. In the United States, the older and newer schools of natural law have contended against each other since the latter half of the eighteenth century, and both have been hotly assailed by positivistic, utilitarian, and pragmatic interpretations of law. Yet appeals to the "natural law" or "a higher law" have recurred often in American politics and jurisprudence; both conservatives and radicals, from time to time, have invoked this law of nature.

The Catholic Church continues to adhere to the classical and Thomistic understanding of the natural law—to an apprehension of Justice that is rooted in the wisdom of the species. Sir Ernest Barker put thus the idea of natural law: "This justice is conceived as being the higher or ultimate law, proceeding from the nature of the universe—from the Being of God and the reason of man. It follows that law—in the sense of the law of the last resort—is somehow above lawmaking."

As mentioned last chapter, the most lucid and popular exposition of natural law it to be found in the Appendix, "Illustrations of the *Tao*," to C. S. Lewis's little book *The Abolition of Man*. Therein Lewis distinguishes eight major natural laws of universal recognition and application, already outlined, together with several illustrations of each, drawn from a wide diversity of cultures, religions, philosophical discourses, and countries. No code of the laws of nature ever having existed, it is ineffectual to try to enforce that body of ethical principles through courts of law; no judge hands down decisions founded directly upon the admonition, "Honor thy father and thy mother, that thy days may be long in the land"—or the Commandment's equivalents in the Babylonian List of Sins, the Egyptian Confession of the Righteous Soul, the Manual of Epictetus, Leviticus, the Analects, or Hindu books of wisdom. Nevertheless, such perpetual precepts lie behind the customs and the statutes that shelter father and mother.

*   *   *

So much, succinctly, by way of definition. Turn we now to the difficulty of explaining natural law to the average sensual man.

Permit me to discourse with you for a little while about natural law and the moral imagination. Incidentally, I am helped here by an unpublished essay by the late Raymond English, who understood and praised the natural law, and understood and despised the claims for "natural right." Let me quote English directly:

> The natural law cannot be understood except through the elements of poetry and imagination in the soul. The poetic and the moral imagination are parts of human reason. For the man who does not feel himself in some sense a child of God, who is not possessed by the 'desire and pursuit of the whole,' and for whom words like *honor* are meaningless, the notion of natural law must be a Mumbojumbo, a bogle to make children behave tolerably well, a fantasy from the adolescence or the childhood of the race. Poets, James Elroy Flecker says, are those who swear that Beauty lives although lilies die; and the natural law is the poetry of political science, the assurance that Justice lives though states are imperfect and ephemeral. Justice is to politics what beauty is to art; indeed, beauty and justice become almost identical at the highest levels of human aspiration.

Permit me to repeat here that the natural law is more than a guide for statesmen and jurists. It is meant primarily for the governance of persons—for you and me, that we may restrain will and appetite in our ordinary walks of life. Natural law is not a harsh code that we thrust upon other people: rather, it is an ethical knowledge, innate perhaps, but made more clearly known to us through the operation of right reason. And the more imagination with which a person is endowed, the more will he apprehend the essence of the natural law, and understand its necessity. If such a one, despite his power of imagination, offends against the natural law, the greater must be his suffering. So I have discovered in the course of a peregrine life. And over a good many decades I have found that most contemners of the natural law are dull dogs, afflicted by a paucity of imagination. As Adam Mickiewicz instructs us:

> *Your soul deserves the place to which it came,*
> *If having entered Hell, you feel no flame.*

Such is the case for the importance of natural law. Permit me to turn now to the case against natural law, as expressed by the legal positivists—most strongly, perhaps, by the German scholar Hans Kelsen. They regard natural law as a body of sentimental fictions; they hold that the state is the only true source of law. The views of John Austin and the Analytical Jurists are similar: all law is decreed by the political sovereign, they hold. Rather than moving abstractly among the several schools of jurisprudence in the twentieth century, I offer you now the contents of a letter I received recently from a German inventor and industrialist who had read in the Bavarian magazine *Epoche* some remarks of mine on natural law. My correspondent is a very intelligent and indeed talented man, considerable of a naturalist in that he studies flora and fauna. In politics, I suppose he may be classified as a German liberal of the old school. His communication, refreshingly innocent of the jargon of jurisprudence and ethics, suggests the mentality that lies behind the denigration of natural law by positivists and secular humanists, who recognize and deride the Christian and the classical origins of the idea of natural law.

"Whether the term 'law of nature' is more frequently used nowadays, or whether *the jus naturale* is an old invention," my German correspondent begins, "I think this term is wrong and misleading. There is no law or legislative system which can be derived from nature. Nature has rules developed during evolution, but there is only a *jus hominis* and no *jus naturale.*"

"In other words," my friend goes on,

> all ethical norms are developed and worked out by
> human beings, in this case mostly by the *homo stultus,*
> *subspecies sapiens....* The order of nature follows in many
> respects the right of the stronger, which, in fact, keeps
> nature with all its plants and animals in excellent shape.
> But mankind has set up ethical rules, good ones and bad
> ones, very different from natural rules. Many of these
> man-made rules are quite bad, sinning against nature....
>
> The very deplorable situation of the species *homo*
> *stultus* comes from wrong ethical rules, which are against
> nature. I am not pleading for the right of the stronger
> between human beings, but for more influence of the rare
> subspecies *sapiens,* especially of those individuals who
> understand nature—which means also the nature of
> human character. Unfortunately Jesus did not under-
> stand the real nature of men; nor do the socialists
> understand it when they expect that people will work for
> the state rather than for themselves....
>
> I offer another example, in which American legislators
> have chosen the wrong solution. There is a law in the
> United States, if I am correct, which forbids the killing
> of foreign heads of state. If I am correct this is concerned
> with clandestine actions, e.g. by the CIA. This law is
> unethical. Assuming that no American president or the
> American government plans to eliminate a foreign dic-
> tator just for fun, but rather because he is a danger to the
> United States or to his own people or both, then remov-
> ing a dictator as soon as possible would save the lives of
> many; and is, in consequence, completely justified.
>
> We should agree that right is an exclusively human

creation. What is regarded as rightful by one group of people within a community, can be regarded as wrongful by another group. I seek a terminology where there is a clean and clear distinction between what comes from nature and what comes from human efforts. Human efforts are aimed very often, with the best intentions, in the wrong direction. I mean 'wrong' in this sense: against nature, for nature cannot be neglected without harming the human race....

Failing to realize that often human character is bad must lead to destroying a society through leniency. We have to determine when our ethical laws accord with nature and when they counteract nature. We must not ignore 'the rule of the fittest,' when we decide to kill a dictator, for instance. We acknowledge the right of every nation to use as much force as possible when fighting another nation to death. The fight between nations follows what could be called natural right, but is better called the rule of nature.

For this German correspondent of mine, you will have noted, "nature" signifies animal nature, Darwinian nature, red in tooth and claw. Therefore he despises appeals to natural law, and believes that not only all positive or traditional law, but all ethical principles, are human creations merely. And these human contrivances, he implies, sometimes may be mistaken; we might be wiser to found our human institutions on the principle of competition, favoring the fitter.

Here, I suggest, we perceive the mentality that lies back of the jurisprudence of Hans Kelsen and certain other positivists: critics of the whole concept of natural law.

Yet in one matter my correspondent does turn to the extreme

medicine of natural law: his commendation of tyrannicide. This is interesting, as it is related to Germany in this century.

German jurisprudence demands that the citizen be strictly obedient to the state, for the state is the source of all law, the omniscient keeper of the peace. No law but positive law has been recognized in Germany since the fall of the German monarchy; natural law has no place at all.

Adolph Hitler, chosen Reichschancellor by lawful means, and confirmed in power by the Reichstag in 1933, was sustained later by national plebiscites. He was the head of the German state, the source of all law, to which all Germans had been taught obedience. Yet certain Germans—army officers, scholars, professional people, chiefly—found his actions evil. By quasi-constitutional means he had subverted the constitution. His popularity had become tremendous, and his military power. Only by death might he be removed.

Therefore a little knot of brave and conscientious men determined to save Germany and Europe by killing Hitler. They had been reared in the doctrine that all citizens must obey the inerrant state. In this exigency, however, they turned to doctrines of natural law for justification. Was there no remedy against an unnatural master of the state? In the teachings of natural law they discerned a fatal remedy. Fatal to them, at least; for nearly all of the heroic men involved in the several conspiracies against Hitler died frightful deaths. I knew well Dr. Ludwig Freund, a kindly professor of political science, one of the two survivors of the first plot to kill Hitler. By nature Professor Freund was a law-abiding gentleman. And being law-abiding, in defense of true law he was prepared to slay the chief of state, perverter of Germany's laws and the laws of man's nature.

I repeat that we have recourse to natural law, as opposed to positive law, only as a last resort, ordinarily. My only service as a jurist occurred in Morton Township, Mecosta County, some decades ago, when for two consecutive terms I was elected—unanimously—justice of the peace. When determining a disputed boundary between two farms, a justice of the peace does not repair to theories of natural law and meditate upon which of two claimants is the more worthy of judicial compassion; rather, the justice of the peace turns to statute, common law, possibly to local custom—and to the files of the recorder of deeds at the county seat. And so it is with the ordinary administration of law at every level. Statute, charter, and prescription ordinarily are sufficient to maintain the rule of law—the end of which, we ought not to forget, is to keep the peace.

Yet to guide the sovereign; the chief of state; the legislator; the public prosecutor; the judge when, in effect, he sits in equity—to guide you and me, indeed—there endures the natural law, which in essence is man's endeavor to maintain a moral order through the operation of a mundane system of justice. Unlike my German correspondent, the sustainer of natural law knows that there is law for man, and law for thing; and that our moral order is not the creation of coffeehouse philosophers. Human nature is not vulpine nature, leonine nature, or serpentine nature. Natural law is bound up with the concept of the dignity of man, and with the experience of humankind ever since the beginnings of social community.

It will not do to substitute private interpretations of natural law for common law or civil law, any more than it would have been well for England, during the Reformation, to have obeyed the "Geneva Men" by sweeping away common law and the whole inherited apparatus of parliamentary statutes, to substitute the laws of the ancient Jews. Positive law and customary law, in any country, grow out of a people's experience in community; natural law should have its high part in shaping and restraining positive and customary laws, but natural law could not conceivably supplant judicial institutions. Yet were natural-law concepts to be abandoned altogether—why, then, indeed, the world would find itself governed by

The good old rule, the good old plan,
That they shall take who have the power,
And they shall keep who can.

*   *   *

Turn we now to relationships between the natural law and the American judiciary. Not since Associate Justice Joseph Story adorned the Supreme Court of the United States, early in the nineteenth century, has any member of the Supreme Court had much to say about natural law. Nevertheless, in recent decades a number of Supreme Court decisions seem to have been founded upon natural-law notions of a sort. I think, for instance, of the Warren Court's decision (the opinion written by Chief Justice Warren himself) that congressional districts within the several states must be so drawn in their boundaries as to contain so nearly as possible the same number of persons within the several dis-tricts—a matter previously left to the discretion of state legislatures. In part, this intervention was founded upon Jeremy Bentham's principle of one man, one vote; but also there seems to have lurked at the back of the minds of justices the notion that exact political equality, as told by numbers, somehow is "natural," whatever state and federal constitutions might prescribe and whatever the opin-ions of the Framers may have been. One might cite, too, the Court's decisions in the school desegregation cases. This question having been raised, let us examine how far we should appeal to natural law against statute and Constitution. Here we turn to an historical example and to the judgment of a leading American political and religious writer who endeavored to reconcile the claims of authority and the claims of freedom.

I refer to the "higher law" controversy of 1850 and to Orestes Brownson, the Catholic scholar and polemicist. In March 1850, on the floor of the United States Senate, William Henry Seward made his famous declaration that there exists "a higher law than the Constitution." He was referring to the Fugitive Slave Law and the Supreme Court. At once a hot controversy arose. In January 1851, Brownson published his review-essay entitled "The Higher Law," in which he refuted the claim of Seward, the Abolitionists, and the Free-Soilers to transcend the Constitution by appealing to a moral "higher law" during debate on the Fugitive Slave Bill.

Brownson agreed with Seward that

> there is a higher law than the Constitution. The law of God is supreme, and overrides all human enactments, and every human enactment incompatible with it is null and void from the beginning, and cannot be obeyed with a good conscience, for 'we must obey God rather than men.' This is the great truth statesmen and lawyers are extremely prone to overlook, which the temporal authority not seldom practically denies, and on which the Church never fails to insist....
>
> But the concession of the fact of a higher law than the Constitution does not of itself justify the appeal to it against the Constitution, either by Mr. Seward or the opponents of the Fugitive Slave Law. Mr. Seward had no right, while holding his seat in the Senate under the Constitution, to appeal to the higher law against the Constitution, because that was to deny the very authority by which he held his seat.... After having taken his oath to support the Constitution, the Senator had, so far as he was concerned, settled the question, and it was no longer for him an open question. In calling God to witness his determination to support the Constitution, he had called God to witness his conviction of the compatibility of the Constitution with the law of God, and therefore left

himself no plea for appealing from it to a higher law.

We cannot be bound, Brownson continued, to obey a law that is in contravention of the law of God.

> This is the grand principle held by the old martyrs, and therefore they chose martyrdom rather than obedience to the state commanding them to act contrary to the Divine law. But who is to decide whether a special civil enactment be or be not repugnant to the law of God? Here is a grave and perplexing question for those who have no divinely authorized interpreter of the divine law.

The Abolitionists and Free-Soilers, Brownson remarked, had adopted the Protestant principle of private judgment.

> But this places the individual above the state, and is wholly incompatible with the simplest conception of civil government. No civil government can exist, none is conceivable even, when every individual is free to disobey its orders whenever they do not happen to square with his private convictions of what is the law of God.

The Church, Brownson writes, is the authoritative interpreter of the divine law. He reminds his readers that the state is ordained of God; but the state is not the supreme and infallible organ of God's will on earth.

> Now it is clear that Mr. Seward and his friends, the Abolitionists and the Free Soilers, have nothing to which

they can appeal from the action of government but their private interpretation of the law of God, that is to say, their own private judgment or opinion as individuals; for it is notorious that they are good Protestants, holding the pretended right of private judgment, and rejecting all authoritative interpretation of the Divine law. To appeal from government to private judgment is to place private judgment above public authority, the individual above the state, which, as we have seen, is incompatible with the very existence of government, and therefore, since government is a divine ordinance, absolutely forbidden by the law of God—that very higher law invoked to justify resistance to civil enactments.... No man can ever be justifiable in resisting the civil law under the pretence that it is repugnant to the Divine law, when he has only his private judgment, or, what is the same thing, his private interpretation of the Sacred Scriptures, to tell him what the Divine law is on the point in question, because the principle on which he would act in doing so would be repugnant to the very existence of government, and therefore in contravention of the ordinance, therefore of the law, of God.

Brownson's argument—which we have not time enough to analyze in full here—in substance is this, in his own words: "Mr. Seward and his friends asserted a great and glorious principle, but misapplied it." It was not for them to utter commands in the name of God. Their claims, if carried far enough, would lead to anarchy. The arguments of some of their adversaries would lead to Statolatry, the worship of the state.

The cry for liberty abolishes all loyalty, and destroys the principle and the spirit of obedience, while the usurpations of the state leave to conscience no freedom, to religion no independence. The state tramples on the spiritual prerogatives of the Church, assumes to itself the functions of schoolmaster and director of consciences, and the multitude clap their hands, and call it liberty and progress!

Brownson advocated compliance with the Fugitive Slave Law, which clearly was constitutional; indeed, obligatory under Article IV, Section 2 of the Constitution. It was his hope to avert the Civil War which burst out ten years later. "Now there is a right and a wrong way of defending the truth, and it is always easier to defend the truth on sound than on unsound principles," he wrote. "If men were less blind and headstrong, they would see that the higher law can be asserted without any attack upon legitimate civil authority, and legitimate civil authority and the majesty of the law can be vindicated without asserting the absolute supremacy of the civil power, and falling into statolatry—as absurd a species of idolatry as the worship of sticks and stones."

*   *   *

Very possibly, you will found in these passages from "The Higher Law" and in Brownson's general argument various considerations highly relevant to our own era.

As Brownson remarks, the natural law (or law of God) and the American civil law are not ordinarily at swords' points. Large elements of natural law entered into the common law of England—and therefore into the common law of the United States—over the centuries; and the Roman law, so eminent in the science of jurisprudence, expresses the natural law enunciated by the Roman jurisconsults. No civilization ever has attempted to maintain the bed of justice by direct application of natural-law doctrines by magistrates; necessarily, it is by edict, rescript, and statute that any state keeps the peace through a system of courts. It simply will not do to maintain that private interpretation of natural law should be the means by which conflicting claims are settled.

Rather, natural law ought to help form the judgments of the persons who are lawmakers—whether emperors, kings, ecclesiastics, aristocratic republicans, or representatives of a democracy. The civil law should be shaped in conformity to the natural law—which originated, in Cicero's words, "before any written law existed or any state had been established."

It does not follow that judges should be permitted to push aside the Constitution, or statutory laws, in order to substitute their private interpretations of what the law of nature declares. To give the judiciary such power would be to establish what might be called an archonocracy, a domination of judges, supplanting the constitutional republic; also it surely would produce some curious and unsettling decisions, sweeping away precedent, which would be found highly distressing by friends to classical and Christian natural law. Only the Catholic Church, Brownson reasoned, has authority to interpret the laws of nature; but the Supreme Court of the United States, and the inferior federal courts, and our state courts, take no cognizance of papal encyclicals. Left to their several private judgments of what is "natural," some judges indubitably would do mischief to the person and the republic. The Supreme Court's majority decision in the case of *Roe v. Wade*—in which a pretended "right of privacy," previously unknown, was discovered—in actuality amounted to a declaration of the "natural right" of a mother to destroy her offspring.

Now it seems to me curiously naive to fancy that American courts always would subscribe to Thomistic concepts of the laws of nature, and abjure Jacobin doctrines of natural right. Courts of law must ordinarily accord with the general legislative authority; otherwise the Book of Judges is followed by the Book of Kings.

In the seventh revised edition of *The Conservative Mind*, I have written that the first canon of conservative thought is "Belief in a transcendent order, or body of natural law. Political problems, at bottom, are religious and moral problems. A narrow rationality, which Coleridge called the Understanding, cannot of itself satisfy human needs.... True politics is the art of apprehending and applying the Justice which ought to prevail in a community of souls."

Now Mr. Robert Bork, whose opinion as to the application of natural-law doctrines by members of the Supreme Court I have just now endorsed with some vigor, has taken notice of this. In an essay entitled "Natural Law and the Constitution," Mr. Bork advises my friend Mr. William Bentley Ball to abjure my exhortation of this sort. "The dictum also is inaccurate," Bork adds, "for it arbitrarily disqualifies as conservatives people who accept and struggle to preserve every conservative value but who do not believe that such values derive from a transcendent order." One might as well say, I suggest, that the Church ought not to emphasize the dogma of the Resurrection because that might alienate some people who are not Christians, but are possible well-wishers.

That federal judges have not been learned in the natural law is one of the educational misfortunes of our age. When the time is out of joint, we can repair to the teachings of Cicero and Aquinas and Hooker about the law of nature, in the hope that we may diminish man's inhumanity unto man. The natural law lacking, we may become so many Cains, and every man's hand may be raised against every other man's.

XVI

The Injustice of Equality

Let me commence with two aphorisms, widely separated in time and substance.

The first is the observation of Aristotle that it is unjust to treat unequal things equally.

The second is the declaration of Marx that to establish equality, first we must establish inequality.

These two assumptions have been at war one with the other during the twentieth century.

What did Aristotle mean by writing that to treat unequal things equally is unjust? He meant that not all human beings are worthy of the same deserts, that not all actions are equally honorable and commendable, that not all works are of equally enduring value; so to confer equal rewards upon excellence and mediocrity would be profoundly unjust to the more deserving of praise. "To each his own."

What did Marx mean by asserting that inequality must be

established before equality might be attained? He meant that the mighty must be pulled down from their seats, the alleged exploiters expropriated, whole classes destroyed—presumably by a general bloodletting—before the earthly paradise of communism might be realized. The bourgeois and all other opponents of socialist progress must be thoroughly discriminated against by the revolutionary proletariat. The bourgeois should be indulged no equality with the son of toil.

The Marxist regime in the Soviet Union fell at last after seven decades of terror and suffering; but the notion that "social justice" means equality of condition still works among us. In this connection, I commend you to three books: F. A. Hayek's *The Mirage of Social Justice;* Helmut Schoeck's *Envy: A Theory of Social Behavior;* and Gonzalo Fernández de la Mora's *Egalitarian Envy: The Political Foundations of Social Justice.* The second book is by a German, the third by a Spaniard; it is a sign of the surviving domination of socialist assumptions about justice in America that these latter books scarcely were reviewed at all in the United States, though editions of both were published here. They deny the notion that there can exist a perfect social justice, attainable by positive law and social engineering; and their authors are agreed that the perfectly egalitarian society would be an unjust society. Let me suggest, also, a keen analysis of socialist errors about justice in a book of yesteryear of which I brought out a new edition a few years ago: W. H. Mallock's *A Critical Examination of Socialism.*

All the four authors I mentioned a moment ago touch upon the vice of envy and its ruinous personal and social consequences. To that vice the Marxists appealed successfully in much of the world. "Why shouldst thou sit, and I stand?" cries incarnate Envy, in Marlowe's play *Dr. Faustus.* "Come away!" Social justice will be attained, the poor are told, when they have unseated the affluent and supplanted them in their possessions. Such doctrines have devastated most of Asia and Africa ever since the Second World

War, causing the massacre of the old leading classes, most hideously in the Congo—now Zaire—Portugese Timor, Portuguese Guinea, Chad, Vietnam, Cambodia, and China. Yet the earthly paradise of social justice did not result from this slaughter: instead, squalid oligarchs and men of blood succeeded to power, and general impoverishment has been experienced. Perhaps we see today the beginning of such a progress toward social justice in the Republic of South Africa.

Until recent decades, nevertheless, socially ruinous envy of this sort was not really powerful in the United States, and did not provoke a powerful political movement for such a restructuring of the economy as would even the scores. During several years of the Great Depression, my parents and my little sister and I lived in an old dwelling near the railway yards at Plymouth, Michigan, my father being a railroad engineman. Our house had no bathroom; its *necessarium* was an outdoor privy, inconvenient under snow. (We had thought we were buying the house on land contract, but it turned out that the man who pretended to sell the dwelling to us had no proper title to it himself, and so my parents lost their investment and went back to renting; they never did succeed in owning any house, lifelong.) Weekly there arrived in our house the newspaper of the Railway Brotherhoods, entitled *Labor*. In almost every issue there appeared a cartoon of a literally bloated Capitalist, in evening dress, smoking a bloated cigar; and such exploiters of the working poor were denounced in editorials.

But these circumstances and publications did not wake envy in my parents. They took it for granted that some people, whether by talent or by inheritance or by mere chance, prosper materially in life, while other people do not; this, they knew, was in the nature of things. They had a subsistence, and kinfolk, and love. The caricatures of the Bloated Capitalist did not rouse my father's wrath; my father did indeed think that the railroads were ill-managed, and that increasing centralization of the economy was to be regretted, and that pride would have a fall on Wall Street, as indeed came to pass; but I never heard my parents utter a word of envy. Things will be as they will be, they took it.

Blessed are those children reared in a household innocent of the deadly sin of envy. Their lives will not be tormented by a grinding resentment that they are not beautiful, or famous, or favored with the gifts of fortune. They will not demand as a natural right or an entitlement a presumptuous personal equality with everybody under the sun; nor maintain that their opinions are as good as anybody else's. They will not covet a neighbor's goods. And thus they may come to know peace of soul. They will perceive the wisdom in these lines of a very early poem in Scots vernacular:

> *I saw this written on a wall:*
> *In what estate, man, that thou fall*
> *Accept thy lot, and thank thy God of all.*

*   *   *

But I do not mean to imply that every form of equality is the work of envy. The Christian doctrine of equality has worked much moral good. This is the teaching that all souls are equal in the ultimate judgment of God; that God is no respecter of persons. Yet God separates the goats from the sheep; in my Father's house are many mansions, but they are not all on the same floor. God's ultimate judgment is not affected by rank and station, wealth or power, here below. All that matters, in the end, is goodness of heart; so sometimes the last, at the judgment seat, shall be first.

And the jurisprudential principle of equal justice under law, too, has worked much social good. The law also is no respecter of persons: the king himself is under the law, as Bracton put it in medieval times. Neither in civil nor in criminal cases, declares the system of law which Americans have inherited from Britain, does any class of persons enjoy privileges or immunities. This doctrine keeps the peace; and to keep the peace is the object of all law.

Whether political equality has worked much good is another matter. In most of the world, attempts at enduring and peaceful democracy have failed. Constitutional democracy of the successful sort has been confined chiefly to English-speaking countries, which have inherited the British historical experience. And even in such countries, who can doubt that democracy, political equality, is in grave trouble nowadays? Is not the United States being converted into a "plebiscitary democracy," with an election of the temporary dictator every four years, actually governed by a centralized bureaucracy nominally under the supervision of a body of squabbling politicians? How much genuine democracy of the sort discerned in America by Tocqueville, what Brownson called "territorial democracy," will remain by the middle of the twenty-first century? Even today, indeed, how much political equality remains in elections determined chiefly by what candidates have the most money to spend on television broadcasts?

But political equality is too large and complex a subject for me to discuss today. I turn, therefore to the subject of equality of condition—that is, equality of incomes and other material rewards, equality in education, equality of mores, manners, lodgings, and tastes. It is this envious passion for equality of condition against which Tocqueville warned his time and ours. The total triumph of the doctrine of equality of condition would be a triumph of injustice. Unthinking demands for an equality allegedly just notwithstanding, a society in which everybody should be precisely in the condition of everybody else would be a thoroughly unjust society.

Zealots throughout the centuries have endeavored to establish communities totally egalitarian; all those endeavors have failed after much suffering. Utopians in the Greek and Roman eras, the Levellers and Diggers of England in the seventeenth century,

Babeuf and his fellow conspirators of 1791, and the communist ideologues who held power in the Russian system for seven decades—these are only some of the enthusiasts for equality who for a time established a domination of equality in misery, collapsing soon or late because contrary to human nature. Yet, as Hegel wrote, we learn from history that we learn nothing from history. What failed disastrously in the late Soviet Union, a good many Americans now seek to enact in these United States.

The instrument of the doctrinaire egalitarian in America is not violent revolution, but employment of taxation—which, as John Marshall declared in the Dartmouth College case, is the power to destroy. A leveller pulls down the more prosperous classes in society through crushing taxation, levied to pay for "entitlements" for an abstraction called The Poor—in effect, to maintain a growing proletariat that contribute nothing much to society except their offspring. Rostovtzeff and other writers on Roman times have drawn the analogy between bread and circuses and the modern dole or "welfare" measures: in the Empire, the emperor with his soldiery united with the Roman mob to extort revenue from the propertied classes—until at last the ancient economy collapsed, and the frontiers could not be defended. Clinton Caesar, eager to placate the Welfare Lobby, proposes to establish new overwhelming "entitlements," particularly medical ones, to be paid for by employers—for of course the wealth of employers is assumed to be inexhaustible. As in the age of Diocletian men fled from public offices, lest they be taxed and regulated to extinction, so by the approaching end of this century employers may be inclined to flee to some other condition of life—but to what?

The mentality of the American leveller nowadays may be sufficiently suggested by a proposal advanced by some of Clinton's inner circle but not presented to the Congress. This was a new tax: a levy upon persons dwelling in large houses. If the residence should contain rooms which might have been rented, had the owner desired, to paying lodgers (or perhaps non-paying homeless persons)—why, the owner of the dwelling would be taxed for the rooms that might have been occupied by other people. This tax would have been a federal levy, not a local real-property assessment. It is just the sort of tax to have been devised by some former hippie, now a bureaucrat, spiritually akin to President Clinton, former hippie himself. The real purpose of this strange proposal clearly was punitive, meant to punish those wicked rich who possessed spare bedrooms. Make them pay through the nose for such undemocratic private possession of domestic amenities! An Englishman's home once upon a time may have been his castle; but now an American's home should be his own only upon the sufferance of the Washington bureaucracy. If such a one should lodge homeless persons in his dining room, say, he might be indulged in a partial remission of taxes. One is reminded of housing in Moscow about the year 1919, when the Communist regime requisitioned even the lavatories of private residences as night lodging for the underprivileged. Envious egalitarianism as implemented by Clintonian zealots might not be satisfied until the whole population of this land should be lodged in immobilized "mobile homes"—a universal rookery of trailer camps. Why should anybody be indulged in domestic comforts not readily available to all citizens?

Have I carried to absurdity my argument against equality of condition? Nay, not so; for the enthusiasts for total equality are not to be satisfied with small concessions. I commend to you a dystopia, a longish short story, by Jacquetta Hawkes, that brilliant Englishwoman of diverse talents, published in her collection *Fables*—which volume appeared in 1952, during Britain's disagreeable experience with a socialist regime.

This fable is entitled "The Unites." God, having sensed no impulses from the planet Earth for a long while, dispatches a humble angel to investigate and report to Him. This emissary, who had visited Earth once long, long before, discovers on this later expedition that humankind has suffered a startling change for the worse. No longer, indeed, do men and women call themselves humans: they style themselves "Unites," for all are united in a kind of subhuman state, everybody precisely like everybody else. These degenerate beings live in some 500,000 Life Units dispersed about the globe, and subsist by primitive agriculture. Private property has been abolished altogether. Every Life Unit consists of four standard tenements: the Pink Block for the young, the Green Block for the cultivators, the Red Block for the industrial workers, the Black Block for the administrators and the governments. Kinship and family life have been swept away, as disruptive of social unity. If equality is the whole aim of existence, why should one person outlive another? There must be equality in death as in life. So on attaining the age of sixty-six, the older Unites are herded into the Finis Chamber of the Black Block, suffocated there, and their bodies incinerated. The only amusement in these Life Unit communes is a colossal sort of motordrome in which some of the performers bloodily perish, to the crowd's satisfaction.

In short, through the doctrine of equality of condition what once was the human race has transformed itself into a moral condition scarcely distinguishable from that of the beasts which perish. And yet a few true human beings, eager to subvert this life-in-death, have survived somehow in Life Unit 1457. The visiting angel learns that this handful of young people are contriving to bring down the dreary system of equality. Indeed their slogan "Equality must be destroyed" prevails; the stupidity of the egalitarian administrators cannot resist the innovators; and in one Life Unit, at least, inequality is happily triumphant. But even so, the angel detects some ideologue of equality plotting already to bring back equal misery; thus the struggle between the forces of individual achievement and the forces of equality runs on in human societies. There are no lost causes because there are no gained causes.

Jacquetta Hawkes's fable or parable is set in a distant future; but in the closing decade of this century we move in that egalitarian direction. Equality is demanded in politics and in monetary incomes; more, it is demanded in formal education. My wife, Annette, fifteen years ago was a member of the Commission on Excellence in Education appointed by President Reagan. She promptly found that many folks in the federal Department of Education, and many educationists in teachers' colleges and teachers' unions, were concerned chiefly for what they called "equity"—that is, equality, sameness, at every level of schooling. Some insisted that American education must have both excellence and equity, a manifest absurdity: for the word "excellence" means to exceed, of course, to do better than others; while "equity," or uniformity, necessarily implies mediocrity. The more equality in schooling, the lower the achievement; and the greater the injustice toward students possessed of some talents. Forty years ago, I resigned a university post in disgust at a deliberate policy of lowering standards in the interest of "equity"—that is, accommodating more students who, from stupidity or indolence, ought not to have been admitted to a university at all. In general, American standards for an education allegedly "higher" have declined still more since I departed from the Ivory Tower.

Egalitarian pressures are exerted in virtually every country to push into the universities most of the rising generation, however dull, bored, or feckless a young person may be. The consequence of this movement is to make the higher learning lower. Avoiding the dullness of most graduate studies in the United States, in 1948 I went abroad for my higher learning—to St. Andrews University, still somewhat medieval in appearance, the oldest of Scottish universities, situated in a charming medieval town. Nowadays St. Andrews is under political pressure to change its character by admitting many more students, which would destroy the tradition of learning there by the North Sea. For what reason? Why, to "give everybody his chance." Perhaps we ought to confer the doctorate upon every infant at birth, and reserve the universities for people really interested in right reason and imagination, so eliminating degree-snobbery and degree-envy. The present disorders of the intellect on most campuses result from the combination of ideologue egalitarians among the professors with ignorant and bored students.

*   *   *

Permit me to suggest some probable long-run consequences of national infatuation with equality of condition.

First, great injury to the leading class that every society requires for its success. This leading class is not identical with sociological "elites"; to ascertain the distinction, read T. S. Eliot's slim book *Notes Towards the Definition of Culture*. This leading class, even in the American democracy, is made up of public-spirited men and women of property; well-educated professional folk, lawyers among them; honest politicians who take long views; publishers and writers who help to shape public opinion on a diversity of matters; the clergy; persons experienced in military affairs, foreign affairs, and the arts of political administration; local leaders in charitable and civic concerns; those people of industry and commerce who know that there is more to life than getting and spending. I am even willing to acknowledge among this leading class some of the better professors of arts and sciences—although Nietzsche reminds us that in politics the professor always plays the comic role.

The authority of this class of persons in America has been declining in recent decades, from a variety of causes; and the decay in public and private morality, the decadence of education, the shallow populist tone of our politics, and a number of other afflictions result in considerable part from that decline of authority. Now a renewed demand for levelling assails this leading class. For one thing, it was possible for members of this leading class to take part in public and charitable concerns, and to set the whole tone of life in their communities, because most of them possessed some private means; they were not daily money-grubbing. Increasingly this class is being pushed to the wall by heavy—nay, savage—taxation. Most people will have noticed how in the past few years various deductions and exemptions have been eliminated from income-tax returns, particularly for persons with incomes exceeding $100,000; for such folk, medical deductions from income are a thing of the past. Now the Clinton Administration imposes new burdens, falling principally upon the class I have just been describing. Many will pay more than half their incomes in taxes—federal and state income taxes, real-property taxes, sales taxes, and the rest. What margin will remain for such people to exercise the functions of voluntary leadership?

The late Michael Harrington, a few years past, was addressing a crowd of poor people. He said that too many affluent people were paying less than half their incomes in income tax. He was surprised by the reaction of his audience. They were indignant at Harrington's proposal that the state should take more than half a man's income, however large that income. "That's just not fair," some of them cried. His audience was right and Harrington wrong. And perhaps some in his audience perceived, better than did Harrington, what would happen to a society—including persons of very modest incomes—in which the Leviathan state should kill the goose that lays the golden eggs.

Already many of us are paying more than half our incomes in taxation. Our time occupied in trying to make ends meet, how much leadership shall we be able to offer? More and more, in such circumstances, the remnant of authority and the power of decision-making are usurped by a centralized bureaucracy—and in the name of "democracy."

Second, an obsession with equality commonly results in general impoverishment, by diminishing saving and capital accumulation, and by "humanitarian" welfare measures that diminish the incentive to work for one's own subsistence. Egalitarian "entitlements" already have so increased the national debt that, as matters are drifting, the amount of interest on the national debt, annually, will come to exceed the total federal revenues collected by the present tax structure!

Decreased economic productivity, caused by a virtual oppression of industry and commerce, will afflict the poor worst of all—even though the mistaken policies of government were undertaken in the name of equality of condition for the alleged poor.

A third consequence of deliberate levelling in society would be grave intellectual damage, already in progress. Over the centuries there was developed in all civilized countries an elaborate edifice of schooling, originally religious in character, meant to impart some measure of wisdom and virtue to the rising generation. Aristotle instructs us that the process of learning cannot be made easy. The higher learning is concerned necessarily with abstractions, in large part; but the common man tends to dislike abstractions. As T. S. Eliot said once, there ought to be many different kinds of education for many different kinds of people; but the egalitarian zealot would enforce uniformity of schooling, perhaps of the "outcomes education" sort to produce conditioned responses, now being pushed in Virginia, Michigan, and other states.

The black-militant outcry against the study of the works of "dead white males" suggests what a thoroughly egalitarian system of schooling would discard. Thought always is painful; so let us get on with the rap sessions.

Those intellectual disciplines that nurture right reason and moral imagination, requiring real thought, are unpopular with the egalitarian, who regards them as archaic and snobbish. The egalitarian much prefers utilitarian schooling and vague "social studies." But both private wisdom and public order require that a substantial number of people be well acquainted with genuine works of the mind. The natural sciences, humane studies, and the philosophical habit of mind neglected, the person and the republic sink into ignorance and apathy; but the egalitarian zealot does not perceive these ruinous consequences until the decline no longer can be arrested. The condition of most of our public schools today, and the inferior performance of most colleges and universities by contrast with their work half a century ago, ought to suggest to us how far, as a people, we already have slipped down the slope toward intellectual failure. What I say of American education is quite as true of British education nowadays, and, with few exceptions of Europe generally. But the educational egalitarian is not deterred—not quite yet: so long as "everybody has equal opportunity" to spend four or five years in an educational establishment professedly higher, social justice has been achieved, he fancies.

*   *   *

In short, I have been arguing that it is profoundly unjust to endeavor to transform society into a tableland of equality. It would be unjust to the energetic, reduced to equality with the slack and indolent; it would be unjust to the imaginative, compelled to share the schooling and the tastes of the dull; it would be unjust to the thrifty, compelled to make up for the losses of the profligate; it would be unjust to those who take long views, forced to submit to the domination of a majority interested chiefly in short-run results.

But I shall not labor this point, already made forcefully by Alexis de Tocqueville and other writers whose talents exceed my own. The egalitarian society, far from satisfying desires for "social justice," would be unjust to the very people who made possible a tolerably orderly and prosperous society. Eric Voegelin remarks that the tolerably just society is one in which the more aspiring natures are free to exercise their talents, but the large majority of people, who desire merely a quiet life, are secured against oppression by the aspiring natures. Mediocre necessarily, the egalitarian society would discourage or suppress enterprising talents—which would result in social stagnation. Life in a social tableland of equality would be infinitely boring.

Yet don't I believe in equality of *opportunity*? No, I do not. The thing is not possible. First of all, genetic differences cannot be surmounted between individual and individual; Thomas Jefferson and the whole school of "created free and equal" knew nothing whatsoever of human genetics, a science of the late nineteenth and the twentieth centuries. Second, opportunity depends greatly upon family background and nurturing; and unless it is proposed to sweep away the family altogether, as in Jacquetta Hawkes's fable, the rising generation of one stock will differ greatly in opportunity from the rising generation of a different family. For instance, I read every evening to my four little daughters, or told them stories; while my neighbors did not so instruct and converse with their children; accordingly, my children have enjoyed superior opportunities in life. It would be outrageously unjust to try somehow to wipe out these advantages of genetic inheritance or familial instruction.

Inequality is the natural condition of human beings; charity may assist those not favored by nature; but attempts to impose an artificial equality of condition and intellect, although in the long run they fail, meanwhile can work great mischief in any society, and—still worse—damage human nature itself.

XVII

The Illusion of "Human Rights"

Human rights, some folk tell us, are not fully realized in El Salvador. Other people have discovered, somewhat tardily, that human rights are not altogether secure in Cambodia. Our national government engages in a curious moral calculus when it essays to weigh the various merits and demerits of regimes in Somalia, Bosnia, Iraq, and Cuba—let alone China.

By what standards are "human rights" to be measured? What, indeed, do we mean by this controversial phrase "human rights?" I offer you some reflections on this subject.

The phrase "human rights" first entered American politics, I believe, when President Woodrow Wilson opposed it to "property rights." President Franklin Roosevelt similarly set human rights against property rights. Presumably President Jimmy Carter had in mind such employment of the term by his predecessors when he set up a bureaucratic apparatus to sit in judgment upon the nations, reproaching client states for not attaining that perfection of human rights enjoyed in the United States of America.

From the first, the odor of demagoguery has clung to the political use of "human rights" language. For all rights are human rights. Does anyone suggest a code of inhuman rights? Dogs and cats do not enjoy rights. States have no rights (despite constitutional arguments); states enjoy powers. God is above rights, and human-kind can claim no rights against God.

And property has no rights, being inanimate and non-human. Human beings, rather, have rights to their lawful property. The right to retain one's real and personal property is among the most important of civil rights; the critic Paul Elmer More declared that so far as civilization is concerned, the right to property is more important than the right to life. President Wilson, well acquainted with political theory and history, must have been aware that he was disingenuous when he opposed "property rights" to "human rights." President Franklin Roosevelt might have pleaded ignorance, had he been accused of this abuse of terms.

I am suggesting, you will perceive, that so vague a term as "human rights" is easily warped to politicians' advantage; and that it may be perilous to employ. Yet behind this feeble term lie old truths and old errors.

When politicians and publicists say "human rights," to what concepts are they referring? Presumably they have at the back of their minds—supposing them to be reflective at all—either the concept "natural law," or the concept "civil rights," or both concepts.

Those two phrases can be defined more readily than can "human rights." Yet at present the tag "human rights" is in vogue. It is incorporated into the Universal Declaration of Human Rights of the United Nations. It even appears in translations of documents issuing from the Vatican. And of course it is beloved by the mass media.

Can we discern some substance behind the tag? Why, the

assumption underlying "human rights" seems to be this: from the nature of man there are derived certain personal immunities that all governments and all people in power ought to respect. This is the doctrine of natural law, as we find it in Cicero and in the Schoolmen. With this natural-law teaching, conferring certain immunities from the operation of power, is bound up the concept of *human dignity*—a belief of mingled Christian and classical origins.

So far as the notion of "human rights" is founded upon doctrines of natural law and of human dignity, it can claim a venerable origin. A few sentences of definition may be useful here.

That term of jurisprudence and politics *natural law* may be defined as a loosely-knit body of rules of action, prescribed by an authority superior to the state.* These rules of natural justice are presumed to be derived from divine commandment, from the nature of man, or from general human experience over thousands of years. From Aristotle, through Cicero and the Roman jurisconsults, a continuity of belief in natural law was imparted to what we call "the West." After the triumph of Christian faith, this doctrine of natural law was interwoven with Christian morality and social thought. It was expounded with especial strength by Saint Thomas Aquinas.

As Sir Ernest Barker wrote of the natural law, "This justice is conceived as being the higher or ultimate law, proceeding from the nature of the universe—from the Being of God and the reason of man. It follows that law—in the sense of the law of last resort—is somehow above lawmaking."

The difficulty of defining natural law closely, and of discovering clear sanctions for invoking it, necessarily involves natural law doctrine in controversy. Yet there remains in the United States and in some other countries a popular attachment to natural-law belief which still possesses vigor.

---

*For an extended definition of "Natural Law" see chapter 15.

In essence, as A. P. d'Entrèves remarks, the doctrine of natural law is "an assertion that law is a part of ethics." Thus, when many people refer to "human rights," they have in mind, vaguely at least, natural-law doctrine: the conviction that a human being is entitled to a certain justice of treatment because by his very nature he is something better than a beast.

This understanding is closely allied to what Pico della Mirandola, five centuries ago, called "the dignity of man": the humanists' aspiration, by a discipline of the reason and the will, to make Man not much inferior to the angels. In short, the politician who employs the phrase "human rights" evokes in some degree, in the popular understanding, ancestral spirits; he conjures up both the Medieval model of Man and the Renaissance model of Man, even though neither the politician nor his auditor may be aware of the sorcery. Ghostly presences, resurrected beliefs, seem to vindicate this incantation of "human rights."

So in November, 1983, addressing the National Assembly of South Korea, President Ronald Reagan declared, "The United States welcomes the goals you have set for political development and increased respect for human rights." Democratic presidents introduced "human rights" to our political discourse; Republican presidents now accept the phrase as conventional political cant. By this employment of the phrase, presumably President Reagan meant "civil liberties."

And when many other people hear the words "human rights," they take the phrase as a synonym for "civil rights" or "civil liberties." Thus American attachment to the concepts of natural law and human dignity is joined with American emphasis upon civil liberties; and these two predilections, merging, seem to confer substance upon the amorphous doctrine of "human rights."

Yet actually the notion of "human rights" is not descended from the natural-law teaching that extends from Aristotle to Burke; nor is "human rights" synonymous with civil liberty. Having just endeavored briefly to define the concept of natural law, now let me say something about civil rights.

A "civil right" is a guarantee that the citizen is protected against certain actions that otherwise the state might take to the citizen's disadvantage. Such rights commonly are stated in the negative— that troops shall not be quartered in private dwellings, for instance, or that punishments shall not be cruel or unusual. Civil rights are understood to entail corresponding civil duties, the most important of which is the duty to maintain the reign of law by which such rights are given flesh.

The extent and exercise of civil rights varies greatly from one culture or political community to another—because "civil rights" are the products of the historical experience of particular peoples. There never has existed a universal code of civil liberties.

The right to trial by jury, for example, so jealously guarded in Britain and the United States, never has prevailed in France. This does not mean that "human rights" are repressed by the French. Instead, it suggests that order and freedom and justice are obtained in diverse ways in different lands and times.

Civil liberties exist under both common law and Roman law, but the particular character of these rights varies from one political system to another. To impose an American pattern of civil rights upon a society of very different origins—upon a Muslim state, for instance—would break down the old pattern of justice without effectually establishing American ways.

To sum up my definitions, natural law is a theory of justice, derived from religious or quasi-religious convictions about the nature of man; while civil liberties are practical immunities at law, derived from a nation's political development over a long period of time. Superficially, the twentieth-century illusion of "human rights" may seem to be the child of these venerable parents. Yet in reality the notion of "human rights" is a bastard idea of recent birth. Its father was the UNO's Universal Declaration of Human Rights, to

which the government of these United States of America has
refused to subscribe. Its grandfather was the Declaration of the
Rights of Man, promulgated by the French Revolutionaries and
Tom Paine—and also rejected, in its time, by the government of
these United States. Friends to natural law and to American civil
liberties would be foolish if they should permit this illegitimate
notion of imprescriptible universal "rights" to be foisted upon them.
The brat might work their undoing.

*   *   *

Rights can take on flesh only if they are derived from some body of
law. The abstractions we call "human rights" have no sanction in the
positive laws of most countries; the Universal Declaration of
Human Rights may receive the formal assent of various governments, but nowhere is that Declaration observed and enforced.

"Rights" are immunities, guarantees that certain things may not
be done to a person against his will. Rights can be secured only in
a civil social order. In a condition of anarchy, no one enjoys rights,
because there exists no just authority to which a person may appeal
against the violation of rights. Therefore what we call the state, or
organized political community, is necessary for the realizing of any
rights.

Yet the government of any state may become oppressive. It may
ignore or virtually extirpate rights of minorities or of majorities. So
enduring rights ought not to be regarded as merely the concessions
of a particular government. True rights find their sanction either in
a theory of human nature or in the long-established customs of a
people. The former of these sanctions is what we call natural law;
the latter, what we call civil rights.

We ought to beware of supposing that all civil social benefits
which citizens of the United States enjoy today are "natural" rights,
universally applicable. Nor should we assume that the civil liberties

of our own country might be exported to, or thrust upon, cultures or countries quite different from our own. It would be inhumane for us to become fanatic ideologues demanding an inflexible universal pattern of "human rights."

In the current confused discussion of human rights in America and abroad, we need to remind ourselves of an observation by Dostoevski, in *The Devils*. Those who begin with unlimited freedom, Dostoevski says, must end with unlimited despotism.

Not everything that men and women desire is their *right*. Politics being the art of the possible, rights do not exist unlimited, in the abstract. Every right is limited by some corresponding duty; and those who claim a right to everything soon find that they are left with a right to nothing.

Near the end of the eighteenth century, in replying to the French revolutionaries, Edmund Burke distinguished between the "real" and the "pretended" rights of human beings. Burke was at once a champion of natural law and a champion of civil liberties in their English form. He declared that the "armed doctrine" (which we now call ideology) was destroying the real rights of men and women even while it proclaimed the pretended rights that cannot be obtained.

There exist certain real rights of all human beings in society, Burke wrote. As he had argued in his prosecution of Warren Hastings, those rights are as valid in India as in Britain. "If civil society be made for the advantage of man," Burke wrote in 1789, "all the advantages for which it is made become his right. It is an institution of beneficence; and law itself is only beneficence acting by rule. Men have a right to live by that rule; they have a right to do justice, as between their fellows, whether their fellows are in public function or in ordinary occupation. They have a right to the fruits of their industry, and to the means of making their industry fruitful. They have a right to the acquisitions of their parents; to the nourishment and improvement of their offspring; to instruction in life, and to consolation in death. Whatever each man can separately do, without trespassing upon others, he has a right to do for himself; and he has a right to all which society, with all its combinations of skill and force, can do in his favor."

Burke emphasized that men also have a right to be restrained by government—that is, a right to be saved from suffering the consequences of their own passions and vices. In effect, Burke argued that the real rights of human beings everywhere amount to the right to live under a rule of law; to the right to be protected in their labor, their property, their inheritance; to the right to religious instruction and consolation; to the right to equality of treatment by the state.

Yet we do not turn ordinarily to these general and abstract claims of right, Burke went on to explain. Rather, when treated unjustly, we appeal first to what Burke called "chartered rights"—that is, the civil rights of our country, as expressed in charters, constitutions, statutes, ancient customs. Statutory and common law, rather than natural law, are the regular means for securing definite rights.

Appeals to natural law are our resort only in times of extreme oppression without regular means of redress; for natural law is not an enforceable code of rules; it is a body of principles of jurisprudence by which we ought to be guided in our construction of positive law.

Although the political and legal forms vary widely from nation to nation, still there endures in every civilization some apprehension of the natural law, derived from an understanding of human nature. All legislators ought to bear in mind the real rights of human beings when they deal with the chartered rights of their country.

Burke's understanding of natural law and of chartered rights has not been altogether forgotten in the United States. Indeed, Burke's thought entered into the Constitution and its interpretation, especially through Chief Justice John Marshall, who was mightily influenced by his reading of Burke. This underlying American affirmation of natural justice and prescriptive civil rights has given to the United States a healthy tension between the claims of order and the claims of freedom. In our domestic politics, at least, we understand that perfect security cannot be attained, nor can perfect freedom: we must balance one against the other. Similarly, we understand reasonably well that every right is married to some responsibility. So the awkward term "human rights" does have behind it, in American public opinion, some substance.

But the twentieth century is a bent time; Burke foresaw the coming of our time of troubles. In country after country, totalist ideology has submerged both natural law and civil liberties. Were it not for the surviving power of the United States, the remnant of order and justice and freedom might be swallowed up by Leviathan Ideology.

In international affairs, nevertheless, the United States needs to beware of what Sir Herbert Butterfield calls "righteousness," a cardinal error in diplomacy—that is, national self-righteousness. The American Republic does not possess virtue and power sufficient to thrust Americans' notions of "human rights" upon all the world. Even a massive assertion of American power, a crusade for "human rights," might destroy more than it could restore. America's undertaking in Vietnam, President Lyndon Johnson's version of human rights, was a salutary lesson in this respect, if in no other.

It is not the mission of the United States to establish universally some imitation of the American political and economic order. Every people must find their own way to order and justice and freedom. As Daniel Boorstin has written, the American Constitution is not for export. He means that our Constitution grew out of the peculiar historical experience of the Americans. So it is with the underlying constitution of every people. We ought not to expect American-type courts of law to be established promptly in Indonesia, say; or great prosperous industrial private corporations to appear abruptly in Russia.

An attempt to impose in short order the American pattern of

rights, aside from being hopelessly impracticable, would have consequences distinctly different from those that most Americans desire. Quite conceivably such forced-draft insistence upon a total program of "human rights," right now, might bring about the triumph of totalist ideologies hostile to both natural law and chartered rights. There is a worse ruler than King Log: he is King Stork.

Consider how the induced demand for "human rights" became a principal instrument for bringing down the Diem government in South Vietnam. That government was engaged in a desperate struggle to repel the aggression of the Communists of the North; simultaneously, it had to maintain itself against factions within its own borders—parties and sects possessing their own armed forces. Despite these overwhelming difficulties, the Diem government was a constitutional order, sustaining a National Assembly and holding elections for both legislative and executive offices. Yet the Left brought against the Diem government the accusation that the regime did not perfectly assure civil liberties, "human rights"; it was said, somewhat vaguely, that Buddhists were discriminated against. Dominant elements of the American mass media repeated these charges until the Kennedy administration abandoned Diem—and made possible his murder. What a triumph for human rights! Now there reigns in Saigon, as in Hanoi, a merciless domination of Marxists who have stamped out the last vestige of civil freedoms. The demand for unlimited freedom has ended in unlimited despotism.

The same process occurred in El Salvador several years ago. Even Mr. Henry Kissinger exhorted the beleaguered government of that unhappy little state—a government democratically elected—to expand its "human rights" in time of civil war, with deadly enemies a few miles from the capital. There exists something even more important than civil liberties: the survival of legitimate governments. I find it a curious notion that the enemies of the state are entitled to full protection of their liberties by the very state they would overthrow. During the Civil War in this Republic, President Abraham Lincoln did not hesitate to reject that sort of disintegrated liberalism: he suspended writs of *habeas corpus*. Constitutions are not suicide pacts.

Has anyone troubled to inquire of the zealots for "human rights" as to precisely what political and social conditions may be regarded as a satisfactory fulfillment of the "human rights" ideal? We may suppose that, as a minimum, all the articles of America's Bill of Rights would have to be observed and enforced most scrupulously; that governments would be carried on by "moderate" or "middle-of-the-road" parties of a social-democratic cast (parties of a kind almost nonexistent in most of the world); that perfect freedom of expression, including street demonstrations by militant factions, would be not merely guaranteed, but encouraged; that a country's armed forces would be reduced to a minimum, if not abolished altogether; that of course secret-police forces would be forbidden, and ordinary police directed by citizens' committees; that universal suffrage would prevail, with frequent elections; that a welfare state would provide a large proportion of the citizenry with generous entitlements; that every demand for more abundant rights would be promptly satisfied. In effect, the "human rights" vision for the world is a latter-day version of the more advanced sentimental liberalism of Victorian England, plus a very considerable dose of socialism.

A principal difficulty of this utopian notion of "human rights" triumphant is that such a society, in most of the world, would be overthrown in very short order by one ideological gang or another—even if it did not collapse of its own weight. The liberal dream began to turn into a nightmare a century ago. The bent world in which we find ourselves will not tolerate such coffeehouse political philosophy. Things will be as they will be; why should we seek to deceive ourselves?

And why should we expect other nations, lacking our political traditions and long-established social institutions, unendowed with America's material resources, to achieve what is imperfectly attained in the United States? Do we Americans enjoy the ultimate fulfillment of "human rights"? To walk the streets with reasonable safety is the most basic of civil liberties; yet millions of Americans dare not step out at night, and some scarcely dare so venture by day. Presumably the safety of children at school is a basic civil right; yet in every American city pupils are assaulted daily, and some killed. Have we no claims of right unsatisfied? Physician, heal thyself.

I do not intend mockery. It is much to be desired that the recovery of order and justice and freedom be advanced throughout the world; we should be thankful, in this rough time, for small mercies. But international politics, like domestic politics, is the art of the possible. To demand that other countries swiftly attain the liberal ideal is to expect what they cannot possibly accomplish; in some cases, it is to expect them to work their own destruction.

Also this is a demand often disingenuous, sometimes hypocritical. The United States has supported by gigantic loans murderous despots in Africa, because now and again they may serve our turn; but our diplomats do not trouble themselves to inquire keenly into their enforcement of "human rights." Similarly, our State Department sedulously refrained from any words that might have annoyed the masters of those countries that usefully served as a bulwark of sorts against the former Soviet Union. We reserve our sermons concerning human rights for such allies and client states as could not or would not break with the United States under any circumstances.

In the affairs of nations, it scarcely can be otherwise. For the aim of foreign policy is to maintain and advance the national interest- not to embark upon moral crusades. We seek an informal alliance with China, and so make large concessions to the oligarchs of Peiping, even to the point of maintaining that the legitimate government of Cambodia is the ferocious Khmer Rouge regime, now driven into Thailand—the domination with the worst "human rights" record in this inhumane twentieth century—merely because such recognition suits Chinese policy. Such is hard realism in diplomacy.

Foreign policy, I repeat, is not an exercise in moralism. We assisted in the conversion of Rhodesia into Zimbabwe, with much fulsome talk about human rights addressed to the former government, because America needs the mineral resources of that country; and our statesmen calculated that it might be possible to detach the major black faction from Soviet influence. However imperfect the fulfillment of human rights in Rhodesia, justice and civil liberty are being extinguished altogether in Zimbabwe. I find it distasteful to cloak the national interest in grandiose phrases about human rights. What we were after, really, was the chromium—not the establishment of a paradise of human rights in the heart of Africa.

Whatever may be done by example and by persuasion to maintain the high principles of natural law and of civil liberty, we ought to do. But we ought not to delude ourselves into fancying that the world can be redeemed by "jawboning"—least of all by jawboning that weakens and offends such governments as are not unfriendly to the United States. And today, we ought not to talk Newspeak. "Human rights" is a Newspeak term, often supercilious, readily employed to advance causes hostile to genuine order and justice and freedom. Let us not hoist ourselves by our own verbal petard.

XVIII

Criminal Character and Mercy

To perceive truth, we require images. As G. K. Chesterton put it, all life is an allegory, and we can understand it only in parable. I am about to offer some observations concerning mercy: that is, mercy toward deadly criminals. I believe that the capital penalty has a compassionate function. I propose to make my point through presenting a series of images—some of them drawn from perceptive works of fiction, others taken from my own experience and acquaintance in the course of a wandering life.

My introductory image is extracted from a memorable novelette by the German writer Stefan Andres, *We Are God's Utopia*. This is a realistic episode from the Spanish Civil War, and it takes place in a desolated convent in a deserted walled town. One faction—the Reds, apparently—have confined two hundred prisoners of the opposing faction in the cells of a convent. These prisoners will be executed if the battle goes against the faction to which the jailers belong.

The captors are commanded by a lieutenant, Don Pedro, who already has committed indescribable atrocities. The memory of the worst of these acts will not permit the lieutenant to sleep—not in this very convent where he tortured the nuns to death.

Among the prisoners here is a former priest, Paco, taken in arms. Don Pedro implores Paco to hear his confession, so that he may sleep again. Although no enthusiast himself for the rite of confession, Paco consents to receive this dreadful penitent. In the course of the lieutenant's confession, Paco learns that Pedro, when a boy, had tortured cats hideously; that he had beheaded the puppets in his own puppet-theater; that he had flung to his death the kindest man Paco ever had known; that he had kept the nuns screaming in agony all night long. Yet Teniente Pedro has taken no real pleasure in these acts; they have made him sad, at the time of their commission and thereafter. He says to Paco, "I dwell in myself as though in a grave!"

The sometime priest absolves Pedro, for at the moment of absolution he is contrite. (Half an hour later, nevertheless, he will direct the massacre of the prisoners.) But before granting absolution, the confessor instructs his penitent, who kneels before him:

> 'I tell you, it would be good for you if you were to die in the war.' The voice was silent; after a pause it went on. 'Yes, pray to God for death. According to the laws of man—but no, you know that!—no sin can separate you from God if you want to come back to Him, but it can separate you from life. For this reason, the death penalty for certain crimes has a decidedly compassionate character. You are a criminal of this sort. Pray to God for death!'

To Don Pedro, death would bring relief from his ghastly sadness and the moral solitude in which he had suffered since childhood;

relief from the tormenting memory of his atrocious crimes; relief from the depravity of his own nature. Like most murderers, Pedro is not totally corrupt: he is capable of some kindly acts and of gratitude. But there is no way in which he can be redeemed or relieved of the torment of being what he is, in the flesh—except through death. To such a one, capital punishment would be an order of release. Sin already has separated the atrocious homicide from true life; yet through grace in death, even the slayer's soul may be redeemed. Death is not the greatest of evils. In the language of orthodoxy, indeed, death is no evil at all.

At this point, it may be objected that I have offered merely a fictitious instance. But great works of fiction are more true than particular incidents of the actual: that is why they are recognized as great. Andres gives us in this story a kind of distillation from mankind's experience of spirit. Those of us who have knocked about the world have encountered our real Teniente Pedros. It is not pleasant to meet them in confined quarters. A friend of mine spent much of his life in the company of conspicuous specimens of such unregenerate humanity. Permit me to offer you, then, a different sort of image: that of my friend the late Clinton Wallace, very much flesh and blood.

Clinton was the most heartfelt advocate of capital punishment that ever I have met. At the age of fourteen, Clinton had run away from a brutal father. Thereafter, until he came to live in my house, Clinton spent his life either on the roads or in prisons. His convictions were for petty offenses against property—usually the pilfering of church poor-boxes—or for endeavoring to escape from prisons. He was a giant in size and strength, and an innocent.

I do not mean that Clinton was a fool: the prison psychiatrists wrote him down as "dull normal," but Clinton was neither dull nor normal. He did not drink, except for one glass of beer on especially convivial occasions; did not smoke; did not curse; did not offend against women or children. His only vice, aside from petty larceny in time of necessity, was indolence. (Like Don Pedro, though, Clinton dwelt in himself, as in a grave.)

Clinton could recite a vast deal of good poetry, could make himself amusing, loved children, and prided himself upon being nonviolent. The worst aspect of life in prison, Clinton told me once, was not the boredom, or even the loss of liberty, but the foul language of the convicts—their every other word an obscenity. In recent years, Clinton added, prison conversation had grown monotonous—everybody discussing interminably the pleas of Miranda and Escobedo.

My wife once asked Clinton—who lived with us for six years near the end of his tether—how many of the men in prison are innocent.

"They're all innocent," Clinton replied. "You only have to ask them." He chuckled briefly. "They're all guilty, really, guilty as sin. Many of them are animals, brutes that ought to be put out of their misery."

From the worst forms of degradation at the hands of fellow prisoners, Clinton had been saved by his size, strength, and stentorian power of lung. But he had not been spared the company of the depraved. For some months, in one prison, Clinton's cell-mate had been a man who had taken off his wife's head. That missing head never had been discovered. Clinton (who, like Don Pedro, had trouble getting to sleep) used to lie awake in his bunk at night, watching his cell-mate in the opposite bunk and stroking his own throat to reassure himself.

Clinton went on, in his kitchen-table conversations with us, to talk of the horror and the danger of existence in company with such men. Any tolerably decent person who had been sentenced to confinement might find himself at their mercy. "They're lower than beasts." Out of compassion for the other prisoners and for the guards, Clinton argued, the death penalty ought to be imposed upon men who had committed deliberately those crimes once called capital.

"Nobody can reform you," Clinton would continue. "There's no such thing as a 'reformatory' or a 'correctional facility.' The only person who can reform you is yourself. You have to begin by admitting to yourself that you did wrong. Then you may begin to improve a little."

Clinton Wallace had concluded from much observation and painful experience that very few deadly criminals possess either the ability or the intention to reform themselves. It is their nature, outside of prison, to prey beast-like upon whomever they may devour; and if confined within prison, these human predators are impelled by their very nature to ruin the other inmates. From the time he first was imprisoned—for truancy, at the age of fourteen—Clinton had been flung behind bars with such men. To make a swift lawful end of them, he declared, would be a work of mercy for all concerned.

My acquaintance with convicts is not confined to Clinton Wallace. For armed robbery, my friend Eddie was sentenced to three to thirty years imprisonment. (It was his first offense, committed under the influence of a kinsman and perhaps of drugs.) Within the walls, Eddie's religious yearnings of earlier years returned to him, and he grew almost saintly amidst the general corruption. As a reward for his good conduct, the warden was ready to assign him to an open-air work detail in the Upper Peninsula of Michigan. "For God's sake," Eddie cried, "don't do that to me! Put me in solitary if you have to, but keep me behind these walls! In a camp like that, I wouldn't have a chance against the gangs."

Eddie was a rough-and-ready young man, a seaman by trade, courageous to the point of recklessness. He did not labor under any illusions concerning the character of the dominant spirits within prison walls. He knew that no adequate punishment could be imposed upon any "lifer" who might take it into his head to do Eddie a mischief—including as "mischief" a knife between Eddie's ribs. So Eddie was no advocate of gentleness with the brutally violent.

Both Clinton and Eddie, flesh and blood though they were, have appeared as characters in short stories of mine—Clinton in my best-known tale, "There's a Long, Long Trail a-Winding"; Eddie in my story, "Lex Talionis." I drew them with affection from life. The final penalty called capital punishment does something to protect those men behind bars, like Clinton and Eddie, who may yet redeem themselves.

I have been suggesting through these incidents and images that captial punishment possesses certain merciful aspects. It may be merciful, first, in that it may relieve a depraved criminal of the horror of being what he is. It may be merciful, second, in that it can help to protect the less guilty from the more guilty. And in a third way, which I am about to touch upon, capital punishment may mercifully protect the guiltless from the more extreme forms of violence.

*   *   *

Here the arguments concerning "deterrence," already widely discussed, may emerge afresh. But let me assure you that I have no intention of returning to the theoretical and statistical considerations advanced so often. Instead I offer you now another image which strongly impressed itself upon my consciousness, early. It is an image formed out of a real happening—the kidnapping of my grandfather.

Although that abduction occurred when I was a small boy, I recollect all the details clearly. As noted elsewhere in this volume, Frank Pierce, my grandfather, was a bank manager, a well-read man, kindly and charitable, the leading spirit of our Lower Town by the great railway yards outside Detroit. During the 1920s he repelled several attempts at robbery of his bank. (He carried a tear-gas fountain pen and kept a pistol handy in a drawer, but always had succeeded in baffling the robbers without using either instrument.)

On one occasion, for all that, my grandfather lost the contest.

As he walked from his house toward his bank, very early in the summer morning, an automobile drew up alongside him, a submachine gun was pointed at him, and he was persuaded to enter the car. His captors were two: a vigorous voluble man and an armed thing muffled in women's clothes which never spoke—possibly a disguised man.

They took my grandfather to his bank, long before any customers would appear, and ordered him at gunpoint to open the safe. He would not do so. The two robbers sat down to converse with Mr. Pierce; there was plenty of time yet. The voluble robber, in rather friendly fashion, recounted the story of his own life. He had been a victim of circumstances, he said; but he had transcended them by taking up the robbing of banks. He held a theory of law and society rather like that of Thrasymachus, it seemed to my historically-minded grandfather: that is, the robber maintained that might is right, and that he was by nature one of the strong, which truth he was presently demonstrating. He then requested Mr. Pierce, once more, to open the safe. My grandfather still refused.

"Then, Mr. Pierce, though I've come to like you, I'm going to have to kill you." The voluble robber explained that for the sake of his very reputation and livelihood, it was regrettably necessary for him to shoot bankers who set him at defiance. How otherwise could he subsist at his trade? So, if you really won't....

Convinced of his companion's sincerity, my grandfather opened the safe. The robbers took the money and drove away with my grandfather to an isolated barn. They left him inside, very loosely tied about his wrists, with the admonition that if he should come out within ten minutes, he would be shot. But my grandfather emerged as soon as he heard the robbers' car roar away. It had been his one defeat.

Years later, in an Illinois prison, a police officer who had known my grandfather happened to talk with Machinegun Kelly, generally believed to have been the author of the St. Valentine's Massacre in Chicago. According to my grandfather's acquaintance, Kelly told him that the Plymouth bank-robbery had been one of his jobs, and that he had taken a liking to Mr. Pierce, the banker. Whether or not there was truth in this confession, certainly the man who kidnapped my grandfather was an accomplished professional criminal without scruples. Against him my grandfather could have been a convincing and convicting witness. Then why did he let my grandfather live? Perhaps because this robber was a highly rational criminal who calculated chances and weighed penalties. Pursuit for a murder is more intense than for a mere robbery, and penalties are heavier.

As others have suggested, the degree of deterrence provided by any severe penalty depends in part upon the calculating intelligence of the criminal—or the lack of reckonings and calculations on his part. From what I have observed, systematic bank robbers and safecrackers commonly are cold, egoistic, calculating persons who rank Number One very high indeed, look out carefully for Number One, and therefore weigh disadvantages and penalties. Fairly often they, like my grandfather's kidnapper, develop ideological apologies for their actions. Upon such mentalities, the final penalty of death may exercise a prudent restraint.

I have digressed at this length to suggest that the death penalty may be merciful toward the victims of certain types of crimes, committed by certain types of persons. In such cases, heavy penalties—and capital punishment especially—tend to deter a rational offender from covering up one crime by committing a worse. The instance of my grandfather's misadventure early fixed in my mind, at least, a certain healthy prejudice in favor of stern deterrents.

Doubtless many people could tell us of more dreadful cases of criminality, within their personal experience, than these three vignettes drawn from my own past which I have just presented. The

breakers of violence sweep ever higher up the beaches of our
civilization. We have supped long on horrors. About four years ago,
my wife was kidnapped—though she escaped, chiefly through her
gift of persuasion. (That episode also has gone into a short story of
mine, "The Princess of All Lands.") Everyone knows how the
previous exemptions from criminal depredations have been can-
celled. That, I suppose, is why we are discussing the possible
restoration of capital punishment.

*   *   *

The meliorists of the nineteenth century took it for granted that by
a century after their time—by the year 1980, say—violent criminality
would be virtually extinguished through universal schooling, better
housing, better diet, general prosperity, improved measures for
public health, and the like. They assumed that capital punishment
was a relic of a barbarous and superstitious age. Capital punishment,
they thought, was merciless; and they were themselves evangels of
mercy. Their intellectual descendents did succeed, by the 1950s, in
abolishing the death penalty throughout most of the civilized world.

But they did not succeed in abolishing hideous crimes of the sort
formerly labelled "capital." In the most affluent of great countries,
the United States, the rate of serious crimes rose most steadily and
rapidly. At a time when the need for restraints upon criminality
appeared to be greater than before, penalties were diminished. All
this was done in the name of mercy.

Yet to whom was this mercy extended? Was it mercy toward the
criminals? The recent insistence of a murderer in this country upon
being executed according to sentence is no peculiar phenomenon.
Doubtless many of the unfortunates being worked slowly to death
in the prison-camps of the Soviet Arctic would find a firing-squad
far more merciful than the pretended mercy of a thirty-year
sentence. But we need not turn to totalist lands.

Is it not refined cruelty to keep alive, in self-loathing, a man who is a grave danger to the innocent and a grisly horror to himself? And to do such a thing in countries long admired for the justice of their laws? Once, walking Dartmoor, I came within sight of Dartmoor Prison, celebrated in so many English detective-yarns, but abandoned since I strolled nearby. At that time there was immured in Dartmoor Prison a little man with a talent for escaping. Although serving a life term there, he had managed to get out four or five times. And every time he contrived to elude his pursuers long enough to find, ravish, and kill a small girl. That done, he would submit in apathy to arrest and return to Dartmoor Prison.

This pitiable, loathsome being, after recapture, would be overwhelmed by remorse and would beg for death—which would be denied him, although yet another sentence of imprisonment for life would be imposed. For what purpose was his life so carefully preserved? His continued existence here below was of benefit only to the gutter press of London, which regaled the public with details of his atrocities. To whom was this policy merciful? To the other inmates of Dartmoor, compelled to associate with this creature? To the rural population of Devonshire, among whom the creature repeatedly committed his depredations? What sort of human dignity was this abstinence from capital punishment upholding?

Georgia's most talented writer of this century, the late Flannery O'Connor, once read aloud to me the most famous of her short stories, "A Good Man Is Hard to Find." Flannery was no sentimentalist and no meliorist; blameless herself, she nevertheless perceived the whole depravity of our fallen nature. In her art, she agreed with T. S. Eliot (who never read her stories) that the essential advantage for a poet "is to be able to see beneath both beauty and ugliness; to see the boredom, and the horror, and the glory."

In "A Good Man Is Hard to Find," Miss O'Connor describes the roadside murder of a whole family by an escaped convict called The Misfit, and his chums. (Flannery told me that she got The Misfit's sobriquet from Georgia newspapers—their appellation for a real-life fugitive from justice quite as alarming as Flannery's character.) The Misfit, like Teniente Pedro in *We Are God's Utopia*, is not without his amiable qualities: he apologizes to the grandmother (whom he kills a few minutes later) for not having a shirt to his back. He is a psychopath who had been "buried alive" in the penitentiary. Like many others of his dreadful nature, he has drifted through existence:

> 'I was a gospel singer for a while,' The Misfit said. 'I been most everything. Been in the arm service, both land and sea, at home and abroad, been twice married, been an undertaker, been with the railroads, plowed Mother Earth, been in a tornado, seen a man burnt alive once,' and he looked up at the children's mother and the little girl who were sitting close together, their faces white and their eyes glassy; 'I even seen a woman flogged,' he said.

After a nightmare conversation about how "Jesus thown everything off balance," the grandmother impulsively touches The Misfit; and he shoots her three times. His helpers return from disposing of the other members of the helpless family.

> 'She would of been a good woman,' The Misfit said, 'if it had been somebody there to shoot her every minute of her life.'
>
> 'Some fun!' Bobby Lee said.
>
> 'Shut up, Bobby Lee,' The Misfit said. 'It's no real pleasure in life.'

Aye, a good man is hard to find; in Adam's fall we sinned all; yet the depth and extent of our depravity varies from one person to another; and for the safety—perhaps the survival—of our species, it was found necessary in all previous ages to put out of their misery such criminals as The Misfit. Their physical presence among us cannot well be tolerated; the ultimate mysterious judgment upon their souls—so Flannery O'Connor implies—we leave to God.

To the Dartmoor child-ravager or the Jesus-accusing Misfit, what sort of mercy was burial alive in a penitentiary? Why, such preservation at public expense is merciful only if the mere prolongation of life here on earth is viewed as the chief purpose of existence; it is merciful only if one assumes that death brings annihilation—in Eliot's lines,

> *whirled*
> *Beyond the circuit of the shuddering Bear*
> *In fractured atoms.*

The abolition of capital punishment, I mean, is one of the products of humanitarianism—that is, of the belief that man's cleverness will suffice for all purposes, without need for knowledge of the transcendent and the divine.

Yet humanitarianism is now a decayed creed, worthless as a defense against the ideologues and the terrorists of our age, insufficient even to induce men and women to perform the ordinary duties which are supposed to bring the rewards of ordinary integrity. In a world that has denied God the Father, God the Son, and God the Holy Ghost—why, today the Savage God lays down his new commandments. The gods of the copybook headings with fire and slaughter return. The humanitarian who finds nothing sacred except (mysteriously) human life (so long as it is a criminal's life, not the life of an unborn infant) soon goes to the wall, throughout most of the world, in our time. Flannery O'Connor, a woman of humane letters, was no humanitarian. She was aware that this brief existence of ours—in her case, a brief life of physical suffering—is not the be-all and end-all. She did not mistake physical death for spiritual destruction.

*   *   *

One of the many consequences of the widespread decay of belief in the resurrection of the flesh and the life everlasting has been the revulsion against capital punishment. But our understanding of the human soul begins to revive—encouraged, strange though it may seem to some people, by the speculations of physicists. No longer does it seem absurd to deny the suppositions of materialists and mechanists; no longer is it a mark of ignorance to declare that man is made for eternity. For a popular treatment of this renewed awareness of the realm of spirit, I refer those interested to Morton T. Kelsey's book *Afterlife: the Other Side of Dying*; I might cite also a score of other serious books, among them certain studies of what time is and of what energy is.

The rejection of capital punishment in any circumstances thus is becoming an attitude which belongs to the intellectual and moral era that is passing. If the deprivation of life by human agency amounts only to opening the gate of another realm of existence—why, Death has lost his sting.

Why do some people retain so extreme an aversion to capital punishment that they would deny the death penalty even to condemned murderers who desire to be executed? Because of the fear of death—the dread of the void, of annihilation. Their dread of extinction—even if repressed in their conversation—for themselves is so powerful that they cannot abide the terminating of others' lives, not even the lives of Don Pedros and Misfits. It is an illogical dread, this terror of the inevitable: for we all die, just the same. John Strachey, as the Labor Party was about to push the

Churchill government out of power, promised the electorate that under socialism, the ministry of health would work such wonders that human life itself would be prolonged indefinitely. This did not come to pass. No statutes can assure immortality, except perhaps for corporations.

Yet why is death so dreadful? On my recommendation, the American Book Awards people chose as one of the five best religious books of 1979 Peter J. Kreeft's *Love Is Stronger Than Death*. "Death makes the question of God an empirically testable question," Kreeft writes. "Death makes the abstract God-question concrete. Instead of 'Is there a God?' the question becomes 'Will I see God?'" Death may give life to much, Peter Kreeft tells us:

> We have lost all our absolutes today except one. Once, we had God, truth, morality, family, fidelity, work, country, common sense, and many others—perhaps too many others. Now, in the age of absolute relativism, one absolute is left: death. Death is the one pathway through which all people at all times raise the question of the absolute, the question of God. The last excuse for not raising the God-question is Thoreau's 'one world at a time.' Death removes this last excuse.

The zealots against capital punishment fear to raise the God-question. Yet death, as Peter Kreeft tells us, can be a friend, a mother, a lover. Those who do not fear to clasp darkness as a bride die well, and are not extinguished. For all of us, in the end, death is the ultimate mercy. I do not understand why we should deny that mercy to slayers whose earthly existence is a grave; nor why we should deny a merciful protection to the guiltless whose purpose in this world may be undone by those guilty slayers.

XIX

Three Pillars of Order:
Edmund Burke,
Samuel Johnson,
Adam Smith

What Matthew Arnold called "an epoch of concentration" impends over the English-speaking nations. The revolutionary impulses and the social enthusiasms that dominated our century since their great explosion in Russia are now confronted by a countervailing physical and intellectual force. Fanatic ideology has been, in essence, rebellion against the old moral order of our civilization. To resist ideology, certain principles and forces of order have been waked, quite as they stirred against French innovating fury after 1790. We have entered upon a time of reconstruction and revaluation; we discern a resurrected conservatism in politics and philosophy and letters.

Britain during Arnold's "epoch of concentration" became, despite its disillusion, a society of high intellectual achievement, the revolutionary energy latent in it diverted to reconstructive ends. That the epoch of concentration displayed moral qualities so powerful, that it did not sink into a mere leaden reaction, Arnold attributed to the influence of Edmund Burke. Indeed Burke succeeded in death, beyond his own last expectations, at his labor of upholding the order of civilization. "The communication of the dead is tongued with fire beyond the language of the living." Let me add to the name of Edmund Burke the great names of Samuel Johnson and Adam Smith; and permit me to suggest to you, very succinctly, how these three men of the latter half of the eighteenth century explained and defended that social and moral order which endures to our own present troubled decade.

Although the three great men knew one another, they were not intimates; Smith and Johnson, indeed, were adversaries. Burke was a practical leader of party, Johnson a poet and a critic, Smith a professor (nominally) of moral philosophy. (Actually, he at once converted his Glasgow appointment into a chair of finance and political economy.) Johnson was a Tory; Burke and Smith were Whigs. Doubtless their ghosts would be astonished to find their names joined amicably near the end of the twentieth century. Yet it may be said of them what T. S. Eliot wrote of the partisans of the English Civil Wars: they "Accept the constitution of silence/And are folded in a single party." What party, nowadays? Why, we may call it the party of order.

All three men were moralists; all were realists and shrewd observers; all gave primacy to order in the commonwealth. I propose to touch briefly upon some of their several convictions, to compare the three, and to suggest their relationships. We turn first to Burke, about whom I have written much—probably too much.

*　　　*　　　*

In 1790, when Burke published his *Reflections on the Revolution in France*, he had been a politician for thirty years. Yet his ambition it had been, in his youth, to succeed as a man of letters, eschewing "crooked politicks." Like Johnson, Burke was a man of letters who derived his politics from his ethics and his knowledge of history (as well as from his intensive practical experience, in Burke's case); but unlike Johnson, he made politics his career. It took the catastrophe of the French Revolution to divert the Whig politician from practical statecraft to consideration of the first principles of the civil social order.

When only seventeen years old, Burke had glimpsed the abyss into which the Enlightenment would tumble. "Believe me," he wrote then to a friend, "we are just on the verge of Darkness and one push drives us in—we shall all live, if we live long, to see the prophecy of the Dunciad fulfilled and the age of ignorance come around once more.... Is there no one to relieve the world from the curse of obscurity? No, not one...." And he quoted Vergil: "The Saturnian reign returns and the great order of the centuries is born anew."

By 1790, Saturn was in arms. Anacharsis Cloots wrote to Burke in May of that year that Europe should have no more Gothic architecture: Notre Dame would be pulled down, and a harmonious Temple of Reason would be erected on the cathedral's site, to be admired by all connoisseurs of the arts. But Burke resolved that the Gothic edifice of European civilization should not be submitted to the wrecker's bar. Against an armed doctrine, a revolution of moral ideas carried on by violence, Burke contended with all his power. His determination it was to refurbish "the wardrobe of a moral imagination." Passions once unchained, abstract benevolence and enlightened poses would not suffice to keep men from anarchy, Burke knew. The obscene and the terrible, the sensual and the dark, rise out of the depths when moral authority is derided. For man comes out of mystery, and is plunged back into grisly obscurity when he presumes to fancy himself the rational master of every-thing on earth. So ran Burke's burning rhetoric in his later years. There are flames of glory, and flames of damnation. We are born into a moral order, Burke told England; and if we defy that order, our end is darkness.

"Burke gives the state a soul," Hans Barth writes. "He makes it personal, he fills it with the values and contents of the individual soul. He wants to make it worthy of devotion and of the possible sacrifice of one's life." Burke perceived that the just state exists in a tension between the claims of authority and the claims of freedom. And love of country, like love of kindred or friends, Burke knew, cannot be the fruit of mere rational calculation. Nothing, he said, is more evil than the heart of a thoroughbred metaphysician—that is, of the "intellectual" who enthrones his ego and his private stock of reason upon the ruins of love, duty, and reverence.

In the Jacobins, Burke perceived the fanatics of the armed doctrine, determined to sweep away Christian love and the old rule of law—the revolt of the arrogant enterprising talents of a nation against property and the traditions of civility. It remained for the men of the Napoleonic era to coin the word "ideologue" to describe this passion for innovation, this violent eagerness to abolish the old morality and the old social order, that the New Jerusalem might be created on principles of pure reason.

To resist the Jacobins, Burke undertook what Louis Bredvold justly called "the reconstruction of social philosophy." Like Plato in another time of disorder, Burke endeavored to adapt the ancient structure of his civilization to the challenges of the age. Knowing that mankind really is governed not by the speculations of sophists, but by a "stupendous wisdom molding together the great mysterious incorporation of the human race," Burke sought to revive the understanding of "the contract of eternal society."

One of the more lively disputes over Burke's meaning has arisen from the question of whether Burke was primarily a man of enduring principles, or a champion of expediency and empiricism; whether he stood in the "great tradition" of classical thought, or was a Romantic irrationalist. This controversy seems to have been stirred up chiefly by a passage in Leo Strauss' *Natural Right and*

History. "Burke comes close to suggesting that to oppose a thoroughly evil current in human affairs is perverse if that current is sufficiently powerful," Professor Strauss wrote; "he is oblivious of the nobility of last-ditch resistance." Although the late Leo Strauss was an admirer of Burke, this observation of his has been carried by others to a general denunciation of Burke as a guide in a time of revolution.

The concluding paragraph of Burke's *Thoughts on French Affairs* (1791) is the source from which Strauss' criticism issues. "If a great change is to be made in human affairs," Burke wrote, "the minds of men will be fitted to it, the general opinions and feelings will draw that way. Every fear, every hope, will forward it; and then they, who persist in opposing this mighty current in human affairs, will appear rather to resist the decrees of Providence itself, than the mere designs of men. They will not be resolute and firm, but perverse and obstinate."

Burke's hostile critics interpret this passage to mean that in Burke's view principles change with times, and morals with climes; and that (anticipating Hegel) we ought not to oppose futilely the March of History. But this interpretation of Burke ignores Burke's actual course. Anyone interested in the matter ought to reread *Thoughts on French Affairs.* Therein Burke does not hint that perhaps the champions of religion and of things established ought to let themselves be swept away by the current of the French Revolution. On the contrary, he says that effectual opposition to the Revolution must be the work of many people, acting together intelligently; he professes his inability, as an old politician retired from Parliament and separated from his party, to do more than to declare the evil. The "mighty current" for which he hopes is an awakening of the men with "power, wisdom, and information" to the peril of the Revolution; he is asking for a surge of public opinion in support of things not born yesterday. Providence ordinarily operates through the opinions and habits and decisions of human beings, Burke had said years before; and if mankind neglects the laws for human conduct, then a vengeful providence may begin to operate. Of all men in his time, Burke was the most vehemently opposed to any compromise with Jacobinism. He would have chosen the guillotine rather than submission—or, as he put it, death with the sword in hand. He broke with friends and party, sacrificing reputation and risking bankruptcy, rather than countenance the least concession to the "peace" faction in England.

Neither an irrational devotee of the archaic, nor an apostle of the utilitarian society that was emerging near the end of his life, Edmund Burke looms larger every year, in our time, as a reluctant philosopher who apprehended moral and social order. Practical politics, he taught, is the art of the possible. We cannot alter singlehandedly the climate of opinion, or the institutions of our day, by a haughty adherence to inflexible abstract doctrines. The prudent statesman, in any epoch, must deal with prevailing opinions and customs as he finds them—though he ought to act in the light of enduring *principles* (which Burke distinguished from "abstractions," or theories not grounded in a true understanding of human nature and social institutions as they really are.)

Burke might have been many things—among those, a great economist. Adam Smith declared that Burke's economical reasoning, as expressed in *Burke's Thoughts on Scarcity,* was closer to his own than that of anyone else with whom he had not directly communicated. As editor of *The Annual Register* for many years, and architect of such elaborate pieces of legislation as the Economical Reform, Burke was intimately acquainted with the science of statistics in its eighteenth-century genesis. Yet Burke often expressed his dislike of "sophisters, economists, and calculators," by whom the glory of Europe was extinguished. Elsewhere in the *Reflections,* he argues that industry and commerce owe much to "ancient manners," to the spirit of a gentleman and the spirit of religion, and would fall without the support of those ancient manners; yet he remarks with some contempt that "commerce, and trade, and manufacture" are "the gods of our economical politicians." Despite the Whigs' commercial connections, Burke remains strongly attached to the agricultural and rural interests. He rebukes obsession with economic concerns, perceiving that society is something vaster and nobler than a mere commercial contract.

Burke reviewed favorably *The Wealth of Nations* in *The Annual Register*, and occasionally met Adam Smith at the Club, in London. Smith was Burke's host in Edinburgh, in 1784, and they met there again in 1785; Smith obtained Burke's nomination to the Royal Society of Edinburgh. They were friendly, in short, but not close collaborators. Many parallels may be drawn between their respective remarks on political economy; but it should be noted that Smith, in his social assumptions, was more of an individualist than was Burke. I suspect that Burke may have been a trifle uneasy with Smith because of Smith's intimate friendship with the great skeptic David Hume, against whose first principles Burke set his face. (For his part, Hume desired Burke's friendship, and it was Hume who first introduced Smith to Burke's writings, telling him to send a copy of his *Theory of Moral Sentiments* to "Burke, an Irish gentleman, who wrote lately a very pretty treatise on the Sublime.")

With Samuel Johnson, Burke's connection was dearer and more interesting. We take up the great man of Gough Square.

*   *   *

"The first Whig was the Devil." A good many people know little more of Samuel Johnson's politics than this witticism, which does suggest, indeed, Johnson's emphasis on ordination and subordination. But Johnson was a political thinker of importance, though no abstract metaphysician in politics.

It will not do to look at Johnson through the spectacles of "the Whig interpretation of history" or on the basis of silly commentaries in popular literature-textbooks which result from ignorance of Johnson's doctrines and milieu. The political Johnson was a reasonable, moderate, and generous champion of order, quick to sustain just authority, but suspicious of unchecked power. If one analyzes his Tory pamphlet *Taxation No Tyranny*, one finds that Johnson merely was stating the long accepted and still valid definition of the word "sovereignty" as a term of politics—not advocating absolutism.

There runs through Johnson's works a strong vein of disillusion and doubt of human powers, a sense of the vanity of human wishes. This is part and parcel of the Christian dogmata that governed Johnson's life. Certainly it shaped his political convictions. Dr. Raymond English speaks of "the rather brutal skeptical streak in Johnson's Toryism. It seems to me that Johnson is rather like Dean Inge in that he combines a profound mystical Christian faith with a fierce pessimism about practical politics. Possibly one should compare both of these to St. Augustine, for whom the fall of man had rendered natural law a somewhat inadequate basis for political authority. In a slightly different way, Fitzjames Stephen plays upon a similar theme."

Neither Burke nor Johnson would have been pleased to be styled a "political philosopher." Perhaps Johnson, in his political aspect, is best described as a "statist"—which word has a neutral character in Johnson's *Dictionary*. What Ross Hoffman said of Burke is even more true of Johnson: "He took his first principles in politics from the Authorized Version and the Book of Common Prayer." Granville Hicks once wrote of Robert Louis Stevenson, "The Tory has always insisted that if men would cultivate the individual virtues, social problems would take care of themselves." This is true in essence of Johnson's view of human nature and society; yet Johnson did not ignore the part of institutions in a tolerable social order. Far from being an absolutist, he stood for the rule of law in a polity, the *libido dominandi* checked by custom and Christian doctrine.

"The Whigs will live and die in the heresy that the world is governed by little tracts and pamphlets," Walter Scott wrote once—Scott, who stood directly in the line of Johnson. Into that heresy Samuel Johnson did not slip. His politics did not come from sixteenth- or seventeenth- or eighteenth-century tracts, but from experience of the world, from much reading of the politically wise over many centuries, and from what Eliot calls "the idea of a Christian society," with its concepts of ordination and subordination, charity and justice, divine love, and mortal fallibility.

Whig magnates and demagogic "patriots," Johnson was convinced, meant to break in upon the balance of orders and powers that was eighteenth-century England—an argument later advanced by Disraeli, in the preface to *Sybil.* For Johnson, the Devil was the first Whig because the Whigs stood for insubordination and innovation; Burke was a "bottomless Whig," in Johnson's epithet, because the Whigs clung to no well-defined principles of social order, but lived by expediency and extemporization. Such ejaculations about Whigs, nevertheless, often extracted by Boswell from Johnson in moments whimsical or splenetic, were not Johnson's deeper reflections. At Boswell's request, in 1781, Johnson set down in writing the distinctions between Whig and Tory:

> A wise Tory and a wise Whig, I believe, will agree. Their principles are the same, though their modes of thinking are different. A high Tory makes government unintelligible; it is lost in the clouds. A violent Whig makes it impracticable; he is for allowing so much liberty to every man, that there is not enough power to govern any man. The prejudice of the Tory is for establishment; the prejudice of the Whig is for innovation. A Tory does not wish to give more real power to Government; but that Government should have more reverence. Then they differ as to the Church. The Tory is not for giving more

legal power to the Clergy, but wishes they should have a considerable influence, founded on the opinion of mankind; the Whig is for limiting and watching them with a narrow jealousy.

As Leslie Stephen wrote, "The Whigs were invincibly suspicious of parsons." Johnson was not so suspicious.

It may be perceived that the first principles of such a Tory as Johnson and such a Whig as Burke were very nearly identical. To both, the new politics of the dawning era, whether the notions of Rousseau or of Bentham, were abhorrent. Both Johnson and Burke recognized a transcendent moral order, subscribed to the wisdom of the species, were attached to custom and precedent, upheld the idea of the Christian magistrate, and adhered to the venerable concepts of Christian charity and community. The narrow contract-theory of Locke, the skepticism of Hume, the tendency toward individualism in the writings of Smith—these were inimical to both the Toryism of Johnson and the Whiggery of Burke.

When, at the end of his career, Burke refuted Goldsmith's playful reproach by giving to mankind what once he had owed to party, the Old Whig's principles were almost indistinguishable from those of his friend Johnson, who had died before the Deluge of 1789. "I can live very well with Burke," Johnson had said; "I love his knowledge, his diffusion, and affluence of conversation." Or, on another occasion, "Yes, Sir, if a man were to go by chance at the same time with Burke under a shed to shun a shower, he would say—'we have had an extraordinary man here.'"

It was otherwise with Johnson and Smith. Walter Scott, in a letter to John Wilson Croker written in 1829, records someone's account of a meeting between Johnson and Smith at Glasgow—or rather, the account of it said to have been extracted not long later from Adam Smith:

Smith, obviously much discomposed, came into a party who were playing at cards. The Doctor's appearance suspended the amusement, for as all knew he was to meet Johnson that evening, every one was curious to hear what had passed. Adam Smith, whose temper seemed much ruffled, answered only at first, 'He is a brute! He is a brute!' Upon closer examination it appeared that Dr. Johnson no sooner saw Smith than he brought forward a charge against him for something in his famous letter on the death of Hume. Smith said he had vindicated the truth of the statement. 'And what did the Doctor say?' was the universal query: 'Why, he said—he said—' said Smith, with the deepest impression of resentment, 'he said—You *lie!*' 'And what did you reply?' 'I said, "You are a son of a bitch!..."' On such terms did these two great moralists meet and part, and such was the classic dialogue betwixt them.

Birkbeck Hill doubts the veracity of this incident; however that may be, it represents well enough the degree of esteem in which the two moral philosophers held each other. We shall touch upon the reasons for this animosity as we sketch the Scots professor.

*   *   *

The unacknowledged debt to Adam Smith's writings is even larger than the influence generally recognized. One finds in the volumes of John Adams, for instance, a very shrewd and seemingly original (so far as any psychology can be called original) analysis of the moral nature of man. At least I took it to be original, until recent years; then I discovered that many of Adams's passages, and indeed the

greater part of his convictions on this grand subject, are borrowed—
almost plagiarized—from Smith's *Theory of Moral Sentiments,*
published in 1759. (Similarly, much of the account of the American
Revolution in John Marshall's *Life of Washington* is lifted from
Burke's *Annual Register.*) America's borrowing from the Old World
did not terminate in 1776.

But it was as a financier, rather than as a moralist, that Smith
moved the men of his time. I possess and use the third edition of *An
Inquiry into the Nature and Causes of the Wealth of Nations,* published
in 1786—the edition owned and so highly praised by Robert Burns.
The great reason for the book's practical success was its combination of genuine learning with a profusion of canny Scottish
commonsensical observations—and the whole written lucidly and
dispassionately. Charles James Fox said of the earlier editions, in an
address to the House of Commons in 1783:

> There was a maxim laid down in an excellent book on the
> Wealth of Nations, which had been ridiculed for its
> simplicity, but which was indisputable as to its truth. In
> this book it was stated, that the only way to become rich
> was to manage matters so as to make one's expenses not
> exceed one's income. This maxim applied equally to an
> individual and to a nation. The proper line of conduct,
> therefore, was by a well-directed economy to retrench
> every current expense, and to making as large a saving
> during the peace as possible.... He should not think that,
> as prospect of recovery was opened, the country was likely to
> be restored to its former greatness, unless ministers contrive
> some measure or other to pay off a part at least of the National
> Debt, and did something towards establishing an actual
> sinking fund, capable of being applied to a constant and
> sensible diminution of the public burdens.

The phrase "applied equally to an individual" on the lips of the profligate Fox may have provoked at least smiles from the opposite benches. For that matter, Smith himself was not much favored with the goods of fortune. (Fox's praise did much increase the sales of *The Wealth of Nations,* so enlarging its author's resources.) To Charles Butler, Fox later confessed that he never actually read Smith: "There is something in all these subjects which passes my comprehension; something so wide, that I could never embrace them myself or find any one who did." Of how many other public men who quote philosophers is Fox's confession true!

Yet what the Arch-Whig could not apprehend, the Arch-Tory did. The younger William Pitt found in Smith the sagacity demanded for financing a quarter-century of war. In his Budget Speech of 17 February 1792, Pitt discussed as one of the causes of the increase of national wealth "the constant accumulation of capital, wherever it is not obstructed by some public calamity or by some mistaken and mischievous policy. Simple and obvious as this principle is, and felt and observed as it must have been in a greater or lesser degree even from the earliest periods, I doubt whether it has ever been fully developed and sufficiently explained but in an author of our own time, now unfortunately no more (I mean the author of the celebrated treatise on the Wealth of Nations) whose extensive knowledge of detail and depth of philosophical research will, I believe, furnish the best solution of every question connected with the history of commerce, and with the system of political economy."

In America, during the same period, *The Wealth of Nations* runs through all of Alexander Hamilton's principal financial reports. Also Hamilton's opponents drew upon the Smith well of economic wisdom for some of their arguments. Ever since that age, on both sides of the Atlantic, those who sit in the seats of the mighty either have given lip-service to Adam Smith or else have employed his great book without bothering to cite the source of their prescience.

Great influence sometimes proceeds from small and obscure origins. Smith's observation of the decline of the small industry of nail-making in his native burgh of Kirkcaldy led him to reflect upon the division of labor; and his analysis of the division of labor grew into *The Wealth of Nations*. Very much the Scottish professor, Smith was so engrossed lifelong by the subject of the division of labor that on one occasion he was nearly extinguished by it. The London *Times*, in its obituary of Smith (who died in 1790), somewhat unkindly recorded one professorial episode of this character. When Charles Townshend, the politician, visited Glasgow, Dr. Smith took him to see a tannery:

They were standing on a plank which had been laid across the tanning pit; the Doctor, who was talking warmly on his favorite subject, the division of labour, forgetting the precarious ground on which he stood, plunged headlong into the nauseous pool. He was dragged out, stripped, and carried with blankets, and conveyed home on a sedan chair, where, having recovered of the shock of this unexpected cold bath, he complained bitterly that he must leave life with all his affairs in the greatest disorder; which was considered an affectation, as his transactions had been few and his fortune was nothing.

Actually, Smith survived this disaster; and his reputation has survived the crash of empires. Not so his Glasgow, or his Kirkcaldy. Until recently, Glasgow was one of the great stone-built cities of the world; but in recent decades public policies for which the most kindly word is "inane" have reduced nearly the whole of the old city to total dereliction or howling slum—by ignoring, along with much else, certain principles expounded in *The Wealth of Nations*. As for Kirkcaldy, where linoleum supplanted nails, an American documentary film about that burgh was produced a few years ago—or rather, a film about Smith's life and work, in which there were scenes of modern Kirkcaldy, represented as a hive of industry of the sort made possible by the triumph of Smith's economic ideas. Kirkcaldy I happen to know too well; and the bustling industry shown in the film is mostly a socialist operation, run at a loss; and Kirkcaldy has one of the highest unemployment rates in Britain; and nearly all the curious old buildings associated with Smith and Kirkcaldy of his time have been thoughtfully demolished, to be replaced by ugliness or by rubble-strewn vacant lots. A prophet is not without honor....

But I digress. Earlier I promised to point out why Johnson did not love Smith. One reason for this is that Smith did not love Johnson. In his early Rhetorical Lectures, Smith proclaimed, "Of all writers ancient and modern, he that keeps the greatest distance from common sense is Dr. Samuel Johnson." On the other hand, Smith once told Boswell that "Johnson knew more than any man alive." Boswell had studied under Smith at Glasgow; on one occasion he mentioned to Johnson that Smith preferred rhyme to blank verse. "Sir," replied Johnson, "I was once in the company with Smith, and we did not take to each other; but had I known that he loved Rhyme as much as you tell me he does, I should have hugged him." The two did meet later occasionally at the Club, in London, and seemingly were civil enough in disputes. But Smith had reviewed Johnson's *Dictionary* in hostile fashion; and for that Johnson did not forgive him.

These small matters aside, a gulf was widening even in the last quarter of the eighteen century between men of intellect who professed Christian dogmata, and men of intellect who had their liberal doubts. Johnson and Burke were of the former party; Smith was Hume's warmest admirer. As Manning said, all differences of opinion are theological at bottom. Smith was no atheist; yet his animadversion on the church, in the first edition of *The Wealth of*

Nations, disquieted even his good friend Hugh Blair, the famous liberal preacher of the age, who wrote to Smith in April, 1776: "But in your system about the Church I cannot wholly agree with you. Independency was at no time a possible or practicable system. The little sects you speak of would, for many reasons, have combined together into greater bodies and done much mischief to society." By such remarks, Smith had raised up formidable adversaries, Blair told him. Johnson was one such, no doubt; and Burke, though an energetic friend to religious toleration, was no admirer of the dissidence of dissent.

Finally, there were differences of temperament and social assumptions among these three. Burke was very much an Irishman, Johnson very much an Englishman—and Smith redoubtably a Scot. His mind was the mind of a Scottish Whig, however urbanely professorial Smith might be. William Butler Yeats, in his poem "The Seven Sages," suggests that Burke, though a Whig nominally and occupationally, deep down detested the whole Whig cast of mind and character:

> *All hated Whiggery; but what is Whiggery?*
> *A levelling, rancorous, rational sort of mind*
> *That never looked out of the eye of a saint*
> *Or out of drunkard's eye.*

Johnson feared Hell and venerated saints; Burke sometimes was facetious in his cups, and read "the fathers of the fourteenth century." Smith appears to have been sober always, and not given to visions of the world beyond the world. It is a great way from Kirkcaldy to Dublin or to Litchfield.

Be that as it may, Burke and Johnson and Smith, in their several ways, described and defended those beliefs and institutions that maintain the beneficent tension of order and freedom. All were pillars of what Burke called "this world of reason, and order, and peace, and virtue, and fruitful penitence"; all knew how men and nations may make choices that cast them "into the antagonist world of madness, discord, vice, confusion, and unavailing sorrow." Such frantic choices are being made two centuries after these three lived and breathed and had their being. So I do not find it at all surprising that some among us, in what we hope will be an era of concentration rather than of eccentricity, are reading afresh Burke and Johnson and Smith.

XX

Libertarians: Chirping Sectaries

Any discussion of the relationships between conservatives (who now, to judge by public-opinion polls, are a majority among American citizens) and libertarians (who, as tested by recent elections, remain a tiny though unproscribed minority) naturally commences with an inquiry into what these disparate groups hold in common. These two bodies of opinion share a detestation of collectivism. They set their faces against the totalist state and the heavy hand of bureaucracy. That much is obvious enough.

What else do conservatives and libertarians profess in common? The answer to that question is simple: nothing. Nor will they ever. To talk of forming a league or coalition between these two is like advocating a union of ice and fire.

The ruinous failing of the ideologues who call themselves libertarians is their fanatic attachment to a simple solitary principle—that is, to the notion of personal freedom as the whole end of the civil social order, and indeed of human existence. The libertarians are oldfangled folk, in the sense that they live by certain abstractions of the nineteenth century. They carry to absurdity the doctrines of John Stuart Mill (before Mill's wife converted him to socialism, that is). To understand the mentality of the libertarians, it may be useful to remind ourselves of a little book published more than a hundred and twenty years ago: John Stuart Mill's *On Liberty*. Arguments that were flimsy in 1859 (and were soundly refuted by James Fitzjames Stephen) have become farcical today. So permit me to digress concerning Mill's famous essay. Some books tend to form the character of their age; others to reflect it; and Mill's *Liberty* is of the latter order.

That tract is a product of the peacefulness and optimism of Victorian England; written at the summit of what Bagehot calls the Age of Discussion, it is a voice from out the vanished past of nineteenth-century meliorism. The future, it turned out, was not to the school of Mill. As Mill himself was the last of the line of British empiricists, so his *Liberty*, with its foreboding remarks on the despotism of the masses, was more an epilogue to middle-class liberalism than a rallying-cry.

James Mill, John Stuart Mill's austere doctrinaire father (what sour folk many of these zealots for liberty turn themselves into!) subjected his son to a rigorous course of private study. By the time he was eight years old, J. S. Mill knew nearly everything that a doctor of philosophy is supposed to know nowadays; but his intellect was untouched by the higher imagination, and for that Mill groped in vain all his life long. J. S. Mill became all head and no heart, in which character he represents Jeremy Bentham; yet in truth, it was Mill himself, rather than Bentham, who turned into defecated intellect.

Mill exhibited but one failing, so far as emotions go, and that not an uncommon one—being too fond of another man's wife. F. A. Hayek has discussed this association and its consequences for Mill and his followers. Mill eventually married this dismaying bluestocking, Harriet Taylor, the forerunner of today's feminist militant. He was devoted to her, and she to humanitarian abstractions. It was under her tutelage that he wrote *On Liberty*. The intellectual ancestors of today's libertarians were no very jolly crew.

"By slaying all his animal spirits," Ruth Borchard writes of Mill, "he was utterly cut off from his instincts—instinct for life, instinctive understanding of nature, of human nature in general and of his own in particular." It might be interesting to examine how these deficiencies in Mill characterized and vitiated the whole liberal movement in English and American thought; and how they affect the vestigial form of nineteenth-century liberalism that now styles itself "libertarianism." But we must pass on, remarking only that this imperfect apprehension of human nature is readily discerned in the pages of Mill's essay *On Liberty*.

Now the younger Mill, in his essays on Coleridge and Bentham, had remarked truly that the cardinal error of Bentham was his supposition that the affairs of men may be reduced to a few simple formulas, to be applied universally and inflexibly—when actually the great mysterious incorporation of the human race is infinitely subtle and complex, not to be dominated by neat little abstractions. Yet into precisely this same pit Mill falls in his *Liberty*. In his introductory chapter, he declares his object to be the assertion of "one very simple principle, as entitled to govern absolutely the dealings of society with the individual in the way of compulsion and control, whether the means used by physical force in the form of legal penalties, or the moral coercion of public opinion. That principle is, that the sole end for which mankind are warranted, individually or collectively, in interfering with the liberty of action of any of their number, is self-protection. That the only purpose for which power can be rightfully exercised over any member of a civilized community, against his will, is to prevent harm to others."

This seems an attractive solitary simple principle. It sufficiently defines the convictions of twentieth-century libertarians, I believe.

But the trouble with it is that solitary simple principles, however tidy, really do not describe human behavior, and certainly cannot govern it.

James Fitzjames Stephen, a forthright man of affairs and a scholar in the law, perceived with irritation that fallacy which makes Mill's *Liberty* a frail reed in troubled times; and in *Liberty, Equality, Fraternity*, which Stephen published in 1873, he set upon Mill with a whip of scorpions. John Stuart Mill, in Stephen's eyes, was hopelessly naive:

> To me the question whether liberty is a good or a bad thing [Stephen wrote] appears as irrational as the question whether fire is a good or a bad thing? It is both good and bad according to time, place, and circumstance, and a complete answer to the question, in what cases is liberty good and in what is it bad? would involve not merely a universal history of mankind, but a complete solution of the problems which such a history would offer. I do not believe that the state of our knowledge is such as to enable us to enunciate any 'very simple principle as entitled to govern absolutely the dealings of society with the individual in the way of compulsion and control.' We must proceed in a far more cautious way, and confine ourselves to such remarks as experience suggests about the advantages and disadvantages of compulsion and liberty respectively in particular cases.

In every principal premise of his argument, Stephen declared, Mill suffered from an inadequate understanding of human nature and history. All the great movements of humankind, Stephen said, have been achieved by force, not by free discussion; and if we leave force out of our calculations, very soon we will be subject to the intolerant wills of men who know no scruples about employing force against us. (So, one may remark, many twentieth-century libertarians would have had us stand defenseless before the Soviet Russians.) It is consummate folly to tolerate every variety of opinion, on every topic, out of devotion to an abstract "liberty"; for opinion soon finds its expression in action, and the fanatics whom we tolerated will not tolerate us when they have power.

The fierce current of events, in our century, has supplied the proof for Stephen's case. Was the world improved by free discussion of the Nazis' thesis that Jews ought to be treated as less than human? Just this subject was presented to the population of one of the most advanced and most thoroughly schooled nations of the modern world; and then the crew of adventurers who had contrived to win the argument proceeded to act after the fashion with which we now are dreadfully familiar. We have come to understand, to our cost, what Burke meant by a "licentious toleration." An incessant zeal for repression is not the answer to the complex difficulties of liberty and order, either. What Stephen was saying, however, and what we recognize now, is that liberty cannot be maintained or extended by an abstract appeal to free discussion, sweet reasonableness, and solitary simple principle.

Since Mill, the libertarians have forgotten nothing and learned nothing. Mill dreaded, and they dread today, obedience to the dictates of custom. In our time, the real danger is that custom and prescription and tradition may be overthrown utterly among us—for has not that occurred already in most of the world?—by neoterism, the lust for novelty; and that men will be no better than the flies of a summer, oblivious to the wisdom of their ancestors, and forming every opinion merely under the pressure of the fad, the foible, the passion of the hour.

It may be objected that libertarian notions extend back beyond the time of Mill. Indeed they do; and they had been refuted before Stephen wrote, as John Adams refuted them in his exchange of letters with Thomas Jefferson and with John Taylor of Caroline. The first Whig was the devil, Samuel Johnson informs us; it might be truer to say that the devil was the original libertarian. "Lo, I am proud!" The perennial libertarian, like Satan, can bear no authority temporal or spiritual. He desires to be different, in morals as in politics. In a highly tolerant society like that of America today, such defiance of authority on principle may lead to perversity on principle, for lack of anything more startling to do; there is no great gulf fixed between libertarianism and libertinism.

Thus the typical libertarian of our day delights in eccentricity—including, often, sexual eccentricity (a point observed by that mordant psychologist Dr. Ernest van den Haag). Did not John Stuart Mill himself commend eccentricity as a defense against deadening democratic conformity? He rejoices, our representative libertarian, in strutting political eccentricity, as in strutting moral eccentricity. But, as Stephen commented on Mill, "Eccentricity is far more often a mark of weakness than a mark of strength. Weakness wishes, as a rule, to attract attention by trifling distinctions, and strength wishes to avoid it."

Amen to that. Passing from the nineteenth century to the twentieth, by 1929 we encounter a writer very unlike Mill exposing the absurdities of affected eccentricity and of doctrinaire libertarianism: G. K. Chesterton. Gabriel Gale, the intuitive hero of Chesterton's collection of stories entitled *The Poet and the Lunatics,* speaks up for centricity: "Genius oughtn't to be eccentric! It ought to be the core of the cosmos, not on the revolving edges. People seem to think it a compliment to accuse one of being an outsider, and to talk about the eccentricities of genius. What would they think if I said I only wish to God I had the centricities of genius?"

No one ever has accused libertarians of being afflicted with the centricities of genius: for the dream of an absolute private freedom is one of those visions which issue from between the gates of ivory; and the dreadful speed with which society moves today flings the libertarians outward through centrifugal force, even to the outer darkness, where there is wailing and gnashing of teeth. The final emancipation from religion, convention, and custom; and order is annihilation—"whirled/ Beyond the circuit of the shuddering bear/ In fractured atoms."

In *The Poet and the Lunatics*, Chesterton offers us a parable of such licentious freedom: a story called "the Yellow Bird." To an English country house comes Professor Ivanhov, a Russian scholar who has published *The Psychology of Liberty*. He is a zealot for emancipation, expansion, the elimination of limits. He begins by liberating a canary from its cage—to be torn to pieces in the forest. He proceeds to liberate the goldfish by smashing their bowl. He ends by blowing up himself and the beautiful old house where he has been a guest.

"What exactly is liberty?" inquires a spectator of this series of events—Gabriel Gale, Chesterton's mouthpiece. "First and foremost, surely, it is the power of a thing to be itself. In some ways the yellow bird was free in the cage. It was free to be alone. It was free to sing. In the forest its feathers would be torn to pieces and its voice choked forever. Then I began to think that being oneself, which is liberty, is itself limitation. We are limited by our brains and bodies; and if we break out, we cease to be ourselves, and, perhaps, to be anything."

The Russian psychologist could not endure the necessary conditions of human existence; he must eliminate all limits; he could not endure the "round prison" of the overarching sky. But his alternative was annihilation for himself and his lodging; and he took that alternative. He ceased to be anything but fractured atoms. That is the ultimate freedom of the devoted libertarian. If, *par impossible*, American society should accept the leadership of libertarian ideologues.

*   *   *

Notwithstanding, there is something to be said for the distintegrated

Professor Ivanhov—relatively speaking. With reference to some remarks of mine, there writes to me Mr. Marion Montgomery, the Georgia novelist and critic: "The libertarians give me the willies. I much prefer the Russian anarchists, who at least have a deeply disturbed moral sensibility (that Dostoevsky makes good use of), to the libertarian anarchists. There is a decadent fervor amongst some of the latter which makes them an unwelcome cross for conservatism to bear."

Just so. The representative libertarian of this decade is humorless, intolerant, self-righteous, badly schooled, and dull. At least the oldfangled Russian anarchist was bold, lively, and knew which sex he belonged to.

But surely, surely I must be misrepresenting the breed? Don't I know self-proclaimed libertarians who are kindly old gentlemen, God-fearing, patriotic, chaste, well endowed with the goods of fortune? Yes, I do know such. They are the people who through misapprehension put up the cash for the fantastics. Such gentlemen call themselves "libertarians" merely because they believe in personal freedom, and do not understand to what extravagance they lend their names by subsidizing doctrinaire "libertarian" causes and publications. If a person describes himself as "libertarian" because he believes in an enduring moral order, the Constitution of the United States, free enterprise, and old American ways of life—why, actually he is a conservative with imperfect understanding of the general terms of politics.

It is not such well-intentioned but mislabeled men whom I am holding up to obloquy here. Rather, I am exposing the pretensions of the narrow doctrinaires who have imprisoned themselves within a "libertarian" ideology as confining and as unreal as Marxism—if less persuasive than that fell delusion.

Why are these doctrinaire libertarians, with a few exceptions, such very odd people—the sort who give hearty folk like Marion Montgomery the willies? Why do genuine conservatives feel an aversion to close association with them? (Incidentally, now and again one reads of two camps of alleged conservatives: "traditionalist conservatives and libertarian conservatives." This is as if a newspaperman were to classify Christians as "Protestant Christians and Muslim Christians.") Why is an alliance between conservatives and libertarians inconceivable? Why, indeed, would such articles of confederation undo whatever gains conservatives have made in this United States?

Because genuine libertarians are mad—metaphysically mad. Lunacy repels, and political lunacy especially. I do not mean that they are dangerous; they are repellent merely, like certain unfortunate inmates of "mental homes." They do not endanger our country and our civilization, because they are few, and seem likely to become fewer. (I refer here, of course, to our homegrown American libertarians, and not to those political sects, among them the Red Brigades of Italy, which have carried libertarian notions to grander and bolder lengths.) There exists no peril that American national policy, foreign or domestic, will be in the least affected by libertarian arguments; the good old causes of Bimetallism, Single Tax, or Prohibition enjoy a better prospect of success than do the programs of libertarianism. But one does not choose as a partner even a harmless political lunatic.

I mean that the libertarians make up what T. S. Eliot called a "chirping sect," an ideological clique forever splitting into sects still smaller and odder, but rarely conjugating. Such petty political sectaries Edmund Burke pictured as "the insects of the hour," as noisy as they are ineffectual against the conservative power of the browsing cattle in an English pasture. If one has chirping sectaries for friends, one doesn't need any enemies.

What do I mean when I say that today's American libertarians are metaphysically mad, and so repellent? Why, the dogmas of libertarianism have been refuted so often, both dialectically and by the hard knocks of experience, that it would be dull work to rehearse here the whole tale of folly. Space wanting, I set down below merely a few of the more conspicuous insufficiencies of libertarianism as a credible moral and political mode of belief. It is such differences from the conservatives' understanding of the human condition that make inconceivable any coalition of conservatives and libertarians.

1. The great line of division in modern politics—as Eric Voegelin reminds us—is not between totalitarians on the one hand and liberals (or libertarians) on the other; rather, it lies between all those who believe in some sort of transcendent moral order, on one side, and on the other side all those who take this ephemeral existence of ours for the be-all and end-all—to be devoted chiefly to producing and consuming. In this discrimination between the sheep and the goats, the libertarians must be classified with the goats—that is, as utilitarians admitting no transcendent sanctions for conduct. In effect, they are converts to Marx's dialectical materialism; so conservatives draw back from them on the first principle of all.

2. In any society, order is the first need of all. Liberty and justice may be established only after order is tolerably secure. But the libertarians give primacy to an abstract liberty. Conservatives, knowing that "liberty inheres in some sensible object," are aware that true freedom can be found only within the framework of a social order, such as the constitutional order of these United States. In exalting an absolute and indefinable "liberty" at the expense of order, the libertarians imperil the very freedoms they praise.

3. What binds society together? The libertarians reply that the cement of society (so far as they will endure any binding at all) is self-interest, closely joined to the nexus of cash payment. But the conservatives declare that society is a community of souls, joining the dead, the living, and those yet unborn; and that it coheres through what Aristotle called friendship and Christians call love of neighbor.

4. Libertarians (like anarchists and Marxists) generally believe that human nature is good, though damaged by certain social

institutions. Conservatives, on the contrary, hold that "in Adam's fall we sinned all": human nature, though compounded of both good and evil, is irremediably flawed; so the perfection of society is impossible, all human beings being imperfect. Thus the libertarian pursues his illusory way to Utopia, and the conservative knows that for the path to Avernus.

5. The libertarian takes the state for the great oppressor. But the conservative finds that the state is ordained of God. In Burke's phrases, "He who gave us our nature to be perfected by our virtue, willed also the necessary means of its perfection. He willed therefore the state—its connexion with the source and original archetype of all perfection." Without the state, man's condition is poor, nasty, brutish, and short—as Augustine argued, many centuries before Hobbes. The libertarians confound the state with government. But government—as Burke continued —"is a contrivance of human wisdom to provide for human *wants.*" Among the more important of those human wants is "a sufficient restraint upon their passions. Society requires not only that the passions of individuals should be subjected, but that even in the mass and body, as well as in the individual, the inclinations of men should frequently be thwarted, their will controlled, and their passions brought into subjection. This can be done only *by a power out of themselves;* and not, in the exercise of its function, subject to that will and to those passions which it is its office to bridle and subdue." In short, a primary function of government is restraint; and that is anathema to libertarians, though an article of faith to conservatives.

6. The libertarian thinks that this world is chiefly a stage for the swaggering ego; the conservative finds himself instead a pilgrim in a realm of mystery and wonder, where duty, discipline, and sacrifice are required—and where the reward is that love which passeth all understanding. The conservative regards the libertarian as impious, in the sense of the old Roman *pietas:* that is, the libertarian does not venerate ancient beliefs and customs, or the natural world, or his

country, or the immortal spark in his fellow men. The cosmos of the libertarian is an arid loveless realm, a "round prison." "I am, and none else beside me," says the libertarian. "We are made for cooperation, like the hands, like the feet," replies the conservative, in the phrases of Marcus Aurelius.

Why multiply these profound differences? Those I have expressed already will suffice to demonstrate the utter incompatibility of the two positions. If one were to content himself simply with contrasting the beliefs of conservatives and libertarians as to the nature of liberty, still we could arrive at no compromise. There is the liberty of the wolf, John Adams wrote to John Taylor; and there is the liberty of civilized man. The conservative will not tolerate ravening liberty; with Dostoevski, he knows that those who commence with absolute liberty will end with absolute tyranny. He maintains, rather, what Burke called "chartered rights," developed slowly and painfully in the civil social order, sanctioned by prescription.

Yet even if libertarian and conservative can affirm nothing in common, may they not agree upon a negative? May they not take common ground against the pretensions of the modern state to omnicompetence? Certainly both bodies of opinion find that modern governments, even in such constitutional orders as the United States, seem afflicted by the *libido dominandi.* The primary function of government, the conservatives say, is to keep the peace: by repelling foreign enemies, by maintaining the bed of justice domestically. When government goes much beyond this end, it falls into difficulty, not being contrived for the management of the whole of life. Thus far, indeed libertarian and conservative hold something in common. But the libertarians, rashly hurrying to an opposite extreme, would deprive government of effective power to undertake the common defense or to restrain the passionate and the unjust. With the libertarians in mind, conservatives repeat Burke's aphorism: "Men of intemperate mind never can be free. Their passions forge their fetters."

So in the nature of things conservatives and libertarians can conclude no friendly pact. Conservatives have no intention of compromising with socialists; but even such an alliance, ridiculous though it would be, is more nearly conceivable than the coalition of conservatives and libertarians. The socialists at least declare the existence of some sort of moral order; the libertarians are quite bottomless.

It is of high importance, indeed, that American conservatives dissociate themselves altogether from the little sour remnant called libertarians. In a time requiring long views and self-denial, alliance with a faction founded upon doctrinaire selfishness would be absurd—and practically damaging. It is not merely that coopera-tion with a tiny chirping sect would be valueless politically; more, such an association would tend to discredit the conservatives, giving aid and comfort to the collective adversaries of ordered freedom. When heaven and earth have passed away, perhaps the conservative mind and the libertarian mind may be joined in synthesis—but not until then. Meanwhile, I venture to predict, the more intelligent and conscientious persons within the libertarian remnant will tend to settle for politics as the art of the possible, so shifting into the conservative camp.

XXI

The Degradation of the Democratic Dogma

I have chosen for my subject the degradation of the democratic dogma, a title I take from the writings of Henry and Brooks Adams. They found American democracy in process of degradation more than a century ago. The decay of the American Presidency from George Washington to Ulysses S. Grant, Henry Adams remarked, refuted altogether Darwin's theory of evolution. To a similar thesis I shall return presently.

But first, indulge me in some observations concerning the present condition of what is called "democracy" near the close of the twentieth century. We are informed by certain voices that soon all the world will be democratic. But whether or not, the American mode of democratic government prevails, the abstract ideology called democratism that any government which has obtained a majority of votes be received as "democratic." Enthusiasts for unrestricted democracy presumably forget that Adolph Hitler, too, was democratically elected and sustained by popular plebiscites.

Alexis de Tocqueville warned his contemporaries against "democratic despotism," twentieth-century writers discuss "totalist democracy."

I am suggesting that democracy—literally, "the rule of the crowd"—is a term so broad and vague as to signify everything or nothing. The American democracy, a unique growth although an offshoot from British culture, innocent of ideology's fury—functioned fairly well in the past because of peculiar beliefs and conditions: a patrimony of ordered freedom, and especially, as Tocqueville pointed out, Americans' *mores,* or moral habits. What is called "democracy" today in most of the world—and nearly every regime represents itself as democratic—bears much resemblance to America's political and social pattern as the oar of the boat does to the ore of the mine. All that these regimes maintain in common is a claim that they rule with the assent of the majority of the people. The tyranny of the majority can be more oppressive, and more effectual, than the tyranny of a single person.

*   *   *

Some neoconservatives' demands nowadays that all the world be thoroughly democratized overnight remind me strongly of a similar enthusiasm not long after the end of the Second World War. Gentlemen such as Chester Bowles then proclaimed that Africa, liberated from European domination, promptly would rejoice in an array of democracies on the American model. The United States took measures, then and later, to accelerate this happy progress— economic restraints upon trade of one sort or another with Portugal, Rhodesia, and latterly the Republic of South Africa. We all know, of course, how blissfully democratic Angola, Mozambique, Guinea, and Rhodesia (now Zimbabwe) are today. America's democracy is not readily transplanted overseas. If anybody emerges alive from the present agony in Somalia, will a peaceful democracy,

told by the nose, soon come to pass there? Was the ejection, after
the Second World War, of the Italian government from part of
Somaliland, and the withdrawal of the British administrators from
another portion of that territory, a victory for democracy in Africa?
Ask the Somali dead.

My point is this, merely to shout the word *democracy* is not to
bring into being a society endowed with order, justice, and freedom.
Those blessings grow but slowly, and by good nurture. The, roots
of the American democratic republic run back through hundreds of
years of American, British, and European experience. While we
prate about exporting American democracy to Eastern Europe,
Africa, and Asia—although, as Daniel Boorstin has written, "the
American Constitution is not for export"—our own political institutions seem to be crumbling. We may sink into the Latin American brand of democracy, class against class, the economy periodi-
cally ruined by inflation, with a semblance of order restored from
time to time by the military.

*   *   *

Sinclair Lewis, late in life, wrote an implausible novel entitled *It
Can't Happen Here*—a fictional affirmation that a fascist regime
might be established in the United States; the book was published
in 1935. The novel was more comical than convincing; but it does
not follow that the American democratic republic will endure for
eternity, as Rome was supposed to last. I remember clearly the
events of the American experience between, and including, the
years 1929 and 1933. I find America's social and economic and
political circumstances today markedly similar to those of that
tumultuous era. Changes still larger than those worked by Franklin
Roosevelt's New Deal may come to pass during the next several
years. Economically, the position of the United States is more
precarious than it was in 1929: our national debt is astronomical in

quantity; personal (family) debt, on the average, is more than four-fifths of a family's annual income; the apparatus of credit is vastly overexpanded; and taxes begin to be crushing. In certain of our cities, ferocious riots far exceed in magnitude the disorders of 1929-1933, and after: those riots really are proletarian risings. This is a time in which, in Yeats's lines, "The best lack all conviction, while the worst / Are full of passionate intensity."

* * *

In 1957, at Bruges, during a conference on Atlantic community, I met Amaury de Riencourt, the author of a book entitled *The Coming Caesars,* published that year, the book was very widely discussed then, but now is forgotten. Unless measures of restraint should be taken, Riencourt wrote—and taken promptly—the United States would fall under the domination of twentieth-century Caesars. Riencourt argued:

> Caesarism is not dictatorship, not the result of one man's overriding ambition; not a brutal seizure of power through revolution. It is not based on a specific doctrine or philosophy. It is essentially pragmatic and untheoretical. It is a slow, often century-old, unconscious development that ends in a voluntary surrender of a free people escaping from freedom to one autocratic master....
>
> Political power in the Western world has become increasingly concentrated in the United States, and in the office of the President within America. The power and prestige of the President have grown with the growth of America and of democracy within America, with the multiplication of economic, political, and military emergencies, with the necessity of ruling what is virtually

becoming an American empire—the universal state of a Western civilization at bay....

Caesarism can come to America constitutionally, without having to alter or break down any existing institution. The White House is already the seat of the most powerful tribunician authority ever known to history. All it needs is amplification and extension. Caesarism in America does not have to challenge the Constitution as in Rome or engage in civil warfare and cross any fateful Rubicon. It can slip in quite naturally, discreetly, through constitutional channels.

Just so. Caesarism slipped into the White House constitutionally, if not naturally, with the murder of President Kennedy in 1963. The plebiscitary democracy would elect Lyndon Johnson president in 1964; but Johnson's military failure would undo him, despite his *panem et circenses;* and a rebellious senator would strip him of the purple. If Caesars do not win their battles, they fall. In this, although not in much else, perhaps it was as well that the war in Vietnam was lost.

On a wall of my library hangs a photograph of myself with President Johnson; both of us are smiling; it is well to be civil to Caesar. It might be thought that Russell Kirk would not have been eager to visit Caesar in the Oval Office of the Imperial Mansion; indeed I was not, but, in collaboration with James McClellan, I had written not long before a biography of Robert Taft; Johnson, as a senatorial colleague, had delivered a funeral eulogy of the famous Republican; and so I was induced by the patroness of the Robert A. Taft Institute of Government to present the president with a copy of the book, at a little White House ceremony.

*   *   *

Present for that occasion in the Oval Office were two Democratic Senators who had been on good terms with Senator Taft—Byrd of Virginia and Tydings of Maryland. Lyndon Johnson towered tall and masterful, clearly a bad man to have for an adversary. The Taft book was presented, and the president exchanged some brief remarks with me; photographs were taken while my irrepressible wife strolled behind the presidential desk, examining photographs of Lady Bird, Lynda Bird, and other folk at the ranch.

True to his reputation if to naught else, President Johnson wheeled and dealt with Senator Byrd and Senator Tydings the while. He knew me for a syndicated columnist, but surely never had opened any of my books. "Stay in school! Stay in school!" Johnson had shouted, over television, to the rising generation. Yet this Caesar had no need of books; he had been the vainglorious disciple of Experience, that famous master of fools.

No, Johnson did not open books: with Septimius Severus, he might have said, "Pay the soldiers; the rest do not matter." Had he not Robert McNamara, creator of the Edsel, to counsel him? Power was all, and surely the power of the United States, under Johnson's hand, was infinite. All the way with LBJ! There came into my head, in the Oval Office, a passage from Amaury de Riencourt:

> With Caesarism and Civilization, the great struggles between political parties are no longer concerned with principles, programs and ideologies, but with men. Marius, Sulla, Cato, Brutus still fought for principles. But now, everything became personalized. Under Augustus, parties still existed, but there were no more *Optimates or Populares*. No more conservatives or democrats. Men campaigned for or against Tiberius or Drusus or Caius Caesar. No one believed any more in the efficacy of ideas, political panaceas, doctrines, or systems, just as

the Greeks had given up building great philosophic systems generations before. Abstractions, ideas, and philosophies were rejected to the periphery of their lives and of the empire, to the East where Jews, agnostics, Christians, and Mithraists attempted to conquer the world of souls and minds while the Caesars ruled their material existence.

All the way with LBJ! *Ave atque vale!*

*   *   *

Every inch a Caesar LBJ looked; he might have sat for Michelangelo for the carving of a statue of a barracks emperor. Experience, nevertheless, had not taught this imperator how to fight a war. To fancy that hundreds of thousands of fanatic guerrillas and North Vietnamese regulars, supplied by Russia and China, might be defeated by military operations merely defensive—plus a great deal of bombing from the air, destroying civilians chiefly, that bombing pinpointed by Johnson himself in the White House! The American troops in Vietnam fought admirably well—how well, my old friend General S. L. A. Marshall described unforgettably in his books— but their situation was untenable. "Imagination rules mankind," Bonaparte had said—Napoleon, master of the big battalions; had Johnson possessed any imagination, he would have sealed Haiphong, as Nixon did later. Only so might the war have been won.

Afflicted by *hubris*, Johnson Caesar piled the tremendous cost of the war—a small item was the immense quantity of milk flown daily from San Francisco to Vietnam, American troops not campaigning on handfuls of rice—upon the staggering cost of his enlargement of the welfare states at home. One might have thought he could not do sums. He ruined the dollar and bequeathed to the nation an incomprehensible national debt. Both guns and butter! It had been swords and liturgies with earlier emperors.

It is with variations that history repeats itself; ignoring history, LBJ was condemned to repeat it.

Morally, he was the worst man ever to make himself master of the White House. The corrupt antics of Bobby Baker and Billie Sol Estes did not bring him down, although he had been intimately connected with both.

In June 1961, an agent of the Department of Agriculture, Henry Marshall, had been found shot to death in Texas. Marshall had been about to expose the criminal wheeling and dealing of Billie Sol Estes, and in that wheeling and dealing Lyndon Johnson, then vice-president, had participated. A justice of the peace declared the murder of Marshall to have been suicide.

But in March 1984, a grand jury in Robertson County would look into the mystery. A federal marshal and Billie Sol Estes would certify before that jury. Estes, under immunity, swore that the killing had been decided upon at a meeting at Vice-President Johnson's Washington residence; Johnson had given the order and directed a hanger-on of his, Malcolm Wallace, to execute it. The grand jury believed Estes, it appears, and concluded that Marshall's death had been a homicide. No one was indicted, for the grand jury presumed that the murderers already were dead.

Such frequently is the way of Caesars. Like some other Caesars, Johnson, from small beginnings, accumulated while in public office a large fortune. No one ever accused him of the vice of scrupulosity. An ill man to deal with, Lyndon Baines Johnson.

Yet Eugene the Poet, Eugene the Giant-Killer, would fetch Caesar down. I do not think that Eugene McCarthy would have converted himself into a Caesar; nay, American conservatives might have been better content with President McCarthy than they would become with President Bush or will be with President Clinton.

*   *   *

During the last election cycle, the American people endured the least edifying of presidential campaigns. No one of the three gentlemen who aspired to the presidential office commanded much respect, and their debates were more concerned with trivia and intemperate accusations than with the great and most difficult public decisions that must be made very soon. The feeblest of the three candidates proposed to refer all of those decisions to the electorate at large, by electronic means of polling—as if every American voter were able and eager to express a considered judgment on what courses should be undertaken in the conduct of foreign policy, on how the national debt should be reduced, on how civil disorders should be averted, on what to do about the American proletariat, on the improvement of public schooling, on the allocation of priorities in public expenditure, on the afflictions of centralization and bureaucracy, on the question of immigration, on the modes of averting an economic collapse on the scale of what occurred in 1929—on these and innumerable other public issues, it is proposed that we take a hasty popular poll! That way lies democratic madness. Why bother with statesmen? Surely the typical American voter is omniscient. We have entered upon the politics of the absurd.

1992's three presidential aspirants seemed absurd to a great multitude of citizens. How had they been selected for candidacy? Mr. Perot selected himself, soon withdrew (but not from modesty), and then selected himself afresh. Mr. Bush and Mr. Clinton were selected chiefly by primary campaigns, the results of which were determined chiefly by the amount of money they were able to spend, respectively, on television advertising. In the case of President Bush, his being an incumbent of the office, with large benefactions to bestow, saved the day for him. *Sic transit gloria mundi;* to them that hath shall be given. Certain Roman Caesars bought the imperial purple. Increasingly, our presidential candidates win by purchasing time on the boobtube.

*　　　*　　　*

The Framers of the Constitution gravely distrusted democratic appetites, as such had been demonstrated by Shays's Rebellion. Also they distrusted arbitrary power in a chief executive. So they endeavored—unsuccessfully, as matters have turned out—to devise a prudent method of selecting presidents, far removed from popular vote. This was the Electoral College. It was assumed by the Framers that within each of the several states there would be chosen (through divers modes) able and conscientious presidential electors, free agents, "men of superior discernment, virtue, and information" (in Senator Thomas Hart Benton's phrases) who would select a strong and good president "according to their own will," regardless of popular sentiment of the hour. This upright intended Electoral College never has functioned as the Framers intended, nevertheless, because with the rise of great coherent political parties came the pledging in advance of electors to the candidacy of some particular individual—Adams, or Jefferson, or Burr, say—and therefore the reduction of the Electoral College to insignificance, except so far as the College preserved the idea of a nation of sovereign states, the presidential electoral vote being cast by the several states according to their representation in the Congress— and not according to the popular vote, nationally regarded.

The Framers of the Constitution conceivably might have revised a different move for the Electoral College that could have survived the rise of great political parties. One such arrangement might have been to make the sitting governors of the several states, if chosen long before the presidential election, the independent choosers of the president, so retrieving the selection from the ephemeral preferences of the great mass of ill-informed voters nationally. But "of all sad words of tongue or pen, / The saddest are these: 'It might have been!'" Now we expect presidential candidates to exhaust themselves, and their supporters' fund, by two overwhelming national campaigns—one the primaries and conventions held in every state, the other the frantic struggle on the eve of the November election every four years. This method is supposed to ascertain the popular will; but in effect it blurs distinctions between parties, the candidates promising to be all things, to all men—and women; and commonly this method gives us demagogues or else bladders of vanity as party candidates. All too possibly it may give us more Caesar-presidents; President Bush endeavored to be one such, causing the deaths of a quarter of a million people in Iraq; but the popularity of that exploit rapidly evaporated. The more we behave as if the president were the embodiment of the American democracy, and do little about the Congress except to revile senators and representatives, the less genuinely democratic this nation must become.

*   *   *

Electronic technology becomes a tool of plebiscitary democracy. As Mr. James M. Perry put it in the *Wall Street Journal* on November 4, hereafter, having upheld the presidential contest of 1992, "Candidates will build on what they saw this year—800-telephone number satellite hook-ups, soft Larry King-style interviews, televised town meetings." It's a brave new world, with words like "teledemocracy" and "interactive communications" being used by the scholars to describe it. Notions like Mr. Perot's "electronic town hall," should they come to pass, would concentrate the national public's attention upon the presidential candidates merely, sweeping aside the mechanism of parties and in effect reducing the Congress (or, on the level of the several states, the state legislatures) to little more than ratifying bodies, pledged to whatever programs the victorious presidential candidate might advocate and decree. The peril to true representative government, and to America's old territorial democracy, is too obvious for me to labor this point. The presidential candidates, in such a novel system, necessarily would have to raise enormous quantities of money from such special interests, pressure groups, and ethnic blocs as might expect to profit from the ascendancy of some vigorous demagogue or some persuasive instrument of oligarchy.

Yet a good many Americans fancy that these developments founded upon television and telephone will bring about "government of the people, by the people, and for the people." At our county Republican convention in my state of Michigan, an amiable young candidate for the office of representative in the Michigan legislature—a person who thought himself conservative—declared himself delighted at the prospect of serving the people "in the new direct democracy." Now direct democracy did not function well in ancient Athens, when the whole electorate's few thousand men could assemble in the agora; it would function disastrously, if at all, in the United States of the twentieth century, with a population of some two hundred and fifty million people. In any event, the people possessing no unanimous collective will on any question, this virtual abolition of representative government would come down to skillful manipulation of the moment's public opinion by a circle of electronic-media specialists in the service of the president: an extreme form of plebiscitary democracy. In effect, the presidency would become a dictatorship achieved without violence and checked only by the necessity of an election every four years. How very democratic!

*   *   *

I speak thus alarmingly only of future possibilities, not of the reign of Clinton Caesar. For Mr. Clinton achieved a majority of the popular vote merely in his own state of Arkansas; he is a plurality president merely, no popular hero empowered by the Demos to shape the world nearer to his heart's desire. Moreover, he has promised all things to all men—free medical care; free college education, or virtually free, for all comers; emancipation from the tiresome restraints of bourgeois morality; more lavish entitlements for such minorities as can turn out the vote; Lord knows what all benefits. These promises cannot be fulfilled; therefore the reproaches which were heaped upon President Bush these past four years will descend upon President Clinton twofold, not long after his inauguration; and he lacks the rhetorical skill and cunning with which Franklin Roosevelt, in highly similar circumstances, deflected or repelled such criticisms. So feebleness, rather than militancy, is liable to predominate during the Clinton years. And if President Clinton presumes to increase income taxes, as he has said he will do—why, the new Congress, mindful of the fate of the late Bush Administration, may turn rebellious. *In fine*, Mr. Clinton will not be crowned with laurel.

Clinton's successors, nevertheless, may have more happy opportunities for the concentration of power in their hands. Increasing military involvement in the European continent, or the collapse of the world economy in a fashion more ruinous than what occurred from 1929 to 1992, might whet presidential candidates' eagerness for power, and public willingness to entrust all to an American Caesar.

Circumstances from Siberia to San Francisco strongly resemble political and social and economic circumstances in most of the world between the two World Wars. The coming of immense inflation of currencies—now quite conceivable—might cause such immense public resentment and distress that executive forces and legislative bodies might be swept out of power, in country after country, and by plebiscites might usher in persons not at all scrupulous in their attainment of power. Such radical changes would be accomplished in the name of Democracy, of course, but what would result would be plebiscitary democracy, ruthless enough.

In the name of Democracy, America's representative government, under the Constitution, might be swept aside, and politics might be debased to contests between hypocritical ideologues, every one of them claiming to be more democratic than the others. What's in a name? In Haiti, "democracy" signifies the arbitrary power of former President Aristide to have rubber tires slung round the necks of his opponents, and they set afire. In the United States, the demand for more democracy might lead to the legalized plundering of the hardworking by those who prefer not to work at all. And a line of American Caesars might be required to preserve any sort of order.

I am arguing that these United States would be only degraded by a submission to an ideological democracy, in either domestic or foreign policy, a Rousseauistic democracy restyled "teledemocracy." What we require is a vigorous recovery of true representative government, one of the principal achievements of our culture, a legacy from centuries of British and colonial experience and from the practical wisdom of the Framers of the Constitution of the United States. Say not the struggle naught availeth.

XXII

The Wise Men Know What Wicked Things Are Written on the Sky

The end of the twentieth century of the Christian era is now only a few years distant, and all about us things seem to fall apart. There comes to my mind the last drawing from the pencil of William Hogarth, who died in 1764: it is a sufficient representation of much of the world today.

Hogarth's final drawing is known as "The Bathos" or "Finis." This word *bathos* signifies the depths, or the bottom; also it is applied to the process of sinking from the sublime to the ridiculous. Hogarth's pencil shows us a devastated and desiccated world in which all things have come to an end. In the shadow of a ruined tower, Father Time himself lies expiring, his scythe and his hourglass broken. In the last puff of smoke from Time's tobacco pipe, one discerns the word "Finis." A cracked bell, a shattered crown, the discarded stock of an old musket, the tottering signpost of a tavern called "The World's End," a bow unstrung, a map of the world burning, a gibbet falling, an empty purse, a proclamation of bankruptcy, the stump of a broom, a broken bottle—this litter lies about fallen Time. In the background one finds a wrecked ship. Overhead, the moon wanes, and Phoebus and his horses lie dead in the clouds. What once was sublime has descended to the ridiculous: thus the world ends, not with a bang but a whimper. A month after he had executed this famous tall-piece, Hogarth himself ceased to be.

This is the bent world of Orwell's *Nineteen Eighty-Four*, and it is the actual state in many lands of what once was a civilized order. Will the wave of the future engulf the remaining islands of refuge? Will the American Republic go down to dusty death?

Perhaps you fear that I am embarking upon a long tale of woe. But I mean to spare you that. Rather, my purpose it is to suggest that you and I are not the slaves of some impersonal force called Destiny or History. I come to you not as a gravedigger, but as a diagnostician. Indeed our whole civilization is sorely afflicted by decadence; yet it need not follow that, already having passed the point of no return, we must submit ourselves to total servitude and infinite boredom. Just as renewal of soul and body often is possible for the individual person, so whole societies may recover from follies and blunders.

Letting some cheerfulness break in, I have taken for the title of this address G. K. Chesterton's long poem *The Ballad of the White Horse*, which has for its setting the age of King Alfred in England. In certain stanzas of the first book of that courageous ballad, Chesterton speaks of Eastern fatalism—as contrasted with Christian hope. Here Chesterton really has in mind those people in the twentieth century who declare that our culture is doomed to destruction. I give you two of Chesterton's stanzas:

> *The wise men know what wicked things*
> *Are written on the sky,*
> *They trim sad lamps, they touch sad strings,*
> *Hearing the heavy purple wings,*

Where the forgotten seraph kings
Still plot how God shall die.

The wise men know all evil things
Under the twisted trees,
Where the perverse in pleasure pine
And men are weary of green wine
And sick of crimson seas.

Truly, many wicked things have been written on today's sky, worse than things written on New York's subway cars. Certainly many millions of Americans pine in their perverse pleasures, glutted with narcotics, pornography, and insane sensuality. A good many people fret themselves over the rather improbable speculation that the earth itself might be blown asunder by nuclear weapons. The grimmer and more immediate prospect is that men and women may be reduced to a sub-human state through limitless indulgence in their own vices—with ruinous consequences to society generally.

The possibilities for efficient corruption, political and personal, are greater in our time than in any previous era: we have devised ingenious instruments to that end. Anyone who thinks seriously upon these tribulations must grow disheartened on some occasions; he may be tempted to confess himself one of those "men of the East" who know all too well what wicked things are written on the sky—tempted to shrug, sigh, and murmur, "What cannot be mended, must be endured."

Yet if most people so resign themselves, indeed all is lost. Public affairs are surrendered to the domination of squalid oligarchies, and private life becomes a fruitless pursuit of sensual pleasure. One may trace such a process through the Roman decadence, but we of the twentieth century have enabled ourselves to carry on the process more swiftly and thoroughly.

Should we submit ourselves to what has been called "the wave of the future," accepting as inevitable the decline of order and justice and freedom? Should we resign ourselves to the decay of public and private morality? Should we say, "Well, the neighbors seem to enjoy their own corruption: who are we to object?" Should we take it for granted that Christian belief is doomed to fade away, to be supplanted by a new morality of "looking out for Number One"? Should we accept a regime of centralized power, general mediocrity, and life concerned wholly with getting and spending? Should we be content to live in a devil's sabbath of whirling machinery, and call it progress?

Must we believe those wicked words of doom and decadence that fatalists see written on the sky? Or is it still in our power as a people, by exertion of our wills and our energies, to renew our vigor and our beliefs? Must we trim sad lamps and strum sad strings, in the gloomy expectation that the forces of evil, those "seraph kings," will work the death of God? Or, given resolution and imagination, may we Americans yet enter upon a time of greatness, an augustan age? Permit me to touch briefly upon such questions.

*   *   *

Of all the forms of pride, the worst is intellectual pride. "Lo, I am proud!" declares Lucifer, in a medieval miracle play. Congratulating themselves upon their own wisdom, various intellectuals of our day fancy that they know to be true those wicked things written on the sky; or at least that those things must come to pass, whether we like it or not. Intellectuals of this stamp take it for granted that the American people must sink into decadence—and enjoy the decadence, if they can.

Pride of this sort presumes to prophesy; and prophecies of that order tend to work their own fulfillment. The seraph kings of

Chesterton's ballad are quick to take advantage of human pride. "Through that fault fell the angels."

Our intellectual resistance to prophecies of decadence, those wicked things written on the sky, is weakened by the growth in our midst of what has been called a "New Class"—although, as Peter Berger and Brigette Berger remark in their book *The War Over the Family*, this body of men and women might better be described as the Knowledge Class. Here is the Berger description of them:

"Put simply, these are the people who derived their livelihood from the production, distribution, and administration of symbolic knowledge. They are not just the so-called intellectuals, who may be seen as an upper crust in this new stratum. Rather, the expanding 'knowledge industry' (as the economist Fritz Machlup first called it) contains large numbers of people who could by no reasonable criterion be called intellectuals: the vast educational system, the therapeutic-'helping' complex, sizable portions of government bureaucracy, the media and publishing industries, and others. What all these have in common is that bodies of symbolic knowledge (as distinct from the knowledge of, say, the physical scientist or the marketing expert) are to be applied to indoctrinate ('educate'), inspire ('help'), and plan for other people. This group, certainly numbered in the millions in America today, fulfills the category of 'class' in a number of specifics: it has a particular relation to the economic system (one important aspect of this relation is that a large portion of this group is either on the public payroll or is publicly subsidized), has particular collective interests (the most important being the maintenance and, if possible, expansion of the welfare state), and also has a particular subculture that is more than a direct expression of its vested interests."

Just so. Recently an able young woman of our acquaintance, enjoying considerable success in the new realm of "computer science," related to us some anecdotes drawn from her experience with this Knowledge Class. They are endowed with academic tenure, frequent leaves of absence, abundant grants, and "gofers" to assist them in routine duties; their labors ordinarily are light. Yet they are given to muttering such malcontent declarations as "Eighty per cent of the wealth is owned by two per cent of the people"—a sentiment, incidentally, which suggests the limits of the knowledge of the Knowledge Class. They seem quite unaware that they constitute themselves a class lavishly endowed with privileges. And they are puffed up with intellectual pride.

This Knowledge Class, the product of our superficial system of public instruction during recent decades, increasingly pines in perverse pleasures under those twisted trees. The Bergers suggest that this large and influential body of persons sets itself against the bourgeois family; for the family stresses personal discipline and ability, which the Knowledge Class detests. The Knowledge Class yearns after a risk-free existence, devoted to the pursuit of pleasures. These are the champions of self-realization, of abortion, of the "gay life-style." Their notion of a risk-free existence persuades them to embrace political leftism, zero-growth and zero-population theories, anti-nuclear and anti-technological sentiments, pacifism, suspicion of patriotism, and dislike of discipline, achievement, and competition. "In the aggregate, this is indeed a constellation of decadence," the Bergers write. "A society dominated by these themes has rather poor prospects in the real world, which is mostly inhabited by people with very contrary norms and habits."

The more this presumptuous Knowledge Class comes to influence public opinion and public policy, the more the nation drifts downward toward decadence. The Knowledge Class fulfills those wicked things written on the sky. A society dominated by such votaries of personal pleasure sinks toward personal and social boredom, life without meaning or challenge. And beyond the frontiers of such a society, the totalist ideologues, on whose faces is no smile, observe the progressive enfeeblement of such a nation, and await opportunities.

I venture to suggest that something must be done about the Knowledge Class. Either we must endeavor to restore right reason and imagination among them—among their successors, I should say, for there is small hope of altering the intellects and characters of most of the present members of this Knowledge Class—or else we must take measures to restrain their influence. The Knowledge Class, neglecting or defying the realm of spirit, would convert us into a spiritless people, impoverished morally and economically, unable (as Robert Frost says of the liberal) to take our own side in a quarrel.

It may be thought that I am doing no more than oppressing you with gloomy vaticinations. But that is not my purpose: I propose to let some cheerfulness break in. Certain prophecies are calculated to work their own fulfillment; I would have us reject those prophecies.

*   *   *

Only death and taxes are ineluctable. The Marxists, like Hegel before them, represent History as a force impersonal and irresistible, decreeing progress toward a foredoomed end: in effect, they deify History. But actually history is nothing of the sort. Mankind makes history, which is merely the written record of what has occurred in mankind's past. The sacred history of Christians speaks of the march of Providence; but that is something different from the Marxist notion of an ineluctable History that foreordains certain stages of development, leading to the triumph of the proletariat, the withering away of the state, and apparently an endless monotony of egalitarian communal existence.

All we know about the future, really, is that the future remains unknowable. Marx's historical determinism is sufficiently refuted by the events of this century: the Communist ideology triumphed not in Britain or Germany, but in Russia, which land Marx detested; far from establishing a sprawl of idyllic communes, the application of Marx's doctrines produced a hideous imperial tyranny maintained by a secret police and a huge army. The Nazis' version of historical inevitability was undone even more swiftly.

Human thought and human actions, unpredictable ordinarily, determine the course of civilizations. Decadence is no more inevitable than is progress. Great civilizations commonly experience certain periods of decay, alternating with periods of renewal. The American nation conceivably may be entering now upon an augustan age of high achievement. As George Washington put it at the Constitutional Convention, the event is in the hand of God.

Nothing is but thinking makes it so. The present mind-set of the Knowledge Class is produced by ideas of the nineteenth and twentieth centuries: vulgarized Darwinianism, socialism, vulgarized Freudianism, winds of doctrine of yesteryear. Mechanism and materialism, scientists' concepts now being undone by physicists of our own time, still lie at the back of the assumptions of the Knowledge Class. The typical member of the Knowledge Class possesses no distinct awareness of the source of his prejudices; nor does he understand that the ground is shifting under his feet: that newer ideas are at work. The presumed wave of the future may drown him.

One thing we can do is this: to refrain from choking up the springs of the moral imagination. If we stifle the sense of wonder, no wonders will occur amongst us; and if wondrous remedies are lacking, then indeed the words of doom written on the sky will become as the laws of the Medes and the Persians, ineluctable. The computerized intellect of the Knowledge Class would deny us wonder; it would deny us fruitful speculation.

Sir Bernard Lovell, the astronomer, recently pointed out that "literal-minded, narrowly focused computerized research is proving antithetical to the free exercise of that happy faculty known as serendipity—that is, the knack of achieving favorable results more or less by chance." This word "serendipity," like that quasi-scientific word "entropy," is a tag attached to the inexplicable: an awkward twentieth-century acknowledgement that now and again, in certain persons, there may penetrate to the imagination perceptions of truth which ordinary rationality cannot attain.

"Computers act as very narrow filters of information," Lovell continues; "they must be oriented to specific observations. In other words, they have to be programmed for the kinds of results that the observer expects." For the past sixteen years, Lovell remarks, no major discovery has been made in radio astrology. "Could it be more than a coincidence that the wholesale application of computers to the techniques of observation is associated with this puzzling cessation of serendipitous discoveries?"

Just so. Computerized knowledge already may have begun to choke the springs of imagination. Of course it is not merely the device called the computer that works this mischief. Rather, it is the mentality of the dominant Knowledge Class, one of whose instruments the computer is. Damage to the imagination—whether we call that mysterious faculty serendipity or intuition or the illative sense—may extend to many other fields than radio astrology. It may extend to attempts at renewal of the person and of the Republic—to the life spiritual and the life temporal. If so, the wicked things written on the sky may be graven upon tablets of stone and set amongst us for our obedience to the commandments of the Savage God.

The Marxist imagination is a mingling of the idyllic and diabolical types of imagination: the dream of the earthly paradise, the vision of triumphant blood-letting. Only the assertion of the moral imagination can thwart the imagination of the ferocious ideologue.

Mankind is governed by imagination: so we are told by Napoleon Bonaparte, master of the big battalions. The moral imagination, the idyllic imagination, and the diabolic imagination are at war in our time. It was a principal delusion of the nineteenth-century liberals that the individual is thoroughly rational, pursuing intelligently his self-interest. Not pure reason, but imagination—the high dream or the low dream—is the moving force in private life and in public. What person chooses a spouse on purely rational grounds—or has opportunity to do so? What successful movement in history was produced by purely rational calculations?

Losing wisdom in a labyrinth of knowledge, losing knowledge in a mass of information, we Americans have saddled ourselves with a Knowledge Class that takes for gospel the wicked things written on the sky—or, at best, has no knowledge of how to erase those wicked things. Fancying themselves wise, the Knowledge Class play with their computers in the belief that they open the way to emancipation from old dogmas and old duties. In reality, they open the way to the bathos—descent from the sublime to the ridiculous. They would subject us to servitude of imagination, of mind, of body; and that servitude would not be mild.

Then let us seek our redemption from outside the ranks of the Knowledge Class. Let us remember, with Burke, that even a common soldier, a child, or a girl at the door of an inn may change the face of fortune. Sometimes we Americans seem trapped in the world of the Flight. It is not economic arguments that will redeem us, nor electoral contests.

If we are to refute those wicked things written on the sky, we must renew our power of moral imagination. This is no easy undertaking; but the alternative is altogether thinkable. It is an antagonist world, in Sir Osbert Sitwell's lines,

> *Without the gambler's hope to a gambler's life,*
> *Where the highest prize is a week in a Butlin camp,*
> *And the forfeit, a star's disruption.*

A shallow schooling, indifferent to development of imagination and of character, produced the mentality of the Knowledge Class.

The imagination neglected, two generations of Americans have been left with security and sensuality as the ends of life. Why wonder at the popularity of hard drugs? The narcotic trance is one substitute for the life of the imagination.

Our private and our public future will be determined by the sort of imagination that gains ascendancy among the rising generation. It is not too late to write some good things on the sky.

*   *   *

For it is not inevitable that we submit ourselves to a social life-in-death of boring uniformity and equality. It is not inevitable that we indulge all our appetites to fatigued satiety. It is not inevitable that we reduce our schooling to the lowest common denominator. It is not inevitable that obsession with creature-comforts should sweep away belief in a transcendent order. It is not inevitable that the computer should supplant the poet.

Despite my warnings against false prophets, I venture now timidly upon modest prediction. It appears to me that this country has entered upon an era of reconstruction and conservative reform, Caesar Clinton notwithstanding. We are settling down after a quarter of a century of turbulence and confusion.

Consider first the moral condition of the American people. Alexis de Tocqueville, a century and a half ago, remarked that there exist three causes of a nation's success: its material circumstances, its laws, and its mores (or moral habits and customs). In circumstances and laws, Tocqueville found, America enjoyed then no especial advantages. The reason for the success of the American democracy, he concluded, as compared with the failure of other democracies, was America's moral habits.

Those old mores appeared to be dissolving during much of the 1960s and 1970s; we have not now any high moral tone. Yet in such concerns we appear to be improving. The crime rate is diminishing in most categories. The narcotics traffic, though still formidable, is less alarming than it was a few years ago. (Cocaine addiction appears to be principally a vice of the Knowledge Class.) The voices demanding "sexual emancipation"—that is, sexual indulgence in its more perverse forms—grow less strident. About half the American population retain some church connection—a higher proportion than in any other great nation of our time. Stricter probity in public office is insisted upon. In schooling, we begin to renew some attention to the development of good character. Our present tendency, in short, is toward the restoration of moral order. We seem to have begun to understand afresh that there can survive no decent social order unless it rests upon a decent moral order.

Consider domestic politics. After a time of political passions and radical enthusiasms, we appear to be settling for politics as the art of the possible. The public has come to desire stability and continuity. Ideological fanaticism distinctly has lost its appeal to the rising generation. Relatively few people desire to enlarge the welfare state. I do not imply that we are about to achieve a perfect political consensus; but I do suggest that the American Republic will endure.

Given imagination, Americans may refute the prophecies of decadence. Whether those wicked things written on the sky will be erased in the age that is dawning, or whether the children of darkness will prevail—why, that will be decided by the rising generation, in whose power it will be to give the lie to the fatalists. The children of light may labor with fortitude, knowing that the struggle availeth.

Such augustan redemption is far from certain. Providence, it seems, is quite as often retributory as it is beneficent, and ordinarily Providence operates through human agency. In the hope of moving the thoughts and the sentiments of some few people who might become, all unwitting or unwilling, Providence's instruments for the renewal of moral and political order—why, in that hope these lectures were delivered.

Index
